At a level accessible to the educated lay reader, this book describes what changes human activities have produced in the global environment from 300 years ago to the present day. It offers a comprehensive and authoritative inventory of human impact in its varied forms – on the land, oceans, atmosphere, and climate – ranging from long-standing alterations to new and surprising ones that have emerged in recent years, from environmental disasters to false alarms to success stories of environmental management.

This balanced, nonpolemical survey will interest all those concerned about the environment and the likely fate of the planet.

HUMAN
IMPACT ON
THE EARTH

HUMAN IMPACT ON THE EARTH

William B. Meyer

Clark University

Published by the Press Syndicate of the University of Cambridge
The Pitt Building, Trumpington Street, Cambridge CB2 1RP
40 West 20th Street, New York, NY 10011-4211, USA
10 Stamford Road, Oakleigh, Melbourne 3166, Australia

First published 1996

Printed in the United States of America

Library of Congress Cataloging-in-Publication Data
Meyer, William B.
Human impact on the earth / William B. Meyer.
p.   cm.
Includes bibliographical references (p.   ) and index.
ISBN 0-521-36356-X (hardback). – ISBN 0-521-55847-6 (pbk.)
1. Man – Influence on nature.   2. Human ecology.   I. Title.
GF75.M456   1996
304.2 – dc20   95-10818
CIP

A catalog record for this book is available from the British Library.

ISBN 0-521-36356-X Hardback
ISBN 0-521-55847-6 Paperback

Contents

v

Preface

In October 1987 a group of some 100 scientists and scholars from around the world gathered at Clark University in Worcester, Massachusetts, for a week-long examination of "The Earth as Transformed by Human Action." Presentations commissioned well in advance from leading experts examined the major forms of human impact on the earth over the past 300 years; the social forces principally responsible for global environmental transformation; and the environmental history of selected regions around the world. The papers prepared for the conference, subsequently revised, appeared in print under the same title as the conference's in 1990.

That large volume forms the basis of this much smaller one. In addition to presenting its contents in a more accessible form, I have done some updating, amplifying, and interpretation of my own in telling more or less the same story: of how human activities have altered the biosphere from the end of the seventeenth century to the present. The authors of the chapters in *The Earth as Transformed by Human Action* are in no way responsible for the use that I have made of, or of course for any divergences I have allowed myself from, their work.

I am most grateful for the assistance of a number of individuals: the steering committee of the Earth Transformed project – Bill Turner, Bill Clark, Bob Kates, John Richards, Jessica Mathews, and Len Berry – for offering me the chance to write this book and for helping along the way; my editors at Cambridge University Press for their patience and helpfulness; and the ninety-odd contributors to *The Earth as Transformed by Human Action*, surely the best team of research assistants an author ever had. Support from the Joyce Mertz-Gilmore Foundation, the Andrew W. Mellon Foundation, and Clark University is also gratefully acknowledged.

1

The Earth as Transformed by Human Action

The human imprint on the earth could be described as unmistakable, were it not often mistaken for the work of nature or natural phenomena for human impacts. Traditional societies that ascribed particular mountains, lakes, and rivers to the deeds of great ancestors had their counterparts in mid-twentieth-century visitors to the Grand Canyon who would remark: "You can't tell me it was made without human aid" (Krutch 1958: 25). Today it is the surrounding desert, and not the canyon, that tourists familiar with the term "desertification" might erroneously see as of human making. The Sahara is sometimes seen that way, and not only by laypeople. At the same time, the Amazonian tropical rainforest is often thought, just as erroneously, to be a pristine natural treasure threatened for the first time by human interference. The accumulating evidence suggests to the contrary that it owes much of its character and richness to a long history of human use.

Yet if it is not strictly unmistakable, the human imprint is often clear enough. It is often profound even when invisible to the naked eye. It is most blatant in cities, where some three billion people – half the world's population – now live. A large city keeps its original topography and climate, more or less, though hills are cut down, river channels shifted, and temperature, precipitation, air quality, storms, and winds altered. The rest of it is plainly the work of humankind. Any further transformations it undergoes are from one human-shaped state to another; efforts at nature preservation give way to historic preservation. But rural areas and even seeming wildlands may also be much altered by past or present human use even if the alteration is not so apparent. Even the most remote and thinly populated regions of the world are not remote enough to have remained unaffected. Haze from fossil-fuel combustion far to the south pollutes the Arctic sky (Soroos 1992). Both poles now receive heightened levels of ultraviolet radiation through a depleted stratospheric ozone layer.

1

Arctic haze and ozone depletion, of course, though of humankind's doing, are not at all of its desiring. They represent purely unintended consequences of actions taken for other ends. So indeed do many of the changes in urban environments; even these are profoundly transformed without being perfectly tamed. Change driven by human action is pervasive but change consciously controlled by it is not. The fear that our impacts are wilder and more random even as they become ever grander in scale is fundamental to contemporary environmental concern. Humankind has become a force in the biosphere as powerful as many natural forces of change, stronger than some, and sometimes as mindless as any.

The earth is today being transformed by human action; it has always been under transformation by these nonhuman forces. Notions of an earth either eternal in form or created recently in more or less its modern shape had a wide currency until recently in the history of thought but have one no more. Geologists now depict an earth in constant flux.

> The most fundamental and dramatic environmental changes over the 4-billion-year history of the earth have been those produced by natural forces, probably including a few cosmic interventions. Such dramatic metamorphoses have included the creation of the biosphere itself, movements of continents and oceans, the evolutionary development and extinction of millions of plant and animal species, and long-term shifts in climatic conditions and zones. (Kates, Turner, and Clark 1990: 10)

Nature has not retired from the construction (or demolition) business, but humankind has in the recent past emerged as a strong competitor. It is now, indeed, the principal agent modifying the earth's surface. The human imprint on the earth's landscapes and processes – representing deliberate and inadvertent change alike – is profound and pervasive and becoming ever more so. The term "global environmental change" is sometimes used narrowly to refer to a couple of apparent or prospective impacts – "global warming" and stratospheric ozone depletion. Human-induced changes of a global magnitude, however, are much more varied than that. For instance:

- Since preagricultural times, humankind has cleared a net area of forest of some 8 million square km, about the size of the lower 48 United States.
- Human activities contribute about 150 million tons per year (the metric ton unit is used throughout this book) to the flow of sulfur through the biosphere, approximately doubling the natural flow and creating pollution problems from the neighborhood to the continental level.
- The annual human withdrawal of water from the hydrologic cycle is now about 3,600 cubic km – roughly a third of its readily available volume. (Kates, Turner, and Clark 1990: 1; P. Rogers 1994)

Not only are many human impacts on the global environment large, but most are very recent. More than three-quarters of the net clearance of forest has occurred in the past three centuries. The annual withdrawal of water has grown 35-fold in the same period. The human contribution to the sulfur budget was negligible as recently as a century ago.

Given these and other changes, it is possible to speak of an earth transformed by human action. From a long-term global perspective, it is apparent that:

- Human-induced change is now, in most of the significant realms of the environment affected, of unprecedented size. Many forms of human alteration have either become significant fractions of natural change or surpassed it altogether.
- Human action now strongly affects the biosphere's principal "flows" of materials and energy as well as its landscape "faces," such as forests and soils, which have been significantly altered for much longer.
- Human-induced change is proceeding at unprecedented rates compared with past human and natural change, and has also reached unprecedented spatial scales, far outstripping premodern change in the proportion of the earth's surface affected.
- The variety and size of modern change mean a new level of complex interactions and feedbacks among these changes and new perplexities in managing them; ameliorating one problem may create another or make another worse.
- Finally, if there has been much change already, there is much more in prospect. Increases in the world's population and the standard of living that that population expects are likely to increase the rates of environmental change even more in the near future. "It appears inevitable that global population will continue to increase rapidly into and through the next century and that the demands upon nature will reach scales never before imagined." (Kates, Turner, and Clark 1990: 1)

That said, several qualifications are immediately in order. Not all aspects of the earth have been affected equally or even much affected at all. Many natural processes operate on a scale that still dwarfs the human input; much of the earth (including the oceans) has been altered only slightly. Nor is explosive change an invariable rule even in the global aggregate. Some human impacts have slowed, not accelerated, in the past few decades. Hardly anywhere below the global scale have net global trajectories of change been duplicated; in many regions at many times, indeed, they have been reversed. Change is not a synonym for damage. The terms "damage" and "degradation" are best reserved for those changes that do, on balance, more harm than good – however harm and good may be measured. Almost any human-induced change in the environment is likely to have some positive as well as some negative effects, and an earth transformed need not mean an earth degraded. Human-induced change, finally, is not exclusively a modern phenomenon. Significant modification of local and regional environments goes back to antiquity. "The use of fire by hunter-gatherers altered

3

flora and fauna; incipient cultivators spread domesticates and cut forests; early civilizations transformed deserts through irrigation" (Kates, Turner, and Clark 1990: 1).

Just as human alterations of the environment are not new, neither is human fear that they have not been for the better. Concerns about damage to the earth "extend back about as far as one is willing to look" (Clark 1986: 8). Many of the Greek and Roman classics mention human impacts ranging from soil erosion to climatic change caused by forest clearance (Glacken 1967). Across most of human history, to be sure, such expressions are vastly outnumbered by observations of improvement. They would be even more so if the fact of improvement had not often been thought to speak for itself. That imbalance may reflect accurate perception as much as the duller sensitivity or awareness of our forebears. Expression of concern is not proof of acuteness; many of the fears of damage expressed in the past have proved ill founded.

With a vast if disorganized and fragmented literature of observation and interpretation on which to draw – and with personal experience both of rapid change in the New World where he had grown up and of long-term cumulative effects in the Mediterranean lands that he had visited – George Perkins Marsh published in 1864 a landmark volume entitled *Man and Nature: or, Physical Geography as Modified by Human Action*. Marsh was a Vermonter by origin and in the course of his life many things by profession. He failed as a businessman, confessed himself "an indifferent practitioner" of the law, spent six productive years in Congress, and served with distinction as commissioner of Vermont fisheries and railways and as U.S. minister to Turkey and Italy. He also supervised the design of the Washington Monument and of the capitol building from which the Green Mountain State is still governed, was a leading authority on the history of English and other languages, and was enough of an authority on history in general to be offered a chair in the subject at Harvard (Lowenthal 1958). It was not for his writings on the environment that he was best known in his day. His authorship of *Man and Nature* earned a single line in his half-column obituary in the *New York Times*. But it is for them that he is best remembered now.

Marsh made no claim of originality in most of the specific points he discussed in *Man and Nature*. At a more general level, he no more discovered the earth to have been modified than Columbus had discovered it to be round, facts well known to their contemporaries and predecessors. In his work of synthesis and interpretation, however, he broke new ground. Though the human impact on the earth had been "incidentally touched upon by many geographers, and treated with much fulness of detail in regard to certain limited fields of human effort," Marsh noted, "it has not, *as a whole,* so far as I know, been made a matter of special observation, or of critical research by any scientific observer" (Marsh [1864] 1965: 13). *Man and Nature* was the first general survey of the effects on the earth, incidental as well as deliberate, of human activities and the first to make it clear that those effects in sum were a cause for concern.

4

The volume has been rightly called "a prodigiously learned discussion of the modifications of the flora and fauna and the destruction wrought on forests, waters, soils, and sands" (Kates, Turner, and Clark 1990: 3). Page by page, it reads today like any classic from another time. It disconcertingly blends errors that have been exploded with insights that have endured. Many of Marsh's speculations, though reflecting the best science of his time, have not aged well. He too readily blamed the existence of deserts, as did many of his contemporaries, on human action rather than on natural forces. He overstated, as many others did then and have done since, the effect of deforestation on climate and floods. Many of his hopes and fears have not been realized. We have not, as Marsh ([1864] 1965: 459–60) expected, begun to prevent earthquakes by drilling shafts to release subterranean forces. Of his suggestion that the earth's axis and magnetic fields might be affected by human modification of the surface, one admirer has written tactfully that it "is still ahead of its time" (Jacobs 1978: 15), and it is likely forever to remain so.

It is impressive, though, how well *Man and Nature* has held up. Much of what Marsh had to say is still worth listening to. His volume remains an extraordinarily valuable collection of important principles, memorably phrased. Few environmentalist sermons are preached even today that could not draw a suitable text from its pages: it remains a source of "insights still unsurpassed" (Lowenthal 1990: 132). Several of them deserve particular mention. Marsh warned that many human impacts, though speedily inflicted, might be irreversible, or at least impossible to repair in the short or medium term. The processes of natural recovery, "under ordinary circumstances, demand, not years, generations, but centuries; and man, who even now finds scarce breathing room on this vast globe, cannot retire from the Old World to some yet undiscovered continent, and wait for the slow action of such causes to replace, by a new creation, the Eden he has wasted" (Marsh [1864] 1965: 228).

Throughout, Marsh also emphasized the secondary and unintended environmental consequences of human actions. The "intentional changes" wrought by humankind, he granted, "constitute, indeed, great revolutions; but vast as is their magnitude and importance, they are, as we shall see, insignificant in comparison to the contingent and unsought results which have flowed from them." "We are never justified," he wrote, "in assuming a force to be insignificant because its measure is unknown, or even because no physical effect can now be traced to it as its origin" (Marsh [1864] 1965: 36, 465). As Marsh stressed, in our actions in the physical world we frequently do not know what we are doing. The earth, as he claimed, has been modified by human action but not always by human intent.

Marsh on this point was more correct about our time than about his own: what he lacked as an interpreter of the nineteenth-century world he made up for as a prophet of the twentieth. Significant impacts in Marsh's day tended to be more visible and straightforward than contemporary ones, shorter in range and more rapidly registered. They affected principally the landscapes or "faces" of the earth. What is distinctive about the twentieth century is the degree to which human impacts have expanded to affect the invisible and far-reaching chemical flows of the biosphere. The secondary, distant, and surprising effects of which Marsh spoke have become commonplace.

His most important lesson was also his simplest: that humankind has unsuspected power to alter the earth, and is indeed an agent so powerful that it could destroy its own home even in the act of trying to improve it. That power, wisely applied, could bring about great improvements, but all too often, whether from simple lack of knowledge or from carelessness about results, it had "brought the face of the earth to a desolation almost as complete as that of the moon. . . ." (Marsh [1864] 1965: 42).

Though it has taken more than a century to be fully appreciated, *Man and Nature* did win immediate recognition as an impressive inventory and analysis of the human impact on the natural world. Of the second edition, *The Earth as Modified by Human Action* (1874), an American journal said:

> It is, in our opinion, one of the most useful and suggestive works ever published, and to those who have never reflected on the various ways in which mankind consciously or unconsciously disturbs the equilibrium of nature, with effects beneficial, indifferent, or disastrous, as the case may be, Mr. Marsh's observations and laboriously collected facts will come with the force of a revelation. (Anon. 1874)

For all its breadth, *Man and Nature* did not exhaust the possibilities of environmental thought even at that time. If Marsh came close to being "the last person to be individually omniscient in environmental matters" (O'Riordan 1988: 25), even he ignored or neglected some. A number of environmental concerns expressed by other observers of the time found no place in Marsh's book.

One such strand of thought was nature preservation, one of its exponents Marsh's New England contemporary, Henry David Thoreau. Marsh urged restraint in modifying nature on mainly utilitarian grounds; Thoreau on other grounds altogether. "Thoreau loved nature but wished it kept wild, Marsh wanted it tamed. Thoreau appealed chiefly to the aesthetic sensibility, Marsh to practicality" (Lowenthal 1958: 272). Theirs was a time not merely of exhortation but of early actions for preservation. In 1864, the year *Man and Nature* was published, Congress granted California a tract of public lands in the Yosemite Valley to be made a park "for public use, resort, and recreation." Eight years later, the Yellowstone region in Wyoming became the world's first full-fledged national park, its scenic features to be preserved "in their natural condition" (Nash 1967).

Attitudes of that time and ours also illustrate some of the enduring pitfalls of preservationism. One lies in the realm of fact: the mistaking of a human-altered landscape for a natural one. From mid- and late nineteenth-century New England dates the myth that the early European colonists of the region found and subdued a "forest primeval," whereas what they had found was an ecosystem dotted with large open tracts and long altered by its Amerindian inhabitants (Bowden 1992; Denevan 1992). Another pitfall lies in the realm of value. Preservationists often urge that natural features be protected for their own sake rather than on "anthropocentric" criteria, but the choice of which features to protect necessarily reflects human values. "In considering whether our impact has been creative or destructive, we can *only* be anthropocentric; whether we deform or destroy aspects of our environment is not good or bad in itself, but only by reference to mutable human values" (Lowenthal 1962).

Devoting more than a third of his book to deforestation, Marsh dealt with it mainly as a cause of secondary effects on climate, streamflow, and soil, and only in passing with it as a form of resource depletion. To the depletion of other resources he paid even less attention. What for him was a peripheral interest was for others a core question. Among Marsh's contemporaries, the British economist William Stanley Jevons (1835–82) best represented this line of thought: a conservationism focused on the ways in which humankind uses up natural resources that exist – as all do – in finite quantities. Jevons attracted much attention with his long essay *The Coal Question,* published the year after *Man and Nature.* He argued that industrial England's prosperity rested upon its coal supply, whose exhaustion, inevitable sooner or later, would necessarily spell national decline.

The Coal Question endorsed and extended to a second resource the earlier argument of Thomas Robert Malthus, that a necessarily limited food supply limited the growth of human numbers and well-being. Narrow and quite parochial in its focus, Jevons's essay remains important as a model of conservationist concern. It is equally important as a case study in the pitfalls of that perspective. Surprisingly, it was the importance of substitution in resource use, one of the central insights of modern resource economists, that escaped Jevons. Britain's coal supply, he insisted after a review of possible alternatives, was essential to the sustenance of its industrial system, an irreplaceable element in national prosperity. One cannot fault Jevons for failing to foresee all of the energy developments of the future. One can fault him for dismissing the likelihood of technological improvement. Some of his contemporaries advanced that criticism, as indeed some of Malthus's had done. In 1860, five years before *The Coal Question,* an American journal countered a gloomy forecast of the consequences of coal exhaustion similar to Jevons's. It cited in rebuttal "the great fact that human invention keeps pace with human necessities, and if the supply of coal should happen ever to give out, its place in the economy of the world would doubtless be supplied by some new and equally efficient agent" (Anon. 1860: 295). John Maynard Keynes, who thought highly of Jevons's other writings, found *The Coal Question* one of his weakest productions intellectually if one of his most striking stylistically: "its prophecies have not been fulfilled, the assumptions on which they were based are unsound, and re-read to-day it appears over-strained and exaggerated." It had not been its author's only failure in resource forecasting:

7

Jevons held similar ideas as to the approaching scarcity of paper as a result of the vastness of the demand in relation to the supply of suitable material (and here again he omitted to make adequate allowance for the progress of technical methods). Moreover, he acted on his fears and laid in such stores not only of writing-paper, but also of thin brown packing paper, that even to-day, more than fifty years after his death, his children have not used up the stock he left behind him of the latter. . . . (Keynes [1936] 1972: 112, 117)

It is a striking case of a tale often repeated – a specific forecast of resource exhaustion falsified by events. If his examples proved ill chosen, however, the themes that Jevons developed around them have had a more lasting significance. *The Coal Question* remains a landmark warning that resources have physical limits and that their depletion may set bounds on economic growth. What is known as the conservation movement – which historians have studied most closely in its turn-of-the-century American incarnation, but was a much wider phenomenon – extended Jevons's concern with depletion and waste to many other resources: timber, soil, metal ores, waterpower, farmland.

Marsh paid almost as little attention to environmental pollution as to resource conservation. Many of his contemporaries paid it much more. At the same time that Jevons warned of the dwindling of the coal supply, some of his countrymen warned of the damage done by its continued use. The term "acid rain" dates back to the 1850s. The British chemist R. A. Smith coined it to describe one of the effects of coal burning that he discovered in studying the London fogs that have been made legendary by Dickens, Conan Doyle, and other writers. Smith's 1872 book *Air and Rain* documented the changes in the atmosphere caused by urbanization and industrialization. It grew out of his work as the government inspector appointed to enforce the Alkali Act of 1863. Parliament had passed the act to control releases of hydrochloric acid, a waste product from factories that produced alkalis for industrial uses. Before being regulated, these acid emissions had made large tracts of neighboring land "as barren as the shores of the Dead Sea." Ten years earlier, Parliament had passed another landmark – though less effective – antipollution law, the Smoke Nuisance Abatement Act, aimed at coal-burning London factories (Brimblecombe 1987: 103, 137–41).

If technological change makes conservationist predictions of resource exhaustion a hazardous enterprise, warnings about pollution have their own characteristic dangers. The invisibility shared by many real and imagined polluting substances makes study of their effects and even assertions of their existence a risky endeavor. By far the most widespread pollution concerns in North America and Western Europe in Marsh's day were not about acid precipitation. They were concerns that have long since been discredited, ones that now belong to the domain of intellectual history and not environmental science. "Anticontagionist" theories dominant in these two world regions during much of the nineteenth century ascribed many diseases not to germs, but to gases – "miasma" or "sewer gas" – given off by decaying organic matter, filth, or stagnant water. In the countryside, such theories offered a powerful argument for wetland drainage and against irrigation and the damming of streams for reservoirs. In cities, they prompted important measures of urban environmental reform. British public health policy in the Victorian era rested squarely on the miasma theory of disease. Miasma – its existence scientifically discredited by the beginning of the twentieth century, now relegated to the museum of imaginary substances alongside phlogiston and the ether – was the one environmental pollutant discussed at length in *Man and Nature*. Marsh noted the importance of trees as agents for disinfecting the air of miasma, the health benefits of wetland drainage, and the danger of flooding fields to grow rice. Catholic doctrine, he argued, had done great damage to the European environment by requiring the consumption of fish at certain times, leading to the creation of fishponds whose stagnant waters poisoned the atmosphere (Marsh [1864] 1965: 361n).

Global-scale changes in the biogeochemical flows of the earth were the focus of a Russian scientist who was Marsh's most important successor in defining the character of human impact on the earth. The American, writing in the nineteenth century, documented the reshaping of the land surface. Writing in the twentieth, Vladimir Ivanovich Vernadsky (1863–1945) documented the subtler transformation of the chemical environment. Vernadsky described this change as the transformation of the biosphere – a term to which he gave its modern currency and meaning, as the thin shell of land, water, and air capable of supporting life – into the noosphere, a realm more and more shaped by the human mind, which had become a powerful new geological force, and a realm more and more open to rational human control, or to unthinking abuse.

In 1955, some one hundred scholars from diverse backgrounds in the humanities and the natural and social sciences assembled in Princeton, New Jersey, to examine "Man's Role in Changing the Face of the Earth." The papers and proceedings of the conference were published in the following year and dedicated to George Perkins Marsh (Thomas 1956). This volume offered a long if unevenly detailed panorama of environmental change since prehistoric times, the second major stocktaking of the human impact on the earth. Environmental concerns had not stood still since Marsh's 1864 assessment. In particular, there had been a widespread sense of ecological crisis in the 1930s that paralleled the socio-economic malaise of the times. Preservation, conservation, and pollution had remained lively currents of thought. With the end of World War II, the possibility of nuclear war aroused new fears. Humankind had developed tools whose power to devastate had no parallels in history. Somewhat insulated from these popular concerns (Lowenthal 1990: 124–26), *Man's Role* represented the attempt of some brilliant and learned individuals to come to grips with human–nature interactions in their long-term history as a way to understand the present and inform the future. Not a work of doomsaying nor of celebration, though each tone dominates some chapters, *Man's Role* "appears to have exerted a much more subtle, and perhaps more lasting, influence as a reflective, broad-ranging, and multi-

9

dimensional work that has informed and sometimes inspired several generations of scholars in the natural sciences, social sciences, and humanities" (Kates, Turner, and Clark 1990: 4).

The attitude of detachment evident at Princeton, unusual even then, would not remain possible for much longer. More change has occurred in many realms of nature and society in the four decades since 1955 than occurred during the near-century that separated Marsh's volume from the Princeton conference. Our attention – both scientific understanding and public awareness – to the changes has grown too. Modern concern over the possibility of global climatic change resulting from accumulation of carbon dioxide and other gases in the atmosphere dates back only about as far as the "Man's Role" conference. Today such "global warming" is a hotly debated issue in international politics and the popular press as well as in the scientific community. Obscure place names unknown to the world at the time of the Princeton conference are now prominent in the gazetteer of environmental disaster: Minamata, Japan, where industrial mercury pollution caused nightmarish damage to the health of fishermen and their customers; sites of chemical pollution episodes such as Bhopal, Times Beach, and Love Canal; nuclear accident locales such as Chernobyl and Three Mile Island; and loci of oil spills culminating in the 1989 *Exxon Valdez* disaster in Prince William Sound, Alaska. Such terms as acid rain, nuclear winter, the ozone layer, and biodiversity loss have all entered the popular vocabulary since 1955.

If the agenda of concerns has lengthened, it has not been by simple accumulation. Many items have disappeared from it as others have been added. A forecast of disaster may fail to come true because it prompted action that succeeded in averting it – the so-called self-refuting prophecy. Other concerns fade because closer study reveals that they are chimerical or at least overstated. The geographer Václav Smil makes an interesting point in this regard. A conference on the Study of Critical Environmental Problems held by MIT in the summer of 1970 identified ten key global pollution issues. When a similar conference was held in Sweden in 1982, only one of the ten remained on the agenda, that of global climatic change resulting from carbon dioxide accumulation in the atmosphere. Many others – formative issues of the Western environmental movement at the time of the first Earth Day – had been either resolved or largely discounted (Smil 1987, 208–09).

More concerns, though, have emerged than have been dispelled during the past several decades. This ever-rising level of worry is reflected in a deluge of volumes and studies. More appear each year than the last. Increasingly the flood of publications is popular as well as scientific. More than ever, "it is difficult to be in the midst of change and to understand it: to separate . . . the profound understandings from the current enthusiasms" (Kates, Turner, and Clark 1990: 14).

A high level of popular concern about environmental damage is apparent and welcome even if its depth remains questionable. To say that environmental changes have become widely publicized is not to say that they have become widely understood. Can they be expected to be? Should they be? A high public level of "environmental literacy" is desirable, certainly, but so is a high level of literacy in other areas – economics, for example; and it may well be that a high level of environmental literacy is more dangerous than none at all if it is not accompanied by an equal knowledge of other fields. Yet there are narrow limits to the material that any individual or any large portion of the public can be expected to master, especially when that material is frequently revised in matters large and small. It is not surprising that though much of the American public professes to believe that global warming is a serious problem, much of the American public also seems to think that it is the result of the depletion of the ozone layer, and to be equally at sea regarding almost anything else about it (Kempton 1991). "It is at best an open question whether environmental education of the general public is a realistic possibility" (Rockwell 1994: 369). All the same, a populace aware that human activities can and perhaps do threaten the environment on which they depend is, other things being equal, preferable to a populace that does not, no matter how foggy it may be on the details.

The current surge of scientific research interest in environmental change makes an equally welcome change from the time – most of the twentieth century – when academic disciplines concerned themselves little if at all with the human relationship to the earth. The environmental dimension of human existence has long been of minimal interest to the social sciences and humanities. Most of the natural sciences for most of their history have largely ignored the human impact on the globe. Yet a proper understanding of environmental change requires the broadest interdisciplinary cooperation. To understand an environmental change – why human action brings about certain environmental effects – it is necessary to understand both why the human action has the physical consequences that it has and why the action was undertaken. The former question is the domain of the natural and the latter of the social sciences. To understand why the change matters, if it does, one needs again to know both its physical characteristics and the complex ways in which they interact with human populations and activities.

Such cooperation is beginning to emerge. The boundary zone between the natural and social sciences was not long ago a desolate and disreputable strip of territory that scholars from either side frequented unwillingly or at their professional risk. Today, transformed, it is a lively and inviting frontier of research; it hosts a thriving cross-border trade in data, methods, and ideas developed on one side and useful but scarce on the other. The terms of trade, to be sure, are not necessarily equal, being typically weighted in favor of the natural sciences. There occurs much dangerous and unsupervised transfer of methods and techniques that require care in use. Once the province of no field, ignored rather than disputed ground, the boundary zone has like many frontiers become a contested and volatile area, as scholars and disciplines stake claims, often overlapping, and fire on intruders. Yet the gains from their lively interaction outweigh the losses.

The data and research tools available to researchers are still far from adequate to many of the questions asked. Yet they far exceed those available even a few decades ago. "At the time of the Princeton symposium in 1955, planning was underway for the International Geophysical Year (IGY) – the beginning of to-day's worldwide scientific efforts to identify and monitor the key global processes and to measure systematically the effects of human activity." The use of such new technologies as remote sensing (including satellite imagery) has greatly ex-panded the data available on environmental change. Indeed, "the stock of exist-ing information . . . often exceeds the capacity of specialists to analyze it and of generalists to synthesize it" (Kates, Turner, and Clark 1990: 4, 5).

The concepts in use have also become more sophisticated. That nature is stable if not disturbed by humankind was long an axiom of environmental thought. To George Perkins Marsh, natural landscapes displayed "an almost un-changing permanence of form, outline, and proportion." With a few qualifica-tions, he held that "in countries untrodden by man, the proportions and relative positions of land and water, the atmospheric precipitation and evaporation, the thermometric mean, and the distribution of animal and vegetable life, are sub-ject to change only from geological influences so slow in their operation that the geographical conditions may be regarded as constant and immutable" (Marsh [1864] 1965: 29, 35). For Marsh, evidence of change all but equaled evidence of human impact. His Victorian confidence in the equilibrium of the natural world suffused *Man and Nature*. It is probably the aspect of the volume that has dated the most.

For many decades after 1864, to be sure, it dated little if at all. Around the turn of the century, the climax theory developed by plant ecologists pictured natural communities as changing, but not randomly – as tending to evolve to-ward a predictable and stable end state. But among ecologists, climax dogma has in recent times been replaced by recognition of the pervasiveness of fluctuation and disturbance in the natural world. In Marsh's lifetime, geologists were just recognizing the most striking evidence of nature's global-scale instability – that of continental glaciation in the geologically recent past. As modern research has revealed, a great breadth and variety of landscape and vegetational changes have occurred even over the past ten thousand years – since the retreat of the last continental ice sheets – in association with further fluctuations in climate (McDowell, Webb, and Bartlein 1990).

Nature without humankind would not be stable nor even slow and regular in its changes. To be sure, the emerging picture is of a biosphere unstable only compared to the previous static picture, not to popular imaginings; science has not come all the way around to accepting Noah's flood or Velikovsky's comets, and equilibria do occur even though they cannot always be expected. But the shift is a real one, and it has important implications. From some angles, the recognition of natural systems as possibly unstable and subject to abrupt change lessens the relative importance of human impact. From others, however, it adds to the fear that human-induced change may provoke responses from natural systems – ones as vast as the oceans or the global climate – that are surprisingly and unmanageably large and rapid. In any case, without a thorough understanding of how the environment fluctuates, the human element in environmental change cannot be separated from the nonhuman. The problems are greater in some realms than others. Climate and marine fish stocks, to name two, vary so much in nature that the human responsibility for changes observed today can be quite difficult to determine.

Yet disturbances of the physical environment have long included human impacts at local and regional scales. Recognition has grown of the depth and antiquity of our alteration of the earth just as it has grown of the instability of nature. Even many landscapes that look untouched by human hands have histories of reshaping by intensive use. Scientists now ascribe to human authors areas and features once thought the unaided work of nature. Large portions of Amazonia are best understood as "culture forests" altered and indeed enriched by intensive human management in pre-Columbian times, not as the purely natural features some activists seek to protect (Balée 1989). "Primeval wilderness – in the sense of untrodden forests or deserts – exists only in our collective imagination" (Richards 1990: 165). Yet awareness of our power to change the environment has sometimes gone too far. We often credit or blame ourselves for features and events in which we had no part. Hideous "badlands" and beautiful landscapes can be the work of either nature or humankind. It is dangerous to approach questions of environmental history armed only with philosophical preconceptions or aesthetic tastes.

The way in which the terms "environment" and "environmentalism" have largely displaced "conservation" or "preservation" reflects the way in which problems now tend to be seen as interconnected syndromes rather than innumerable isolated challenges. Conservation and preservation had fairly clear and narrow meanings. They denoted, respectively, concern for the efficient use of natural resources and for the protection of natural landscapes and communities. Both dealt largely with changes of a direct and visible nature. "Environmentalism" suggests concern with the entire surroundings of human life. Still more so does the newer term "global environmental change," where "global" has two senses, both apt: world-scale and all-encompassing. The boundaries of the system to be studied and managed have become ever harder to draw, the full consequences of an action ever harder to gauge. Such complex, wide-ranging, and often subtle impacts as pollution, species loss, and climatic change – and their own many further consequences – that figured at most marginally among the concerns of preservationists and conservationists are central to environmentalism.

Marsh's emphasis on the many, varied, and unforeseen results of human actions has been amply borne out in a "growing recognition that everything connects with everything else in an indivisible causal web" (Lowenthal 1990: 127). This recognition sets daunting challenges for research and for management. It becomes difficult to explain any occurrence because of the multitude of near and distant factors – of natural and of human origin – that may have entered into it. Doing something about environmental problems thus becomes harder yet. It is difficult to predict the results of actions in the environment because of the many unforeseen factors that can alter and even reverse the expected outcome. Hence a rational response to an apparent environmental problem is hard to choose because of the unpredictability of its consequences. Some unpleasant surprises are likely to follow even the best-intentioned and best-informed attempts to make a difference for the better.

During the 1960s and 1970s ecologists emphasized to great effect the complexity of the natural world and the possibilities for unforeseen consequences when humankind interferes with it. A sequence of events repeated in many places became a classic ecological cautionary tale. Technologically sophisticated programs of pest control were introduced in agricultural communities, involving chemical spraying to eradicate the insects that damaged crops. New pests appeared and thrived, their usual predators having been thinned severely by the pesticides. Before long, new strains of the old pests emerged that had evolved resistance to the sprays. New chemicals had to be adopted, and the cost of pest control steadily increased even as the value of production declined.

The lesson that ecologists drew was simple and compelling: to try to make the environment better is to risk making it worse. The principle was not a novel one. *Man and Nature* had offered a similar warning based on a similar story a hundred years before. Farmers often persecuted birds who fed on their crops, until it was realized, as Marsh wrote, that "in many instances, the destruction of wild birds has been followed by a great multiplication of noxious insects." It was, Marsh thought, "no longer open to doubt . . . that even the species which consume more or less grain generally make amends, by destroying insects whose ravages would have been still more injurious" ([1864] 1965: 80–81). The point appeared in the book not as a new discovery but as a bit of commonplace environmental wisdom. It had been remarked upon by Benjamin Franklin in the 1750s (Lowenthal 1958, 372–73); it was the basis of Henry Wadsworth Longfellow's 1863 poem "The Birds of Killingsworth" and of bird protection laws in many American states throughout the nineteenth century.

If nature is a complex system, so is society. Perverse effects, unforeseen consequences, and planning disasters are as ubiquitous in the annals of the applied social sciences as in the environmental. Where the two spheres overlap, the complexities of the nonhuman realm are multiplied by those of the human:

> Profoundly complicating our assessment of past human impacts on the environment, or estimates of future ones, is the prevalence of indirect, or second-order, interactions. Much recent policy-oriented research makes us increasingly conscious of them and of resultant uncertainty as to the connection – if any – between intentions and outcomes. In the social sciences, reductionist paradigms are giving way to more pessimistic appraisals of the extent to which the results of large-scale planning and intervention are ever truly predictable. (Adams 1990: x)

Of course not all harmful environmental outcomes are unforeseen, any more than all beneficial outcomes are intended. Arguments about unintended consequences do not owe all of their influence to their intrinsic merit; they doubtless owe some to their usefulness in allowing those responsible for harm to evade responsibility. Not all damage, environmental or social, is inadvertent. It may be done consciously because the doer cannot afford not to do it or because the damage is inflicted on someone else. Outcomes that were not foreseen would not necessarily have been guarded against if they had been. The lesson of unintended consequences is rather that even the best-intentioned of all possible worlds would not necessarily have the best environment unless that world were also perfectly informed about the systems with which it had to deal.

Environmental improvement by human intervention, at any rate, was long seen as the typical case and damage as the exceptional. Certainly it was seen that way at the time of *Man and Nature*. What is "natural" has long been cited rhetorically as a standard of value and a guide to human action. Yet rarely has it been preferred for its own sake. Against the supposed superiority of the natural to the "artificial," John Stuart Mill, Marsh's contemporary, cited alterations of nature that nearly all had to agree were improvements: "the junction by bridges of shores which Nature had made separate . . . the excavation of her wells, the dragging to light of what she has buried at immense depths in the earth; the turning away of her thunderbolts by lightning rods, of her inundations by embankments, of her oceans by breakwaters." And in the moral sphere, argued Mill, there was no point in taking lessons in conduct from nature when "a single hurricane destroys the hopes of a season; a flight of locusts, or an inundation, desolates a district; a trifling chemical change in an edible root, starves a million of people. . . . Everything, in short, which the worst men commit either against life or property is perpetrated on a larger scale by natural agents" (Mill [1874] 1969: 381). When William James in the early 1900s coined the phrase "the moral equivalent of war," it was to urge his countrymen to join "the army enlisted against *Nature*." Even in cultures such as China and pre-Columbian America that have professed or been ascribed a high regard for nature, it is not clear that actions have been any less fervently directed than elsewhere toward reshaping it to meet human wants (Tuan 1968; Smil 1987: 199–200; Turner and Butzer 1992). Around the globe, the physical environment remodeled by human action has long and overwhelmingly been preferred to nature raw. American pioneers of the eighteenth and nineteenth centuries, like those of many other times and places,

> found the untouched environment repugnant, the forests "howling" and "dismal," the prairie a "trackless waste" to be "transformed into fruitful farms and flourishing cities." . . . As it was their mission "to cause the wilderness to bloom and fructify," Genesis 1: 28 was invoked to "subjugate" the "enemy" – the wilderness. Pioneer goals transcended personal gain; they "broke the long chain of savage life" and replaced "primitive barbarism" with "civilization, liberty, and law." . . . (Lowenthal 1990: 122)

15

Such attitudes blinded many to the damage done in the transformation of the land, though never as completely as is sometimes supposed. But the climate of opinion has changed since 1864. One can hardly speak today of the earth as modified or transformed by human action without implying condemnation. It has become a core element of cultural literacy in at least the developed world that the natural is better than the human-altered. We nowadays "take [it] for granted that the notion of conquest [of nature] is deplorable." Environmental change connotes environmental damage; "the most troglodyte industrialist could no longer celebrate mastery over nature as an unalloyed virtue" (Lowenthal 1990: 132). The idea of progress has given way to the idea of decay, or if the exploitation of the physical world is still seen as progress, it is as progress toward an abyss. The notion of some distant past as a lost era of harmony between humankind and nature has flourished in recent times. It is widely recommended that we adopt the supposed environmental attitudes of that time to solve the problems of our own, that we acknowledge that nature knows best.

Marsh's subtitle, "Physical Geography as Modified by Human Action," may have suggested a celebratory theme to his readers in 1864, "modified" implying "conquered" or "tamed" or improved for human use. Yet the volume it headed took no such triumphalist view. Marsh was unusual – though not unique – in his time in emphasizing the waste and the damage inflicted on the earth by human action. Even so, he regarded the earth as necessarily humankind's to modify. For Marsh, the unforeseen consequences of environmental modification taught "the dangers of imprudence and the necessity of caution" ([1864] 1965: 3); the lesson was not to cease modifying but to learn to foresee better. In assessing human impact, he took an admirably balanced and dispassionate view. Documenting and analyzing environmental damage and recommending caution and restraint, he stood apart from the assumptions of a time when to speak of the earth modified by human action was to suggest another rung up the ladder of progress. Though the pendulum has swung to the other side, his middle perspective is no less appropriate today than it was in 1864.

One of the lessons of environmental and social complexity is that sweeping generalizations can easily mislead, because the environmental and social consequences of actions can, and usually do, mingle the positive and negative. All changes are connected, but they are not all connected in the same direction, though it seems often to be supposed that they are. The British elementary school students questioned by Francis et al. (1993) erroneously thought that "keeping beaches clean," "using lead-free petrol," protecting endangered species, and reducing the size of the world's nuclear arsenals would all lessen the greenhouse effect. The older they were, the more certain they were that nuclear energy would make the greenhouse effect more severe than coal would, again apparently classifying all environmentally "undesirable" activities together as equally undesirable in every way, and all "desirable" activities as effective against all problems. It would be nice to believe that good things, environmental and social alike, do naturally go together: that alleviating one environmental change will never make another worse, today's solution never becoming tomorrow's problem; that democratic government is always better for the environment than authoritarianism, or that income equality always benefits and war always harms the environment, that raising the standard of living of the world's poorer countries will bring environmental benefits rather than an environmental price tag, and so on, any of which may be true in many or most cases but cannot be taken for granted. War sometimes devastates environments, but sometimes interrupts peacetime activities that were devastating them. As the economist Robert Solow (1974: 8) observes, concentrated monopolies, however undesirable on economic and political grounds, are "the conservationist's best friend." Because they raise prices, they lower resource demands. It remains a much-debated matter whether and in what circumstances poverty increases or lessens pressure on the resource base. A reasonable assessment of environmental changes can be achieved only by studying them with an open mind as to whether the changes are for the better or the worse – and for what and for whom. Marsh's independence before the assumptions of his time remains one of the most valuable lessons to be learned from reading *Man and Nature*.

Global environmental change is now receiving unprecedented attention because most of it is seen as environmental degradation. But how do we know degradation from simple change or from improvement? From what is sometimes called a "geocentric," a "biocentric," or an "ecocentric" perspective, degradation represents any change from the natural state of the environment. As human observers, though, we are condemned to an anthropocentric viewpoint. In trying to see from nature's point of view, we see all the more like people for attempting not to. If degradation means change for the worse, it cannot be defined ecocentrically because degradation is a standard of value and nature has no such standards. Degradation can be measured only by a yardstick that we make ourselves – which is not to say that wealth or profit or human well-being is the only thing that it can be used to measure. (Even if it did make sense to talk about nature's aversions – and it does not – they clearly would not include global climate change, soil erosion, the creation of deserts, or the extinction of species. All of these human-induced processes are likewise routine natural processes.) Change from the natural state would not be a reasonable definition of degradation even if we could usually define what was or would be the natural state independent of our presence and our past impacts. Clearly there is much in the physical environment that we prize and should prize and much that we do not and should not. Some aspects of nature threaten our very existence and others underpin it. To reify "Nature" – what has been called "the most complex word in the language" (Williams 1976) – and then make it a standard of good or of bad is a guarantee of confusion.

The varied strands of modern environmental thought "have converged, though incompletely, on an emerging, widely shared ethic: to do minimal harm to the biosphere." (The goal might once have been phrased, with a different emphasis, as making sure the biosphere does minimal harm to us.) This ethic has various sources: "in an ontology of the unity of nature . . . in a morality that demands human stewardship . . . or in a pragmatism that acknowledges our dependence on nature's life-support systems" (Kates, Turner, and Clark 1990: 3). But it is less an answer than a restatement of the question. What is harm, and where is the line separating the minimal from the unacceptably large? Consensus in the case of any particular change is not to be expected. To reify "society" or "humankind" and then ask what are or should be its relations with nature is to invite confusion compounded. Different people and groups often have different interests in environmental changes. What is for the conservationist the "excessively" rapid depletion of nonrenewable resources is a short-term boon for the consumer, for whom it means lower prices. Landlocked countries have little to fear from sea-level rise caused by global warming; high-latitude ones can look forward to an expansion of their arable land and an extension of the growing season.

Hence one definition of degradation is any action whose total costs – however calculated – exceed its total benefits – however calculated. A different criterion for distinguishing acceptable change from unacceptable damage, and perhaps the most widely endorsed, is the one known as "sustainability" or "sustainable development." By this standard, environmental degradation equals the unsustainable use of the environment. Yet what it means is exceedingly difficult to specify. The World Commission on Environment and Development, which popularized the term in its 1987 report *Our Common Future,* took "sustainable development" to mean "development that meets the needs of the present without compromising the ability of future generations to meet their own needs" (WCED 1987: 43).

The definition, appealing enough in the abstract, leaves many questions open as to how it is to be applied and over what time scale. "Unsustainability" is equally difficult to define though perhaps easier to illustrate. Writing in the mid-nineteenth century, Marsh ([1864] 1965: 52) drew on the classic imagery of the earth as the home of humankind to offer his readers perhaps the most evocative image ever advanced of unsustainability: "we are," he wrote, "even now, breaking up the floor and wainscoting and doors and window frames of our dwelling, for fuel to warm our bodies and seethe our pottage. " A century and a half has done little to make the concept more rigorous, for the problems in doing so are substantial. Forests can be cut for timber or for fuel faster than they grow back or fisheries be harvested more rapidly than they reproduce. Such rates of use are clearly unsustainable, but only if the goal is to maintain the use. The management term "sustained yield" refers to an amount of a renewable resource that can be extracted without jeopardizing future extraction. It long predates "sustainable development" (and is essentially a conservationist notion where "sustainable development" has an environmentalist dimension to it), but it has a place on the intellectual family tree of the later concept. Some of the practical problems of managing for sustained yield are also those of defining sustainable development. Natural systems fluctuate in ways that managers cannot predict. Fish stocks occasionally explode or collapse without human interference; forests succumb to new pests or diseases or to high winds or fire; unexpected droughts bedevil water-supply managers. If natural processes cannot yet be reliably predicted, the social changes that alter the nature of natural resources – and hence the sustainability of their value and use – are more elusive yet.

Zimmermann (1951: 9–11) countered the belief that "resources are" with the assertion that "resources become." Changes in technology and social organization create and define usefulness and scarcity in biophysical features of the environment. And not only do resources become, but through the same social processes, they cease to be; they are destroyed as resources without ceasing to exist physically. To maintain or sustain a resource about to be devalued by technical innovation makes no more sense than to hold onto stock in a company that one knows is about to go bankrupt. If the welfare of the future is the issue, one will pass on more wealth by doing the opposite. The strong possibility exists that a natural resource will not run short before it is no longer needed. Or if a shortage does become apparent, it will send price signals that will encourage the development and adoption of substitutes. (There is, to be sure, an ambiguity to be kept in mind in the use of terms like "scarcity." In the economic sense, all resources are always scarce because human wants are unlimited, yet at the same time the "supply" of any resource, however small the quantity that exists, never fails to meet the "demand," considered as the amount exchanged at the price agreed upon.)

A half-century ago, the economist Joseph Schumpeter (1939: 242) knew of only "one major case . . . in which a raw material had time to approach exhaustion before being replaced by something else." It had occurred in early industrializing England, a "scarcity of timber that entailed high and rising prices." Responses included both "various measures for the protection of forests" and the replacement of wood by coal and by iron for different uses. Even in this case, the resource shortage may have done little more than hasten what would have occurred anyway. At the time the substitution was made, "both the use of coal and the use of iron without wood would have been profitable without [the timber scarcity]." There have been other examples, if perhaps not "major" ones in Schumpeter's sense. Yet large-scale shifts in resource use seem to have been, and seem still to be, much more often pulled by technical change than they are pushed by resource depletion. In the modern world, resource extraction is doubtless more rapid than ever before, but so are the innovation and substitution that keep the pressure of extraction shifting from one resource to the next.

The twentieth-century story of one tract of land neatly illustrates the theme. The Harvard Forest lies in the north-central Massachusetts town of Petersham (50 km from Worcester, the site of the "Earth Transformed" symposium). At the turn of the century the forest was "a pioneer research and education program and an early American center for experiments with new notions of sustainable yields and multiple use in forestry. As a major research station, it drew upon the very best in scientific forestry; as a gift to Harvard University, it was required to be self-supporting." "The early managers tried to maintain the forest as they found it . . . not understanding at the time that they were actually trying to stabilize a forest in succession. Even where they succeeded in maintaining pine stands, they husbanded them, cutting only an equivalent to the portion grown on a sustainable basis from year to year." Unexpected natural disturbances interfered, one of them catastrophic: "The bulk of this carefully maintained inventory was lost in the hurricane of 1938. The economic worth of the forest fared just as poorly. When Harvard took over the forest, it was within the center of the country's wooden-box industry. The timber continued to grow in value, to a high in 1923, but was worth virtually nothing by 1940" as a result of industrial and technological changes that made the valuable resource valueless. In short, even "the very best scientists of any time may only poorly understand the fundamental processes governing nature, society, and the relations between them" (Kates, Turner, and Clark 1990: 14–15).

This tale is not a counsel of despair but a goad to do better. Viewing the environmental changes of the present in the light of the past is not sufficient for understanding and managing the future, but it may offer insights that are necessary for that endeavor. The goal of the *Earth Transformed* project and volume was to undertake a broad overview of the human impact on the biosphere. A global-scale, long-term assessment of the full array of important impacts offers a valuable perspective on the nature of contemporary change. The relative weights of different transformations, let alone strategies for their management, cannot be determined by looking individually at one seeming crisis after another; instead, one must examine the net impact over the long term on the various realms of the environment.

An approach that is global in both senses of the word – that is, both world-scale and integrated – offers some of the same opportunities and pitfalls that accompany a long time scale of inquiry. Globally significant environmental changes cannot be properly assessed in an anecdotal approach with its appeal to illustration and example that may be typical or characteristic but may be quite exceptional. Changes that provide the most striking illustrations may yet pose insignificant threats to human well-being at the world scale. Resources for managing risks are always scarce, and only a comparative and broad-focus approach can hope to give priority to the direst threats. Rarely, however, does a global scale of inquiry suffice. Even the global changes that are most physically uniform across the globe – such as the evenly diffused increase in carbon dioxide levels – will vary considerably in their regional impacts according to the differing physical and social systems with which they interact. And most changes of a worldwide magnitude are quite unevenly distributed. If a global view is necessary to address some questions, so is a constant contrasting of the global aggregates with regional and local variations.

After several decades of intensive study, the materials existed in the late 1980s for another inventory of the human impact on the earth, one more quantitative than *Man and Nature* or *Man's Role*. "The exact measurement of the geographical changes" brought about by human action, Marsh wrote, is "impracticable, and we possess, in relation to them, the means of only qualitative, not quantitative analysis" ([1864] 1965: 19–20). Today it is less impracticable even if not perfectly attainable. The *Earth Transformed* project's goal of a global, three-century stocktaking of change was an ambitious one. Here and there the assessment proved impossible to achieve in quantitative terms. Difficulties exist even in making reliable estimates of the current size of some resource or flow, to say nothing of estimating how much it has been changed from some prior condition. Yet in many if not all important areas, the general story of how humankind has remade the planet on which it lives can be recovered and told, and that story forms the core of this book.

2

Changes in Population and Society

That humankind profoundly alters its terrestrial surroundings is not a new idea. How and why it does so is no new question. The search for the human driving forces of environmental transformation, especially of environmental damage, is an ancient one. "Environmental catastrophism" is David Lowenthal's term for the fear that people's unwise actions or even their impious thoughts will devastate the natural world on which they depend. It is a long-standing fear; as Lowenthal observes, "many premoderns attributed environmental change more readily to human agency than to nature, God, or chance" (Lowenthal 1990: 121). In early Christianity and well into the Renaissance and the Reformation, the earth was seen as a world in decay, its fallen condition a result and a reminder of Adam's sin. The notion still had some currency, in seventeenth-century Europe, that the earth's axis had been straight before the Fall; divine punishment had taken the form of global climate change. A character in Shakespeare (*As You Like It*) spoke of "the penalty of Adam, / The seasons' difference." Milton dramatized the idea in *Paradise Lost*. When Adam sins, the earth's axis, previously straight, is tilted, and where once "the Spring / Perpetual smil'd on Earth with vernant Flowers," the fallen planet is now afflicted with "cold and heat / Scarce tollerable" (Carey and Fowler 1968: 959–61).

In short, "we are far from being the first civilization to realise that our environment is at risk" (M. Douglas 1975: 230). "Most tribal environments are held to be in danger in much the same way as ours. . . . Always and everywhere it is human folly, hate and greed which puts the human environment at risk." So too, many modern lists of driving forces of environmental change resemble nothing so much as the catalog of the seven deadly sins. Lust appears as overpopulation, envy and gluttony as affluence or mass consumption, pride as Western technological hubris elevating humankind over the natural world, and so on. The moral dimension is important in arousing concern. Support is more easily mobilized

22

when there are clear villains than when there are not, even if they turn out to be us. But unexamined, moralizing can also be an important source of confusion. It carries with it a tendency to confuse good or bad intentions with good or bad results, and irrelevant considerations with vital ones.

The most useful attempts to locate the human sources of contemporary global change invoke not personal sins of thought and behavior but the broader (and more manageable) variables of collective organization. The physical transformation of the earth has been accompanied and driven by social changes no less remarkable. Three hundred years ago, the earth was the home of about 700 million people; more than seven people are alive today, and at a vastly higher standard of living, for every one alive in 1700. Less than 10% of the population then lived in cities; close to half now do. The largest city of 1700, Istanbul, contained 700,000 people. Today's largest urban complex, the Tokyo region, holds 23,000,000, and there are hundreds of cities more populous than Istanbul was in 1700. Distant places are more closely linked than ever; during the past century alone, the tonnage of international seaborne freight per capita has increased about sevenfold. Per capita energy use has grown by about 10 times. The world's industrial capacity has grown by 20 times since 1900 and by 75 since 1800. Other changes in global society cannot be so simply quantified but represent or have represented real transformations nonetheless: the industrial and technological revolutions, the eras of global exploration, colonialism, and decolonization, the spreading democratization of political life, the successive world primacy of various nations, economic depressions and wars of growing spatial scale, the simultaneous spread of market systems and growth of state power and authority. Many separate changes can be summed up as two: first, growth – demographic, technological, and economic, all tightly interwoven; and second, "globalization," the closer connections and mutual impacts of all parts of the earth's surface.

Individual societal changes have many obvious and many subtle connections to environmental change, but some sorting out of the more from the less important ones would be useful. What are the main human driving forces of global environmental change? The most influential line of argument identifies them as humankind's growth in numbers, in affluence, and in technological capacity. The most influential alternative arguments insist in various ways on the importance of economic, political, and social institutions.

POPULATION, AFFLUENCE, AND TECHNOLOGY

One formula for distinguishing the sources of human impact was introduced by Ehrlich and Holdren (1971) and is now widely used. It notes that human pressure or impact on the environment, I, is equal to demand on the earth's resources per person (A, for affluence) times the number of people (P, for population) times the impact per unit of resource use, a factor of technology (T): $I =$

23

PAT. In that form, it is simply a mathematical identity, but it has often been taken in a broader sense as indicating that high levels of impact are likely to be associated with large and/or affluent human populations. Higher populations and standards of consumption (high values of *P* and *A*), the formula indicates, lead – all else being equal – to greater impact on the environment. Changes in technology (*T*) can independently raise or lower impact by making resource use more or less efficient.

Prevailing trends in population, affluence, and technology have long represented the three most persuasive arguments for the reality of social progress. Belief in progress, for centuries a cornerstone of Western thought, found its securest prop in the material advances embodied in the extraction of resources and the transformation of the landscape to support growing numbers. The horrors of what people did to one another might persist, but what they did to the world around them represented all but unassailable evidence of improvement. For most of modern history, increases in numbers, wealth, and technological capacity have been seen as unalloyed advances. If they caused environmental change, it was change for the better. They now tend to be seen as the three horsemen of environmental apocalypse, the most prominent candidate causes of environmental change seen as change for the worse. No longer does the earth seem vast and inexhaustible in the face of the demands that they can place on it.

POPULATION

The simple curve of world population growth over the past ten thousand years suggests that ours is a period of dramatic and unprecedented change (see Figure 2.1). We have indeed been fruitful and multiplied. It took the vast span of prehistory plus most of recorded time for human numbers to reach one billion (the American billion, equal to 1,000 million, is used throughout this book), early in the nineteenth century. Hardly more than a century was then required to add the second billion. The earth's population doubled between 1950 and 1985, from 2.5 billion to 5 billion, rising to 5.8 billion by 1995. Some 8 billion is the figure that is conservatively projected for the year 2020, and demographers do not expect population growth to cease short of 10 to 12 billion – about twice the present total.

There is no doubting the rough accuracy of these figures. Yet although population data are better than most data on global environmental or social change, they are less than perfect. Censuses go back centuries in some parts of the world, but regular and reliable ones are modern phenomena. Where such figures are not to be had, population must be estimated on other bases. Some of the methods of estimation, used for prehistory, are very indirect indeed, and often dependent on contentious assumptions. Still, archaeological relics or the traces of settlement and cultivation can give rough ideas as to the size of the groups

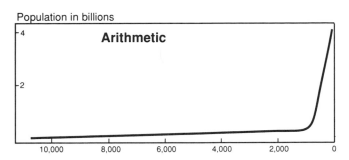

Figure 2.1 World population growth since 10,000 B.P. (arithmetic plot). Source: Demeny.

involved. The reliability of the estimates often diminishes the farther back we go. They may vary widely. Modern scholarly estimates of the aboriginal population of the New World in 1492, for example, have ranged from 14 million to 72 million (Whitmore et al. 1990: 37n). (Numbers toward the higher end of this spectrum are now considered the more likely.) It is an extreme case, but it illustrates problems that are widespread. Prediction of the future and "postdiction" of the past, though, are aided by the inertia, continuity, and predictability of demographic change, at least as compared with other social phenomena. Yet forecasts remain always subject to revision as the complex determinants of demographic behavior change.

Today it is for most people an almost automatic assumption – and indeed a safe one – that the population of the world and of any major region within it is larger at a later time than earlier. Population increases, like price increases, are taken for granted, with the difference that whereas real prices more often fall than rise over time, demographic expansion is genuine and not merely apparent. Such confidence in rising numbers – pessimism, it may seem now – was not so common in the Europe of several centuries ago. The notion dated back to classical times that the earth was a world in decline already long past its peak years of childbearing. It retained currency even in the eighteenth century. Hume ([1752] 1907) could allude in the mid-1700s to the notion of "that superior populousness of antiquity, which is commonly supposed." He devoted an essay to attacking the widely accepted claim of his contemporary, the French political philosopher Montesquieu, that "there are not now, on the face of the earth, the fiftieth part of mankind, which existed in the time of Julius Caesar." The world total in 1700, in fact, was higher than it had ever been, and has never ceased to grow since, but the numbers to prove it were not available at that time. Fresh in Europe's collective memory were examples of severe regional declines: at home, from the Black Death and other epidemics and from the Thirty Years' War, in the New World, in the melting away of indigenous populations after contact. Local overpopulation and pressure on resources were far from unknown, as were folk

25

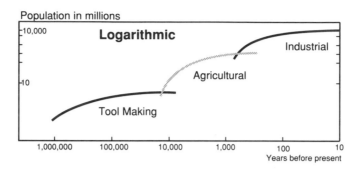

Figure 2.2 World population growth since 1,000,000 B.P. (logarithmic plot). Source: Whitmore et al. 1990.

means for keeping birth rates low and limiting the numbers of the community to a level that their use of the land could support. Yet situations existed too where keeping up the level of population presented real challenges.

In no large region of the world is it a challenge today. At mid-century and still in the mid-1980s, the average annual rate of increase in the world population was 1.8%. We live in the midst of an episode of growth never before known and that it is hard to imagine ever being repeated. The modern global arithmetic curve of population makes a compelling image of worldwide growth out of control. The mathematics of exponential expansion are familiar enough. A population rising at the constant rate of 1% per year will double in 70 years; at 2%, in 35; at even the seemingly modest rate of 3%, in a mere quarter-century. "Two populations, starting with the same initial stock but one growing at a 2 percent annual rate and the other stationary, will be, in 100 years, in a 7:1 numerical ratio to each other. In 250 years, the growing population would be 148 times larger than the stationary population." In short, "over time, seemingly glacial change can rapidly cumulate into major shifts in size and structure" (Demeny 1990: 42).

Yet some different perspectives on the same data qualify the first overwhelming impression of unmanageable growth. One comes from the work of Deevey (1960). He graphed the rough data and projections of long-term world population on a logarithmic rather than an arithmetic scale (see Figure 2.2). What appears is not a slow and steady rise culminating in a modern explosion, but a pattern of two past and one ongoing global period of expansion and leveling off. The rises coincide with the three great technological revolutions in human society: the invention of tools, the development of agriculture, and the Industrial Revolution beginning in the eighteenth century. A possibility that this picture raises is that each great transformation of society may raise the globe's human carrying capacity to some new plateau. Population rises to that height and stabilizes; what happened twice in the past may happen again.

But Deevey's picture too is a global aggregate one. The regional disaggregation of global totals and trends almost always offers insights that qualify broader-scale approaches. Demographic history is no exception. Long-term reconstructions of population change within particular areas reveal episodes of severe decline as well as of rapid growth over the past several thousand years. Whitmore et al. (1990) document "millennial long waves" of human numbers in four ancient-settled regions: the Tigris-Euphrates lowlands, the Egyptian Nile Valley, the Basin of Mexico, and the central Maya Lowlands. Each experienced at least one substantial and sustained demographic collapse from a previous peak during pre-modern times. The population of the Tigris-Euphrates, for instance, dropped from 1.5 million in A.D. 550 to a mere 10% of that figure 750 years later. In the Basin of Mexico, a halving of the total between A.D. 650 and 1150 prefigured the fall, much larger in both absolute numbers and proportions, that the region would experience during the sixteenth and early seventeenth centuries after the Spanish conquest. Modern numbers in three of these areas have considerably outstripped the previous peak totals. The central Maya Lowlands of the Yucatán Peninsula, on the other hand, peaked at some three million inhabitants during the Maya Classic Period in A.D. 800; the area's population was less than seven thousand at the beginning of the twentieth century and even in the late 1980s did not exceed a hundred thousand. (It is an unusual case, to be sure.)

Regional declines of comparable size have not occurred in the modern era, though smaller areas have experienced depopulation for various reasons: disease, emigration, war. The world population over the past three centuries has not declined at all. Its expansion can be divided into two unequal eras (see Figure 2.3). The first spanned the two and a half centuries from 1700 to 1950. It saw total numbers increase from almost 700 million at the outset to 2.5 billion. The most dramatic change was the substantial expansion of the population of the Western Hemisphere. North America – "a virtual demographic vacuum in 1700" (Demeny 1990: 44) – rose to a respectable place on the world population map, and the South and Central American population more than recovered from its fall from the pre-Columbian peak. Changes in other parts of the world helped to smooth, though by no means did they erase, the density gradients across the globe. The population of Africa only doubled, dropping from 16% of the world's total to less than 10%; the population of Europe, on the other hand, grew by four times and that of the twentieth-century USSR by six. This growth swelled a large outflow of European migrants to other regions, largely to the Western Hemisphere (Demeny 1990: 43–45).

The second major era – which has also been one of much better data collection – began after the end of World War II. An unprecedented global rate of growth brought about a doubling in world population, from 2.5 to 5 billion, in the three and a half decades from 1950 to 1985. Part of this rise, though a minor part, stemmed from the brief upturn of birth rates in the developed countries, where they had declined – the phenomenon known as the baby boom in the United States – though rates then fell again after a decade or two. Far more

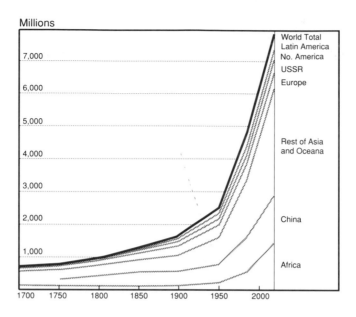

Figure 2.3 World population growth, 1700–1985 and projected to 2020. Sourcer: Demeny 1990.

significant globally was a "radical acceleration" in growth in the developing world. Between 1950 and 1985, annual rates of increase in Africa, Asia, and Latin America exceeded 2%, in contrast to much slower growth in the wealthier world: 1.2% in North America, less than 1% in Europe and the Soviet Union (Demeny 1990: 47–49).

Such trends formed nearly a mirror image of what the earlier growth patterns had been. Between 1750 and 1800, for example, North America, Europe, and Russia led the world in expansion. Between 1850 and 1900 those three regions, along with Latin America, again exceeded the world average growth rate. Asia and Africa fell below it; indeed, the population of China, ravaged by war, disaster, and famine, did not increase at all during that half-century. Today growth is near zero in the developed world, even as numbers in the developing nations continue to rise rapidly. Projections for growth through the year 2020 sharply differentiate the developing regions – roughly, Africa, Asia, and Latin America – from the developed world (see Figure 2.4). It is in the former that virtually all of the growth expected to occur between now and then will occur.

The continents have waxed and waned in their relative shares of the world's numbers in the past three centuries, but have preserved some relative stability. Asia has never held less than half of the world's population and in 1800 held only a hair less than two-thirds; its modern share is about 58%. China alone in 1850 was the home of a third of the world's people and still holds more than a fifth.

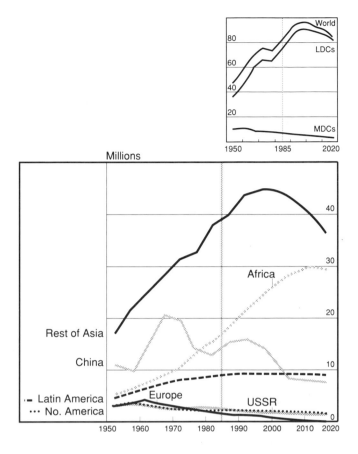

Figure 2.4 Average annual population increase (millions), 1950–85, and projections, 1985–2020. Source: Demeny 1990.

North and South America together, on the other hand, have never held as much as 15% of the world total (Demeny 1990).

What accounts for the modern changes in numbers? Global population changes are simply the sum of the birth rate and the death rate (regional ones also include in- and out-migration). The modern global explosion in numbers reflects a more rapid overall drop in mortality than in fertility. A conceptual framework known as the theory of the demographic transition offers the most coherent available synthesis of population history. Developed from an interpretation of the experience of Western Europe, the theory postulates three phases. In a *premodern* phase, high birth and death rates stand in approximate balance; the high mortality imposed by circumstances is just matched by a high level of births to maintain or at most slowly increase the size of the population. In a *modern* phase, for a variety of reasons mortality falls while fertility remains high, resulting in rapid growth. *Postmodern* fertility falls to a level again more or less in balance with mortality, and numbers stabilize.

Like Deevey's graph, this theory suggests the existence of a natural regulatory mechanism, a means by which explosive growth will eventually subside. At the global level, something of the sort has indeed been occurring, without by any means having completed its course. In 1950 and 1985 alike, the global rate of increase was 1.8%. In the earlier year, it was the sum of birth and death rates of 38 and 20 per thousand; in the later, of the much lower rates of 28 and 10. Birth rates have been falling, though thus far only fast enough to keep up with reduced mortality. Have the subpopulations of the world followed the predicted pattern, and if so, has it been for the reasons that the theory suggests? On ever-closer inspection, the adequacy of the demographic transition model has been brought into question. As Demeny (1990: 46) writes of the period before 1950:

> That this stylized model captures some essential features of world population history . . . is evident. Mortality typically led the process of change, fertility decline lagged, and the growth potential inherent in [high] premodern fertility levels was triggered. . . . It is equally clear, however, that the pattern of transitions, country by country or region by region, exhibited variations too great to permit simple generalizations about the path already travelled, let alone to encourage confident predictions concerning developments to come.

These regional and national variations have remained significant. In the past several decades, rapid fertility declines have occurred in Asia and in Latin America – as the theory would predict – and yet high fertility has persisted in Africa, the third of the largely developing continents. Different nations within each region also show considerable variation.

The changes driving the first stage of the transition, that of declining deaths and continued high births, are supposed to be ones of improved nutrition brought by intensification of agriculture, increased social and personal wealth, and improved public health. The most controversial aspect of the theory is the predicted modern-to-postmodern decline in fertility. In modernizing urban-industrial societies, it is usually argued, children become much less of an economic asset and more of a liability than they were in premodern, largely agrarian ones. Their upbringing becomes expensive compared to the value of their labor. Deeply entrenched premodern norms that had favored numerous births erode, and rates of birth decline toward those of death. The "demographic transition" thus occurs from a phase of explosive growth to one approaching stability. In the light of wide variations in fertility patterns, however, many factors other than the level of economic development have become apparent that encourage smaller families. They include improvements in the status and reproductive rights of women, the availability of reliable social security systems that lessen the need to have many children as a form of old-age insurance, and the availability and ac-

30

ceptability of reliable contraceptives. The map of these factors, and hence of their demographic consequences, is far more complex than a simple one of supposed stages of development.

As for the evaluation of change, the prospect of underpopulation or of too slow growth has for much of human history evoked fears at least as strong as those that overpopulation now produces. Most of the time in most places during the past three centuries, pronatalist policies and attitudes directly encouraging a high birth rate have been the rule, though it is not clear that they have been very effective. Governments have typically thought it to their advantage to have more taxpayers, workers, and soldiers. Much of population-related thought and policy has emphasized the nationalistic, ethnic, and racial importance of increasing "our" numbers against "theirs" and of increasing or at least maintaining "our" share of the world or regional or local total. Yet concern over excess numbers is not new. Island dwellers, and indeed other groups living in lands of clearly restricted resources – which is to say, much of the premodern world population – long had ways, ranging from contraception to infanticide to warfare, to balance births and deaths when natural checks did not prove adequate. Educated opinion in postmedieval England swung back and forth for several centuries on the question of whether the kingdom held too many people or too few. Interest in overseas colonization as a government policy was strongly stimulated by a belief in the sixteenth and early seventeenth centuries that England was overpopulated (Knorr 1944). "Our multitudes like too much blood in the body, do infect our country with plague and poverty, our land hath brought forth, but it hath not milk sufficient in the breast thereof to nourish all those children which it has brought forth," ran a typical complaint in 1609. Opinion went to the other extreme after the mid-seventeenth century. It then reverted to a fear of overcrowding in the first half of the nineteenth century, in part under the influence of the writings of Thomas Robert Malthus. With Malthus and his focus on the food supply, in the *Essay on the Principle of Population* (first edition, 1798), that theme – whether accepted or disputed – became the organizing principle of debate.

Malthus's model of the population–resources relationship exceeds even the demographic transition theory in simplicity (also, not surprisingly, in its ability to arouse controversy). The English thinker began with a few basic principles: population has an inherent tendency, rooted in human nature, to increase. It is capable of increasing in the short term much faster than the means for its subsistence can be increased. The upward pressure of numbers will thus always be hitting painfully against the ceiling of food supply in recurrent crises of subsistence. The disasters of famine will be varied only by those of war or disease – or, to Malthus, the morally objectionable ones of birth control – bringing population back in line with the capacity of the land to support it.

Malthus holds a commanding position in the conservationist tradition of concern over the earth's supply of a scarce and vital resource. Modern "neo-Malthusian" arguments extend the pessimism of the British thinker beyond the realm of

31

food supply to suggest the limits of any number of vital resources, including the earth's capacity to absorb pollutants. They blend a wider conservationism with a modern environmentalism. Neo-Malthusians cite the "population explosion" as the prime cause of environmental crisis and the most basic threat to the sustainable occupation of the earth. For Ehrlich (1968: 66–67), writing in the late 1960s, there was unity beneath the seeming diversity of our problems: "The causal chain of the deterioration is easily followed to its source. Too many cars, too many factories, too much detergent, too much pesticide . . . inadequate sewage treatment plants, too little water, too much carbon dioxide – all can be traced easily to *too many people.*"

Even lists of the basic driving forces of environmental transformation that deal with other contributing factors usually begin with population growth. The editors of the *Earth Transformed* volume felt that "it is difficult not to conclude that population growth has been the first-tier driving force of environmental change throughout the history of humankind" (Kates, Turner, and Clark 1990: 11). Many, perhaps most, authorities would agree. The rationale is simple. If all else – per capita consumption, technological capacity, and so on – remains equal, every increase in numbers increases the demand on the earth's resources and the emission of wastes; it subtracts further from a finite store of what we need and adds to a mounting stock of what we discard. Furthermore, any increase in per capita consumption or waste emission is multiplied by the size of the population. It lies beyond a reasonable doubt that the human population that the earth's resources – however ingeniously used – can support is limited. It is equally incontestable that where population nears that global "carrying capacity," whatever it may be, any increase in the level of consumption would reduce the population that could be supported, and vice versa. Not only is the argument for population's role plausible, but it has some support in the few studies that have sought to correlate environmental against demographic change. Over the past three decades, for example, a near-perfect mathematical relationship has been claimed between annual global population and the annual rise in the atmospheric concentration of carbon dioxide (Newell and Marcus 1987).

Clearly, however, the matter is not as simple and mechanical as such a finding might suggest. Not only population, but other possible social forces of change have increased immensely in the pressure that they put on the biosphere over the same period. At the very least, the impact of every new member of the human species cannot be equated with a fixed average level of demand, because per capita resource use and waste emissions vary greatly across the planet. Even those most insistent on the importance of population depict environmental impact as a function not of population alone, but of consumption and technology: hence the $I = PAT$ formula rather than simply $I = P$. And if population growth increases demands on the environment if other things remain equal, whether other things do remain equal in the face of population growth is another question and not an unimportant one.

The phrase "limits to growth," popular in the 1970s, reflected the neo-Malthusian position. That ultimately such limits exist is questioned by few, but whether that concept offers the best approach to explaining human–environment relations in the recent past and the present is not clear. One criticism, distrustful even of the notion of set natural limits to growth, derives from what is sometimes called the cornucopian view. It sees population not as the ultimate depleter of resources but as itself "the ultimate resource" (Simon 1981), population as a driving force of environmental change but of change for the better. A world of 6 billion people is a world incomparably superior to the long-distant one of a few million hunter-gatherers; the increased levels of population are at once the effect and the best evidence of an earth greatly improved by human action, and a higher population means a greater amount of labor and ingenuity available to meet problems and provide solutions in the future. As for limited resources, the resources available to the future cannot be specified in any way that would justify a prediction of scarcity, because our very knowledge of the resources we possess is closely conditioned by our need to investigate them and by the techniques that we have available to exploit them. A second criticism of neo-Malthusianism attributes most poverty, most famines, and most evidences of resource scarcity not to any physical limits or shortages of absolute supply, but to inequities in distribution. Many countries experiencing famine are not overpopulated beyond their carrying capacity, for they export food at the same time. The sustenance that they require physically exists but exceeds the purchasing power of their inhabitants. Both criticisms represent significant challenges; both can be pressed too far. The latter comes close to arguing that because shortages in some cases are not purely physical they are never physical at all; the cornucopian position, that because growth in numbers is desirable in some contexts it is always so.

AFFLUENCE

In the $I = PAT$ formula, affluence has a specific meaning: per capita consumption. Multiplied by the number of consumers and the technological impacts of their activities, it produces the total drain on the earth's resources, the total burden of wastes on the earth's absorptive capacity. Like population in the same equation, affluence in this sense indeed makes a plausible driving force: surely the more that people extract from a finite earth, the more the earth will be altered and the more it will be depleted.

Like population, per capita consumption has risen dramatically in the past three centuries, and like population, it is today quite unevenly distributed over the earth's surface. The most basic measure of affluence or poverty is food consumption. It can be assessed in terms of amount and in terms of reliability. By both measures, the standard of living has increased across the world in the past three centuries, and both measures show substantial variation across space today. "Before the growth of agricultural productivity and real incomes in Western Europe during the nineteenth century, few countries had supplies over 2,300 calories per capita per day" (Grigg 1993: 253). The figure for the developed world today is about 3,400. For the developing countries, on the other hand, it is only about 2,400, and a much higher proportion of the daily fare is made up of starchy staples – cereals and roots (Grigg 1993).

Differences in food consumption across time and space are relatively modest; there are biological limits on how much even the most affluent person can eat. Per capita levels of consumption of other resources show much wider disparities: timber, energy, minerals, metals. As regards commercial energy, for example, today, if impact is equated with level of consumption,

> a baby born in the United States registers twice the destructive impact on Earth's ecosystems and the services they provide as one born in Sweden, 3 times one born in Italy, 13 times one born in Brazil, 35 times one in India, 140 times one in Bangladesh or Kenya, and 280 times one in Chad, Rwanda, Haiti, or Nepal. (Ehrlich and Ehrlich 1990: 134)

It follows that a low and meager standard of living, if not desirable in itself, is nonetheless not undesirable environmentally. It follows also that countries with a high standard of living may make disproportionately large contributions to global environmental change even if their populations are relatively small. International environmental polemics often pit developed-world claims that population growth is the principal threat to the globe against developing-world claims that the principal threat is developed-world consumption.

But if affluence makes a plausible driving force, so in some ways does its opposite: poverty. Countries with high rates of consumption tend also to be ones that have been relatively successful in protecting their environments: in preserving or replanting their forests, in safeguarding threatened species, in conserving soil and water resources, and in controlling pollution and other environmental health risks; whereas the most serious environmental problems today are concentrated in less affluent countries: the Third World and the former Eastern Bloc. The wealthier a country, the better able it is to pay for environmental protection, and the more important environmental protection is likely to seem once other basic needs have been satisfied. What are sometimes called "postmaterial" values depend on a high level of material assurance. If the *PAT* formula suggests that everyone ought to become less affluent, this line of argument concludes that everyone should become more so. There is not lacking a response: that the developed world keeps its own nest clean only by fouling the developing world's and sustains its resource base only by plundering the rest of the globe; that for the entire world population to live at the standard expected by the wealthy countries would be environmentally catastrophic. It is argued in turn that industrialized-world mass consumption supports Third World economies and that a sudden shift to frugality would devastate them. Again, as with population, the role of affluence defies easy formulations that will fit all cases. Again, though, as there undoubtedly exist limits to the numbers that the earth can support, so too must the material level at which they can be supported be finite.

TECHNOLOGICAL CHANGE

The principal reason for identifying the driving forces of damage is to seek to reverse them. Affluence seems to be by far the least promising of the *PAT* variables to try to stem. It is almost by definition something that people who lack want to have and that people who have want to keep. By contrast, technology, whether or not it is the best target for intervention, certainly makes the most appealing (Commoner 1994: 76). Efforts abound to restrict technologies that magnify environmental impact and to encourage those that reduce it.

A satisfactory definition of technology is not easy to come by. Too narrow a scope obscures the range of human activities that can be grouped under that title as having an essentially common character. Too broad a meaning makes the term a vacuously inclusive one simply synonymous with purposeful or rational human action of any sort – walking or breathing, for example. In the $I = PAT$ formula, it is the independent environmental impact associated with the ways in which resources are processed for use and disposed of as wastes. Technology "is a means whereby humans use nature for their own benefit" (Headrick 1990: 55); it is the knowledge of cause-and-effect relationships that allows people to bring about desired changes in their physical environment. At the same time, it is always partial and incomplete knowledge. As such, it leads people in using it to effect other changes that they do not desire or did not foresee.

If world population is said to have "exploded," there is no term adequate to describe the growth of technology. A quantitative measure, though, is not easily found. Industrial capacity is one convenient if imperfect index of society's technological capacity; as mentioned already, it has grown 20-fold during this century alone (see Table 2.1). Energy use is another; global per capita energy consumption between 1870 and the mid-1980s rose more than 10-fold (Simmons 1991: 38). Yet energy use is a particularly inadequate surrogate, for new technologies that reduce energy need are increasingly important and valuable aspects of innovation as energy becomes more costly in itself and in the secondary impacts of its generation and use. Innovation, a more elusive thing, is what one would want to measure.

If a world curve could be drawn for the degree of technical innovation over the past three centuries, it would no doubt look a good deal like those for population and affluence. We live in an age when invention is produced almost as rationally and predictably as any other social output, heavily financed and encouraged by governments and corporations alike. And like the curves for population and wealth, that of innovation would presumably also show significant differences if regionally disaggregated. Explaining technological change as a driving force is a complex matter and one outside the realm of this volume. It

Table 2.1. *World total industrial potential, 1750–1980 (U.K. in 1900 = 100)*

	1750	1800	1830	1860	1880	1900	1913	1928	1938	1953	1963	1973	1980
DEVELOPED	34	47	73	143	253	481	863	1259	1562	2870	4699	8432	9718
U.K.	2	6	18	45	73	100	127	135	181	258	330	462	441
Germany	4	5	7	11	27	71	138	158	214	180	330	550	590
France	5	6	10	18	25	37	57	82	74	98	194	328	362
Italy	3	4	4	6	8	14	23	37	46	71	150	258	319
Russia/U.S.S.R.	6	8	10	16	25	48	77	72	152	328	760	1345	1630
U.S.A.		1	5	16	47	128	298	533	528	1373	1804	3089	3475
Japan	5	5	5	6	8	13	25	45	88	88	264	819	1001
THIRD WORLD	93	99	112	83	67	60	70	98	122	200	439	927	1323
China	42	49	55	44	40	34	33	46	52	71	178	369	553
India	31	29	33	19	9	9	13	26	40	52	91	194	254
WORLD	127	147	184	226	320	541	933	1356	1684	3070	5138	9359	11041

Source: Bairoch 1982: 292,299; reprinted from Headrick 1990.

Notes: These figures include handicrafts as well as industrial manufacturing. Figures are rounded off. Triennial annual averages except for 1913, 1928, and 1938. India includes Pakistan.

requires an explanation not only of the innovation itself – for which the old saw "necessity is the mother of invention" is anything but adequate – but also of its adoption on a large enough scale to have important environmental effects.

Humankind's major direct impacts on the environment can be classed roughly as those of agriculture and industry. Technological change has played a major role in both. Agricultural technologies have been evolving since the domestication of plants and animals in prehistory, accelerating in the past several centuries. Deliberate transfers of species from one locale to another for cultivation have redrawn the map of the world's biogeography; irrigation and drainage through ever-more powerful machines have opened up vast new areas for farmland. The very line between agriculture and industry has blurred as the highly mechanized cultivation on which today's populations depend has become yet another branch of intensive science-based technology. Such key elements as artificial fertilizers, pesticides, and now biotechnologically engineered crop strains (plus such affiliated advances as transportation improvements that link producers to new markets) have been central to the expansion of production to meet new demands. They have had manifold environmental consequences, large and small, of their own.

The history of industrial technology proper at a world scale for the past three centuries is that of the successive development and spread of several clusters of innovations. The first is the one that has gone down in history as the beginning of the Industrial Revolution; it had its origins in late eighteenth-century Great Britain. The innovations that distinguished it were primarily in textile manufacturing, still dependent on water or wind or animal power. The second phase of the Industrial Revolution saw the application of steam power to a variety of activities: manufacturing, transportation (railroads and shipping), pumping water, and so on. Toward the close of the nineteenth century, a cluster of three new industries – steel, chemicals, and electricity – made its appearance, the center of innovation and early development shifted from Britain to other nations in Europe and to the United States, and innovation and industry became closely tied to a strong auxiliary program of scientific research. Just as the steam engine had revolutionized many activities, so did the next key innovation, the internal combustion engine, most prominently through the automobile and the airplane. The fifth and most recent phase is less energy-demanding than its immediate predecessor. It centers on "the production of electronic devices (e.g., computers and television) and a plethora of services (e.g., education, entertainment, defense, finance) that make heavy use of these devices." These phases of invention and diffusion have had their environmental effects on the areas associated with them, most pervasively in the developed-world countries where industry has remained, though decreasingly, concentrated (Headrick 1990).

The use of technologies affects the environment in three basic ways: in the harvesting of resources, in the emission of wastes during the production process, and in the emission of wastes in the consumption of the good or service produced. Technological changes can lessen environmental impacts as well as create or exacerbate them. There usually exist different techniques for reaching the same goal, and which one is chosen may be quite environmentally significant. The replacement of one technology by another may end the resource harvesting and the waste depletion associated with the one abandoned, or it may increase either.

In the $I = PAT$ formula, the T factor diminishes impact when it makes it possible to produce and consume the same goods or services with smaller inputs of resources and smaller outputs of wastes. In practice, any technological change is likely to have some benign and some harmful consequences. What Gray (1989) calls "the paradox of technological development" lies in the fact that technology both solves and creates environmental problems. It may even do so at the same time. The narrow "linear view" of the use of technology emphasizes "solving the immediate problem without necessarily assessing the wider impacts of that solution" until events may make them impossible to ignore (Headrick 1990: 65). That innovation and adoption have accelerated much more than has the discovery of many of their side effects is probably the most troubling aspect of technology's impacts on the environment. The theme of technology as a driving force of damage is often that of "careless technology" (Farvar and Milton 1972) or of unintended and inadvertent side effects.

Innovations, of course, do nothing themselves, they merely expand the possibilities open for actors desiring to do things. Technologies don't damage ecosystems, so to speak; people damage ecosystems. Hence to attribute environmental degradation to the technological innovation that made it possible is in a sense to miss the point. Yet the point is largely a semantic one; in a given situation, changes in the technology available will change environmental impact, and in that regard, technological change differs little from other posited driving forces. Furthermore, because so many of the impacts of a technology are unforeseen and, given the state of knowledge at the time, unforeseeable, to shift the responsibility to the actor employing the technology is no more realistic. We sometimes do not know what we are doing; we sometimes could know but are not obliged to find out because our effects can be externalized to others. But it is the surprising and unforeseen effects that are the most worrisome, especially given the current rate of technological innovation and adoption – though that speed at the same time means the rapid obsolescence and abandonment of other damaging technologies.

Systems of energy generation illustrate some of the unexpected environmental gains and losses associated with technological transitions. Where different technologies provide energy for the same process, their different impacts point up technology's role as a driving force. The dams and water mills that powered the initial stages of the Industrial Revolution in Britain and New England blocked fish from migrating upstream, created ponds that harbored disease, and flooded valuable farmland. The coal-burning steam engines that took their place in the Industrial Revolution's second phase reduced these effects but produced the classic smoke pollution and acid rain of the nineteenth-century city. Automobiles, the villain of much of today's urban environmental literature, were welcomed at the turn of the century as alleviating the serious pollution stemming from a dependence on horse-drawn transit (Tarr 1971). Today the use or the abandonment of nuclear power replaces one diversified portfolio of pollutants with another. It is not clear that until recently these transitions have occurred mainly for environmental reasons. It is certain, though, that they have long had environmental effects.

As technology can be a factor either of mitigation and improvement or of damage, to picture environmental deterioration as the product of "technological change" or of "technology" is to paint with too broad a brush. Innovation sometimes creates new demands on resources or increases existing ones; it also can and does lessen demands by increasing the efficiency of use or by providing substitutes. Equally it can lessen as well as increase the amount or harmfulness of wastes emitted or the harm that they do. Technology is sometimes the problem, sometimes the answer. It is sometimes, moreover, essential even to the recognition of the problem. Without the refinement of some technologies, we would still be ignorant of many of our environmental woes. Technological change has contributed to changes in the composition of the atmosphere; the fossil fuel combustion that has powered the Industrial Revolution has been a major force in increasing the level of carbon dioxide (CO_2) in the atmosphere from 275 parts per million to well over 350 today. Yet it is only other technological advances that have even made the problem apparent. If trace gases could only be measured to the nearest hundredth of a percentage point, the concentration of CO_2 would only just now be showing any change, from a starting level of 0.03% to one today closer to 0.04% (Houghton and Skole 1990: 401). One of the most striking and worrying environmental changes discovered during the 1980s, the stratospheric "ozone hole," has been traced to a particular set of chemical innovations, the invention and large-scale release of compounds known as chlorofluorocarbons (CFCs). Again the problem is the result of the invention and large-scale use of a new substance long before its many consequences could be foreseen; again, the discovery is the fruit of other technologies, those of atmospheric monitoring and remote sensing, and the medium- and long-term solution is likely to come through the development of substitutes for CFCs that possess their virtues without sharing their faults.

POLITICAL-ECONOMIC ORGANIZATION

Closely intertwined with human numbers, affluence, and technological capacity as driving forces of change are many variations in the ways that human beings organize their relations with one another and with the natural world. The use of technology by population to acquire affluence is always conducted and mediated through the institutions of society. The key ones related to the environment are those that Bennett and Dahlberg (1990) classify as the rules of property, exchange, and regulation – institutions so closely intertwined that they can hardly be discussed save together. It is in these institutions, rather than in the *PAT* variables, that many social scientists prefer to seek the human roots of environmental change.

Views of what constitutes environmental degradation – as opposed to environmental change – differ a good deal, of course. The best-developed body of social theory addressing environmental issues, neoclassical economics, avoids the question by deflecting it. It posits no standard of what is desirable other than the aggregate desires held and paid for by the members of the public. Environmental value is measured not by measuring the environment as such but by measuring what people want of it, where what they want is measured ultimately by their willingness to pay – in money, in time, in energy, in other competing desires forgone. What people value in their physical surroundings, relative to other scarce goods that they also value, is the value of the environment. On this view, to blame "the market" or "economics" or "economists" for not valuing a feature of the environment enough to protect it from "degradation" is to shoot the messenger and not the culprit.

Environmental and resource economics and political economy deriving from this tradition offer a number of concepts regarding exchange, property, and regulation that make useful starting points for the analysis of many problems. They note, to begin with, that every activity that people undertake in the environment is a source of both costs and benefits – to them and to others. Suppose that the total well-being of society is to be measured by the total value that it commands (a disputed approach, but again a useful point of departure). Any activity that adds to the total is desirable and can be described as an efficient use of resources. Any that subtracts from it – that incurs more costs than it provides benefits – is undesirable and inefficient.

Four kinds of situations are then possible. The first two are unproblematic: the case where benefits exceed costs and the activity is undertaken, and the case where potential costs exceed potential benefits and the activity is forestalled. Not so those two paradoxical situations in which the market signal is not heeded. The first of them involves activity that is inefficient (producing more damage than benefits) yet continues. Such is most likely to occur when the costs of that damage are inflicted on someone other than the person reaping the benefits; the activity is thus rational and profitable for the latter person, but not for society as a whole. The second involves activity that would be efficient (returning more in net benefits than in costs) yet is not undertaken. This situation is most likely to arise when the person who would have to bear the costs of the improvement could not also capture its benefits; the activity would be rational and efficient for society overall but is not so for any of its members. Either case represents what is called "market failure" and imposes what are called social costs; each promotes environmental degradation, damage being rewarded and improvement discouraged.

The spillover effects underlying such market failures are called *externalities*. They occur in two forms. Positive ones are the benefits that accrue to someone other than the actor bearing the costs of an action. Activities with significant positive externalities are often classed among what economists call public goods – ones that the private sector is unlikely to provide efficiently. A lighthouse is a familiar textbook example. Negative externalities are costs imposed on someone other than the actor reaping the benefits of the action. Some classic textbook illustrations are the factory whose smokestack befouls the property and pollutes the air of its neighbors and the ranch whose straying livestock eat or damage the crops of the farmer next door. Where costs can be readily externalized, an activity damaging to the environment will continue that would not otherwise continue, at least to the same extent.

Externalities of this sort may be dealt with in several ways. One possible response is not to respond at all. Though the externality is a source of inefficiency, the loss it causes might be less than the net loss that any available remedy would produce – for remedies themselves are costly to design and implement, and the resources they would consume might be better used in solving a different problem. Second, property owners might be ordered not to act in such a way as to injure the property of others. On a literal application of the principle, the actively offending party would be compelled either to control the harm done – to add a filter to the smokestack or a spark-catcher to the locomotive or to build a fence to contain the cattle – or, that failing, to cease operation.

On another view, this approach is inefficient. It can allow individuals, even for frivolous reasons, to block or to burden activities that are valuable to the community if somewhat annoying in their immediate neighborhood. "It is necessary to weigh the harm against the good that will result. Nothing could be more 'anti-social' than to oppose any action which causes any harm to anyone" (Coase 1960). If the goal is to maximize the value produced, it is inefficient to force a rancher to build a protective fence that costs more than the value of the crops beyond it. A net loss to society occurs only if the loss borne by the neighbor exceeds what it would cost to put matters right. It makes more sense, on this line of reasoning, to tax the offender the amount of damage caused; only if the activity is still a source of net profit will it then continue. Yet that amount is extremely difficult, especially for a regulator unfamiliar with the details of the actual situation, to calculate. Moreover, it can be argued that to blame only one party is to miss the point that the problem results from the activities of both. The factory smoke and the straying cattle cause damage only because the neighbor and the farmer are located next door to a possible source of harm.

The ideal solution, from the economic point of view, is to bring the externality within the market, for market failures are less failures of functioning markets than they are failures to have markets. What distinguishes externalities from efficient exchanges of costs and benefits is precisely that they do not occur within a system of prices and free exchanges between holders of property rights. It is because no property rights exist in the atmosphere that the factory can pour its smoke with impunity on its neighbor instead of being liable to the owner of those rights for trespass. It is when the farmer does have secure title to his own land that the cattle-raising neighbor can be sued for the cost of the crops that the invading cattle eat. Thus externalities would be dealt with by assigning clear and definite property rights to all possible sources of costs and benefits; the workings of the market system would then maximize the value of goods produced.

There exist three broad possible regimes of access to – which is to say, of property in – environmental resources. (Property in resources includes the right to pollute, which is access to the environment as a sink for wastes.) The first is that of *free access* to environmental resources. No would-be users of the resource can be barred from exploiting it to whatever degree they wish. Air has long been such a good; anything free is proverbially likened to it. The second regime is that of resources as *private property,* whereby the resource domain or, more precisely, the stream of benefits arising from it, is divided into privately owned parcels; their owners have more or less exclusive control over their share of the resource, including the right to exclude others from its use. Free-access resources are those through which externalities can arise; private property is traditionally the form favored by economists as the most efficient.

A third regime is that of *common property,* where there is ownership or control not by an individual but by a collectivity. Title, control, and regulation are vested in a social group or in some branch of the state; the resource is not divided into privately controlled parcels, but neither is its use free to all, for use can be restricted and managed by the decisions of the collectivity that owns it. To some degree, how a resource is recognizable as belonging to one or another of these categories is a matter of scale. An offshore marine zone claimed by one nation-state may be common (state) property from the point of view of that nation's citizens; at an international scale of analysis, where the "actors" are not individuals but governments, it might be better regarded as a privately owned resource controlled by one actor who has the right to exclude the others.

A failure to distinguish between common property and free access has long plagued the environmental literature. Much of it goes back to a classic article by the biologist Garrett Hardin (1968), "The Tragedy of the Commons." What Hardin (following some earlier writers) described as a phenomenon of common-property systems was essentially the problem of wasteful depletion under a regime of free access. His chosen example was a medieval village's common pasture, and he assumed that all of the villagers had free access to it to graze their livestock. Hardin suggested that it would have been in the interest of each villager to increase the size of his herd until the pasture was destroyed by overuse. All would calculate that the profit of increasing their herd size would bring them a gain exceeding their immediate share of the damage done thereby to the pasture. To refrain from doing so would only let others benefit the more. The sum of such individual calculations would be disaster for all as all increased their herds well beyond what the pasture could support, even though the good of each and of all would have been better served by general self-restraint. Many environmental problems, Hardin claimed, reflected this "tragedy of the commons." Wherever access is free, only by exploiting the resource can one claim it as one's own; only by rushing to harvest it – in a frenzy of inefficient and unsustainable depletion – can one see to it that others do not claim it first.

In fact, the medieval common grazing area was usually, as the name might suggest, a common-property resource for the villagers and not a free-access one (Cox 1985). Rules limited the sizes of the herds that villagers could pasture on it, thereby avoiding the rapid depletion that Hardin postulated and that might indeed have occurred under free access. What Hardin himself prescribed for the management of contemporary environmental realms that he likened to the common pasture was government regulation making them a form of common property. The same lands could also have been managed without such depletion by being – as they often were under enclosure acts – converted to private property.

The arguments for private property in natural resources are the classic arguments for the superiority of private over group ownership in anything. Ideally, it imposes the costs of the wise use or the degradation of the resource on the same person who reaps the benefits, which is both efficient and equitable. It frees resources from the constraints of community management and allows them to reach their most useful employment following the signals of market demand. The rationales for common property in land and its resources are the classic ones for the superiority of the common good over individual interests. Common property – again, in the ideal – preserves the access of members of the community to essential inputs and blocks the selfish short-term depletion of resources for private profit; the privatization of those resources into individually owned parcels leads to growing disparities in wealth and power and to marginalization, landlessness, and dependency among large numbers. Yet it would be a mistake to suppose that privatizing common lands is always a project of the rich and powerful. In Revolutionary-era France, for example, the poorest peasants in many areas were the main advocates and defenders of privatization, resisted by the wealthier (Cobban 1964: 113–17).

Studies suggest that common ownership works well where a long period of trial and error has led to the development of rules that sustain the resource, and that it works best on the local level, where community pressures to comply with the rules are most effective and where monitoring of behavior to spot infractions is easiest. Even when narrow economic efficiency is the criterion, a regime of common property is sometimes the best: when the costs of necessary transactions among users are high, and when the resources are relatively sparse and diffuse (Ostrom 1990). A regime of free access is sometimes the most efficient. When resources are plentiful relative to population, neither private nor common property makes as much sense as free access does. Oxygen and sunlight so abound relative to demand in most places today as to be under no threat of depletion. Placing them under either private or common management would be a pointless waste of resources. Even resources that can be depleted by overuse may be most efficiently managed by free access if the costs of patrolling their use exceed the benefits to be gained by their careful management. Technical innovation, of course, may make monitoring cheaper. A realm where private ownership was once unfeasible may become one where it can be efficiently undertaken.

What are known as common-pool resources are a special case but an important one environmentally. They are ones that can be depleted yet cannot be efficiently used under private ownership because excluding other users is too difficult or costly. What is nominally private ownership would prove in practice to be a regime of free access. If an underground oil field can be pumped from any of the landholdings on the surface above it, the oil is for those landowners a free-access resource. If the overlying land is fragmented into many parcels, the pool is a likely candidate for the rapid and wasteful competitive depletion of the tragedy of the commons. At the international scale, ocean fisheries offer another example. In the open seas, beyond the zones legally controlled by coastal nations, fish stocks effectively exist under a regime of free access. The global atmosphere, another common pool, is in a sense a free-access sink into which emissions of such waste gases as carbon dioxide, methane, and CFCs can be dumped with no more cost to the dumper than to anyone else. The costs of reaching and monitoring global arrangements for the atmosphere, compared to the apparent benefits to all parties of such prospective arrangements, have slowed the development of controls on the build-up of greenhouse gases.

In this sense, common-pool resources merely illustrate in an extreme form a problem that exists everywhere. As Coase (1960) pointed out, the transactions that must be carried out among parties to a possible arrangement are not costless. Under some conditions, they can be so costly as to frustrate what would otherwise be efficient and mutually beneficial market exchanges. Transaction costs are defined by Coase as those incurred in efforts "to discover who it is that one wishes to deal with, to inform people that one wishes to deal and on what terms, to conduct negotiations leading up to a bargain, to draw up the contract, to undertake the inspection needed to make sure that the terms of the contract are being observed, and so on." Through these procedures, a common-pool resource could be privatized just as efficiently as any other if the costs of these procedures were not in their cases prohibitive. Attention to these costs helps to understand many other situations of resource and environmental use. The problem of transaction costs is a considerable one even at the local scale. It becomes monumental by the time we reach such global problems as stratospheric ozone depletion or the accumulation of greenhouse gases. The most difficult problems, and the greatest transaction costs, are those of finding out just what the consequences of environmental change will be. It is not known what even the physical outcomes of increased carbon dioxide in the atmosphere will be, let alone who will gain or lose by them and by how much.

While orthodox economics locates environmental degradation in inappropriate – usually nonmarket – institutions for exchange and ownership, markets themselves are blamed for the same phenomenon in other schools of thought. Market exchange, usually equated with capitalism, is said to tend inherently toward environmental destruction and away from sustainability; or, in milder forms of the argument, the imperfections in markets that economic logic tends to obscure are by contrast highlighted, especially the pervasiveness of externalities and the obstacles that transaction costs pose to their resolution by the market. Selective regulation at the minimum is urged to guard against particular threats or to repair market failures.

Criticisms of markets overlap considerably with criticisms of economics as an approach. First, those who believe that particular features of the environment have inherent value naturally dislike seeing them weighed and balanced in monetary terms against other goods. And because the weighing is done in monetary terms, markets respond to demands according to the wealth of the participant. Second, the economist's tendency to assume away key facts for the sake of theoretical elegance can lead to policy prescriptions unsuited to the complexities of the real world. None of the characteristic assumptions of economic analysis is less suited to questions of global environmental change than that of perfect information. Rarely is it known with confidence what will be the physical consequences of a large-scale human intervention in the environment. Still less often is it known how those physical consequences will translate into social ones. To use a distinction drawn by the economist F. H. Knight (1921), global change is less a matter of "risk" – where the probabilities of different outcomes can be calculated and insured against – than it is one of "uncertainty," where they cannot. The risks of catastrophic outcomes are sometimes large enough to suggest the need for intervention to stay on the safe side and guard against such possibilities. Finally, orthodox economics has long tended to relegate distributional questions – who gets what – to secondary importance, when it has addressed them at all, behind questions of how much in sum there is to distribute. Distributional questions remain, understandably, of great and indeed paramount concern to those directly involved; it is hard to understand how people will in fact behave in a certain situation without considering them.

There are inequities in distribution in time as well as in space. Many forms of environmental damage can be interpreted as a matter of shifting costs into the future: the depletion of nonrenewable or exhaustible resources (fossil fuel burning, species extinction) or the release of persistent and cumulative pollutants (carbon dioxide into the atmosphere or toxic pollutants into groundwater). They pose issues of equity between rather than within generations. It is now widely argued that pure market systems are incompatible with long-term environmental sustainability and with the interests of the future.

45

Markets tend to discount the future value – and hence the preservation – of resources as opposed to their present use at roughly the prevailing rate of interest. Discounting has two sources. The first is that of human time preference. In general, the consumption of a good at the present will be preferred to its consumption in the future; hence the future value of the good must be discounted. The second is the productivity of capital; what is put now to a productive use will become more valuable than what is not. To preserve environmental features and resources, environmentalists thus tend to argue in cost–benefit analyses for the application of a rate of discount for their use or preservation below the market rate. There are, however, paradoxes in the argument; it has been necessary in some cases to advocate a high rate where it would discount the future benefits of a development project, such as a dam, that would alter a valued natural setting.

The setting of the discount rate is but one technical manifestation of a more general issue. To remove environmental actions from the control of the market is necessarily to put them under some other kind of control. The question is not whether the market does a bad job in managing the environment but whether it does worse than another agency would do. The agency usually asked to do better is the state; the assumption is often made that it will produce better outcomes than markets will. Government regulation may indeed improve the use of the environment by replacing the immediate and selfish incentives of private profit with management for the common good. Or it may damage environmental quality further because the price incentives to minimize costs and damage are removed and the selfish interest or the ignorance of the managers takes over instead. The interests of the state may be even more antithetical than the market is to long-term sustainability, or even more biased toward the concerns of the wealthy and powerful, and unlike the pressures of a free market they are backed by coercive authority. There are nonmarket failures as well as market failures. There are political as well as economic temptations to externalize costs in space and time and to waste resources in short-term development. Does a regulated or command economy necessarily accord more value to the future than one driven by aggregated individual choice? As the economist Robert Solow (1974: 12) writes, even in a democratic system,

> realistically speaking . . . when we say "public intervention" we mean rough and ready political action. An only moderately cynical observer will see a problem here: it is far from clear that the political process can be relied upon to be more future-oriented than your average corporation. The conventional pay-out period for business is of the same order of magnitude as the time to the next election, and transferring a given individual from the industrial to the government bureaucracy does not transform him into a guardian of the far future's interests. . . . At a minimum, it suggests that one ought to be as suspicious of uncritical centralization as of uncritical free-marketeering.

46

There have been and are regimes that reject market allocation, directing ex-changes instead by state planning. Do such systems produce notably better or worse environments than ones in which markets play a larger role? Like any question in comparative social science, it is an immensely difficult one to answer in a rigorous fashion. In the 1960s and 1970s, data began to suggest that the Soviet Union and the Eastern Bloc suffered from problems of pollution and natural resource waste just as did the Western nations. Some took it to mean that industrialization or "industrial society" was the basic source of environmental damage and that political systems mattered hardly at all. Evidence has since indicated that during the post–World War II era, pollution and resource waste in the Soviet Union and the Eastern Bloc were, if anything, a good deal worse than in Western Europe and the United States (Carter and Turnock 1993; Peterson 1993). The state did not use its monopoly over allocation to protect the environ-ment as it often claimed to do. In its drive for increased production and in its abandonment of market rationality, it did just the opposite.

Some have taken these facts simply to mean that greater wealth allows coun-tries to deal better with their environmental problems, by regulating them or sending them elsewhere: some, that a strong degree of government, rather than market, control tends to worsen environmental problems; others, that the de-gree of popular participation in decision making (high in democracies, low un-der authoritarian regimes of left and right) is the key factor. And high participa-tion indeed allows popular environmental concern, when it exists, to be heard, to bring pressure, and to mold policy. On the other hand, a government suscepti-ble to public pressure is likewise susceptible to pressure for rapid development and other policies antithetical to environmental protection; there is no guaran-tee that public opinion will prefer conservation to exploitation. How do political scale and structure affect environmental outcomes? Is small-scale, localized gov-ernment better than a centralized system because it is more responsive to envi-ronmental concerns? Or is the opposite true, because larger units possess more resources to deal with problems and because smaller units competing with one another compete standards of environmental protection down to a minimum in a "race to the bottom"? These questions cannot be answered with confidence.

Exchange has its spatial dimensions as well as its social ones. An important trend in the human history of the globe over the past three centuries is that of the growth in long-distance trade, or of what Michael Chisholm (1990) defines as "the increasing separation of production and consumption." Trade has for many centuries been an important aspect of the world's economy. Its modern increase, therefore, is a quantitative rather than a qualitative change, but it is an impressive one nonetheless. Freight flows have grown much faster than global population during the twentieth century (Chisholm 1990: 94). The reasons lie partly in improvements in technology that have lessened the "friction of dis-tance" by steadily lowering the cost of transporting goods over long distances.

Even with population growth and technological change, as we have seen, disagreements exist even as to the overall direction of influence on the environment – harmful or beneficial – of changes so broad. The implications of the growth of long-distance trade are also in dispute; the impacts are likely to depend heavily on the context. Certainly most environmental change, and most harmful change as well, has occurred at the same time that long-distance trade has become a steadily larger part of the world's economy. Yet "the significance of the increasing separation of production and consumption is not a matter that can be treated in *a priori* terms, in isolation from other changes" (Chisholm 1990: 99). Trade may lessen environmental damage by permitting regional environments to be used in the ways most suited to their physical base rather than for production of all things needed. When railroads linked nineteenth-century New England to the farms of the Midwest, much upland acreage in New England that had been cultivated to feed the region reverted to forest. Environmental improvement thus occurred, though it did not occur for environmental reasons. Regional specialization can make for a greater economy and efficiency in the use of resources, and it creates markets not only for the principal resources of an area but for their by-products. Marsh ([1864] 1965: 37n) wrote,

> One of the greatest benefits to be expected from the improvements of civilization is, that increased facilities of communication will render it possible to transport to places of consumption much valuable material that is now wasted because the price at the nearest market will not pay freight. The cattle slaughtered in South America for their hides would feed millions of the starving population of the Old World, if their flesh could be economically preserved and transported across the ocean.

The opposed view parallels the criticism of market exchange within nations, seeing regional integration into a global economy as a source of environmental damage and not of protection. It equates the spread of international trade with the spread across the globe of markets or capitalism, and it views capitalism as a system inherently damaging to the natural environment. Traditional societies not incorporated into the world market, so runs the argument, practiced conservationist strategies of resource use that were sustainable over the long term. Today, the primacy of the profit motive compels the abandonment of ecological sustainability for short-term gain, however destructive the results may be. The unequal power relations of nations in the world system translate into the exploitation – economic and environmental – of some areas by the rest. Poverty and powerlessness may force some countries to use their resources unsustainably and unhealthfully just as some peoples within particular countries may be forced to do the same; in this way, environmental damage is continually being "exported" by the haves to the have-nots. If some forms of damage are lessening in the developed world while worsening in the developing countries, the fault lies not with the policies or populations of the latter but with the wealth and high per capita demands of the former, whose effects are masked by being transferred in space.

Certainly some industries have sought "pollution havens" in the Third World where regulations are lax; certainly use has been made of underdeveloped countries as dumping grounds for wastes. Environmental arguments now figure prominently among those advanced against free trade. Yet again there are exceptions and paradoxes to consider; it is also, for example, the case that "the outflow of damaging productive activities has at least as often been resisted as promoted by residents of the wealthier nations – though often with little success – through trade barriers and agricultural subsidies" (Meyer and Turner 1990: 470).

A discussion of the possible sources of environmental change would not be complete without a mention of the role of beliefs and attitudes. Many have been blamed for degradation. They range from the Judeo-Christian tradition, for separating humankind from nature, to the Western scientific tradition or capitalist market rationality, for mechanizing and despiritualizing the environment, to a patriarchal ethos that equates women with nature and seeks to dominate both. Unquestionably attitudes play a part in the human use of the earth. Beyond that statement it is difficult to be specific about their importance. Research has not satisfactorily demonstrated the clear importance of attitudes on a par with the other driving forces (Rockwell 1994). Professed attitudes are not necessarily consistent with behavior, either because they are not strongly or sincerely held or because social and economic constraints outweigh them. Nor, even when attitudes and behavior are consistent, is it clear that attitudes drive behavior and do not instead follow it. A reverent or a fatalistic attitude toward the environment by those lacking the numbers or the technology to transform it could, to put it crudely, be a case of sour grapes. Finally, it is not clear, even when environmental attitudes do drive environmental consequences, that they drive them in the expected direction. Attachment can have effects as damaging as indifference or hostility. Perhaps the greatest threat to many high mountain environments today is mass tourism, driven not by dislike of their scenery – a dislike prevalent in Western attitudes until the nineteenth century – but by appreciation of it.

CONCLUSION

The ancient search for an answer to the question, What are the human causes of environmental change? has been above all a complex and contentious pursuit. The answers have varied widely. Indeed, particular trends of change in each of these categories have been identified not only as causes of degradation but as causes or at least reflections of improvement.

Not surprisingly, each of these sets of variables is used not only to explain the bulk of environmental change but to explain the other social variables. Some writers claim population growth to be the principal mover of human history, constituting a driving force for technological innovation and for the elaboration and rationalization of market and regulatory structures. Economic interpretations of history, on the other hand, have viewed population increases as ultimately the consequence of social changes that offered incentives or support for increased human numbers and technological innovation and adoption as likewise the responses to the structure of economic incentives. Technological determinism explains all other major social changes as the result of technological innovations. From some neo-Marxist perspectives, population increase results from political and economic inequalities and thus, though it may be statistically associated with environmental degradation, it is not its real cause but only a mechanism through which the real cause acts. Disagreement about fundamentals is the contemporary state of the social sciences, no less when they consider environmental matters than when they remain purely within the social realm (Sack 1990).

In short, none of the social changes put forward as driving forces can be clearly identified as the real and prime root cause of global change, either singly or in combination with particular others. Most or all, on the other hand, have clearly played a part. The chapters that follow are not, to borrow an image from Blaikie and Brookfield (1987: 27–8), a mystery story in which one of the suspects will finally be exposed as the culprit. It would be convenient indeed if the world proved to be so simple, but experience suggests the contrary. Indeed, social factors that drive some environmental changes may well lessen others. Each of the major candidate forces evidently is important to some degree globally and perhaps is dominant in some environmental changes in some regions and situations. The variety of cause–consequence situations will become apparent in the chapters that follow.

3

The Land

Land covers 130 million square km, or 29% of the globe. Little if any of it can be considered unaffected by human action, though on much of it the human mark is still not profound. Much of it will not support the ordinary forms of settlement and use that most transform the environment. Antarctica and Greenland, both mostly shielded by ice sheets from any kind of human imprint, together account for more than a tenth of the world's land area. There are other vast regions too dry, too wet, too cold, too remote, too steep, or too bare of soil to support any but the scantiest level of human occupance. Only about a fifth of the global land area is considered suitable for agricultural use, and it is largely the area used intensively for other purposes as well.

The price at which it has been used to date is not readily calculated, but may be enormous in terms of the degradation of the earth's potential. Certainly "the useful product obtained from the world's lands every year is far greater at present than it was three centuries ago," and unprecedented numbers of people are supported at rising average standards of living. Yet "systematic investment in sustained productivity on the land" seems to be rare, suggesting that "worldwide capital investment in the land is less than the demands put on it." If so, "the long-term world trend is a cascading loss in capacity (i.e., degradation) in every broad category of land use" (Richards 1990: 176–77) even as rising needs will call for ever-higher output for the foreseeable future.

Still, any generalizations about the balance of gains and losses and about the sustainability of uses must remain tentative. The vastness of the world's land area that makes many human impacts insignificant in a global view also impedes our knowledge of what aggregate changes – expanse of land under cultivation, area of forest removed, amount of soil degraded or eroded – have taken place. It is embarrassingly difficult to say how large is the current world forest, to take but one example. The uncertainties are greatest, of course, for the distant past, but

51

the earth in many respects, though we can view it whole from space and in detail in atlases, is a *terra incognita* even today and urgently in need of a new era of exploration and mapping.

LAND AND SOCIETY

"Land" denotes both physical objects and social institutions, a bundle of earth materials and vegetation cover and a bundle of legal rights to their use. A discussion of the human impact on the land is a discussion of how the latter affect the former: of how human land uses alter the biophysical land cover.

Much land today, though much less than at one time, is held, or managed, as common property – cropland, pasture and range, woodland, hunting and fishing grounds. As already noted (Chapter 2), common lands are not the free-access, first-come-first-served resource domains of Hardin's "tragedy of the commons." Rather, they are areas collectively controlled and managed. Individuals belonging to the community use their resources but under the community's rules. That control can be exercised does not, of course, guarantee that it will be. Nor does it guarantee that it will be exercised to the benefit of the community and its environment. The powerful members of the community may manage the land for their own gain and the loss of others. But the network of institutions constraining the use of common property does, like private ownership but by different means, make management possible to prevent the overuse that can destroy or devalue free-access resources.

The last three centuries, on the whole, have been an era of the conversion to private ownership of lands once held in common. European exploration and colonization coincided with widespread enclosure in Europe itself. Scholars still argue over the latter's consequences in Great Britain. Some emphasize the increased productivity and efficiency of land use, some the violation of traditional land-use rights and the destruction of the rural community. The Swedish case was similar. Three broad measures enacted in the late eighteenth and early nineteenth centuries swept into history the nucleated village, on which the nation's old order had centered. Cultivated landholdings had been fragmented and grazing and forest area held in common. The new landscape that took form after the redistribution acts, one of individually owned and consolidated holdings, was meant to promote initiative, expansion, and productivity. What followed resembled the sequel to enclosure elsewhere in Europe: the stimulation of agricultural output, along with population increase, growing landlessness, and migration to the cities and abroad (Hägerstrand and Lohm 1990: 608–10).

Policies of enclosure developed in tandem with the theory of the superiority of private land tenure. European colonizers used such arguments to justify the dispossession of indigenous peoples in Europe's "Great Frontier." Those who held lands in common and migrated periodically from one area to another had no claim, it was argued, against those who could make more socially productive use

52

of the land by parceling it out to permanent settlement and farming it more intensively. With no private title, no permanent cultivation and occupance, there was no right of ownership. John Winthrop said of the Indians of New England in the early seventeenth century that because "they inclose noe Land, neither have any settled habitation," their territory "lay open to any that could and would improve it."

In nothing is the global influence of Europe more marked than in the expansion of European land tenure systems centered on the institution of private property (Richards 1990: 175). But if privatization has been one global trend, increased public regulation of land use has been another. The reasons have been varied. Absolute individual ownership, if it is generally consonant with economic efficiency, is under some circumstances highly inefficient itself. The state often intervenes directly in the land market to dislodge holdouts and transfer parcels of land to more productive uses frustrated by the costs of transactions. Pure private enterprise could never have spun the world's web of roads and railroads. In the Anglo-American world, the state routinely delegated its power of condemnation to turnpike and rail companies so that they could assemble the parcels of land needed to construct the shortest and least costly routes; in other countries, the government built the rail network itself. By holding back in an entirely free market, individuals along a planned line might have demanded exorbitant payment for their land, or they might have blocked the project by refusing to sell at any price. Western law, following Roman concepts of property rights, gave the owner of a parcel of land ownership of all the resources below it to the earth's core and of the sky above as far up as the stars. Yet it did so only as long as the right carried little practical importance. Absolute subsurface rights were the first to go. Mining enterprises pursuing the winding paths of ore bodies could not be bothered to negotiate as they went with the owners of the various tracts under which they found themselves; their needs led to various infringements on the power of landowners to bar intruders from deep below their holdings. Rights in the sky have also diminished, more recently but also more completely. The Roman rule would have allowed landowners to bar balloons, airplanes, and even satellites from overflying their property without permission. It did not outlive the adage that if man were meant to fly he would have wings. In terms of the volume of space involved, the legal change represented the largest uncompensated dispossession of property owners in human history.

In the age of wooden warships, the strategic value of a timber supply for naval construction gave nation-states another reason to regulate land use – to ban unrestrained forest cutting or to reserve the larger trees for government use. Such regulations appeared in Elizabethan England and later in Britain's American colonies, in Russia and Sweden at the beginning of the seventeenth century. Many land uses damage neighboring lands in a way that seems to call for strict regulation. Forest burning has long been controlled because of its tendency to leap property lines and consume other holdings; forest cutting has sometimes been restricted with the goal of preventing floods downstream, and sometimes in the belief that it threatened to damage the regional climate.

The authors of early land, forest, and soil conservation measures have won the side benefit of election to conservation halls of fame, while those who had to bear their often high costs have not usually been so lucky. Most of these controls have been deeply resented: flouted or ignored when possible, sometimes resisted by force (Grove 1990). Rarely were they imposed with any attention to the role of the forest in the subsistence or the commercial needs of the nearby population. Eighteenth- and nineteenth-century French rural discontent with Paris's regulation of forest use smoldered in routine acts of disobedience and sometimes flared into violent uprisings. Official measures for soil conservation in Europe's overseas colonies, also designed with little attention to the resource needs of the native population, aroused much resentment and resistance. So too throughout history has any restriction on the expansion of settlement into inviting frontier zones. There are many more reasons for the state to intervene in land use than simply maximizing the land's net return to society: the rewards available to corrupt officials should not be underestimated as a force in land use, nor should mismanagement by authorities (Repetto and Gillis 1988).

If neither efficiency nor equity always governs state action, neither does sustainability. Policies promoting land conservation seem to have been – and perhaps remain – far less frequent than ones promoting development: forest clearance, settlement, wetland drainage, cultivation, the conversion of land cover and the intensification of land use. A varied bundle of carrots and sticks encourages development: free land to settlers, subsidies and tax relief for land conversion, forced resettlement, and, perhaps most effectively, the opening of transportation routes, permitting new occupants to reach the zone in question and to ship their produce out. Taxes levied on subsistence farmers force them into the cash economy and may require more intensive use of their land.

CHANGES IN LAND COVER

The key global land-use/cover classes are cultivation, forest, grassland, wetland, and settlement. Land uses change land covers in two ways (Turner and Meyer 1994). The first is conversion, a change of the cover from one class to another: forest clearance for pasture, wetland drainage for cultivation, cropland conversion to urban settlement. The second is modification, an alteration of the existing cover that does not convert it to a different cover type. Globally, cultivation has pushed out less productive land uses – forest, pasture, rangeland, and "wastelands" of various sorts; at the same time, cultivation itself has suffered the same fate – though only in miniature – as the still more lucrative land uses of sprawling urban areas devour cropland. Besides these forms of conversion, modification has also been important: forests have been thinned, grass cover has been nibbled down or improved, cultivation has been intensified, urban infrastructure has been redeveloped.

Land-use and land-cover change occurs most rapidly and dramatically in zones of frontier expansion:

> Virtually all human societies have experienced that dynamic form of changing land use referred to as a frontier. The frontier is that period and area in which a peripheral region is created or extended. We are all familiar with the transient frontier epoch during which time forests, grasslands, and even deserts are transformed into agricultural, pastoral, and urban landscapes of settlement and sedentary agriculture. Populations of diverse human "tribal" societies – hunter-gatherers, pastoralists, shifting cultivators – succumb to the urgent claims of pioneer settlers backed by the modernizing state. Populations of wild animals are displaced by domesticated draft and grazing animals or are eradicated altogether. (Richards 1990: 165–66)

How many frontiers one counts in the past, Richards notes, is often a matter of the time and space scales that one decides to use. The number might range from just one over the long term to many hundreds of short duration. "The global frontier is in its last decades after a five-century run. . . . Frontier episodes, when seen at the level of an individual county, might be as fleeting as two to three decades." In any case, the future is not likely to add many large areas to the list. The expansion of the past few centuries has spared few if any of the world's large remaining tracts of sparsely settled usable land: "Our states, markets, and people search for, but will no longer find, new frontier lands" (Richards 1990: 166). The zones that have opened up since World War II are likely to be among the last great settlement frontiers of world history. The lowland rainforest of the vast Amazon River Basin attracts settlers not only from Brazil but from the crowded mountain regions of the other countries that hold territory in Amazonia (notably Bolivia, Peru, Ecuador, and Colombia) (Salati et al. 1990). Other modern frontiers – the rainforest of Southeast Asia (Brookfield et al. 1990) and the lowland Terai zone of Nepal – are, like Amazonia, undergoing rapid population influx and transformation of a classic but today unusual kind.

Behind the original frontiers advance what Richards calls secondary and tertiary frontiers, ones of intensified rather than transformed use. Frontier-type cultivation using little labor, machinery, or fertilizer gives way to intensive land management. Small tracts originally bypassed become valuable for exploitation once the prime lands nearby have been taken. As open lands have dwindled, the postwar spread of cultivation has occurred "increasingly [on] marginal lands found in the interstices of settled areas" (Richards 1990: 174).

Conversion is sometimes followed by backsliding. Forests have not only retreated before the plow but occasionally pushed it back. Grasslands and wetlands have done the same when cultivation is abandoned – because of crises of drought, flood, and epidemic, because of war or social disorganization, or simply because of competition from better lands opened to production elsewhere. Land abandonment also occurs because the land has been degraded by misuse.

Table 3.1. *Global land use, 1700–1980*

Regions	Vegetation types	Area (million ha)					Percentage changes from:				
		1700	1850	1920	1950	1980	1700 to 1850	1850 to 1920	1920 to 1950	1950 to 1980	1700 to 1980
Tropical Africa	Forests and woodlands	1358	1336	1275	1188	1074	−1.6%	−4.6%	−6.8%	−9.6%	−20.9%
	Grassland and pasture	1052	1061	1091	1130	1158	0.9%	2.8%	3.6%	2.5%	10.1%
	Croplands	44	57	88	136	222	29.5%	54.4%	54.5%	63.2%	404.5%
North Africa/ Middle East	Forests and woodlands	38	34	27	18	14	−10.5%	−20.6%	−33.3%	−22.2%	−63.2%
	Grassland and pasture	1123	1119	1112	1097	1060	−0.4%	−0.6%	−1.3%	−3.4%	−5.6%
	Croplands	20	27	43	66	107	35.0%	59.3%	53.5%	62.1%	435.0%
North America	Forests and woodlands	1016	971	944	939	942	−4.4%	−2.8%	−0.5%	0.3%	−7.3%
	Grassland and pasture	915	914	811	789	790	−0.1%	−11.3%	−2.7%	0.1%	−13.7%
	Croplands	3	50	179	206	203	1566.7%	258.0%	15.1%	−1.5%	6666.7%
Latin America	Forests and woodlands	1445	1420	1369	1273	1151	−1.7%	−3.6%	−7.0%	−9.6%	−20.3%
	Grassland and pasture	608	621	646	700	767	2.1%	4.0%	8.4%	9.6%	26.2%
	Croplands	7	18	45	87	142	157.1%	150.0%	93.3%	63.2%	1928.6%
China	Forests and woodlands	135	96	79	69	58	−28.9%	−17.7%	−12.7%	−15.9%	−57.0%
	Grassland and pasture	951	944	941	938	923	−0.7%	−0.3%	−0.3%	−1.6%	−2.9%
	Croplands	29	75	95	108	134	158.6%	26.7%	13.7%	24.1%	362.1%
South Asia	Forests and woodlands	335	317	289	251	180	−5.4%	−8.8%	−13.1%	−28.3%	−46.3%
	Grassland and pasture	189	189	190	190	187	0.0%	0.5%	0.0%	−1.6%	−1.1%
	Croplands	53	71	98	136	210	34.0%	38.0%	38.8%	54.4%	296.2%
Southeast Asia	Forests and woodlands	253	252	247	242	235	−0.4%	−2.0%	−2.0%	−2.9%	−7.1%
	Grassland and pasture	125	123	114	105	92	−1.6%	−7.3%	−7.9%	−12.4%	−26.4%
	Croplands	4	7	21	35	55	75.0%	200.0%	66.7%	57.1%	1275.0%
Europe	Forests and woodlands	230	205	200	199	212	−10.9%	−2.4%	−0.5%	6.5%	−7.8%
	Grassland and pasture	190	150	139	136	138	−21.1%	−7.3%	−2.2%	1.5%	−27.4%
	Croplands	67	132	147	152	137	97.0%	11.4%	3.4%	−9.9%	104.5%
USSR	Forests and woodlands	1138	1067	987	952	941	−6.2%	−7.5%	−3.5%	−1.2%	−17.3%
	Grassland and pasture	1068	1078	1074	1070	1065	0.9%	−0.4%	−0.4%	−0.5%	−0.3%
	Croplands	33	94	178	216	233	184.8%	89.4%	21.3%	7.9%	606.1%

	1700	1860	1920	1950	1980					
Pacific developed countries										
Forests and woodlands	267	267	261	258	246	0.0%	-2.2%	-1.1%	-4.7%	-7.9%
Grassland and pasture	639	638	630	625	608	-0.2%	-1.3%	-0.8%	-2.7%	-4.9%
Croplands	5	6	19	28	58	20.0%	216.7%	47.4%	107.1%	1060.0%
Total										
Forests and woodlands	6215	5965	5678	5389	5053	-4.0%	-4.8%	-5.1%	-6.2%	-18.7%
Grassland and pasture	6860	6837	6748	6780	6788	-0.3%	-1.3%	0.5%	0.1%	-1.0%
Croplands	265	537	913	1170	1501	102.6%	70.0%	28.1%	28.3%	466.4%

Source: Richards 1990.

Note: The estimates in this table for 1700 were drawn from R. A. Houghton et al. Changes in the Carbon Content of Terrestrial Biota and Soils Between 1860 and 1980: A Net Release of CO_2 to the Atmosphere. *Ecological Monographs* 53 (1983): 235–62, Table 1, 237. I have combined the areas for seven classes of woodland and shrubland for the forest and woodland figure and for five categories of grassland, shrub land, and pasture land for the grassland and pasture figure. These are estimated figures arrived at by assigning areas of natural vegetation to each world region and then reducing that vegetation by the assumed area of agriculture in 1700. The latter figure was calculated by estimating the extent of agriculture in each region on the basis of the population estimates in C. McEvedy and R. Jones, 1978 *Atlas of World Population History*. Middlesex, Eng: Penguin Books. The remaining values in the table are taken from World Resources Institute, 1987 *World Resources 1987*, Table 18.3 "Land Use, 1850–1980", 272. New York: Basic Books. R. A. Houghton and D. Skole supplied the modeled values for this table for the report. The sources for this table included "four sets of information: maps of natural vegetation, population size and growth data between 1700 and 1980, literature on historical land use and cover, and recent (post-1950) land-use data collected by the United Nations Food and Agriculture Organization (FAO)" (p. 273). The primary driving force in land conversion was presumed to be expansion of sedentary agriculture. Extension of agriculture drew land from natural ecosystems in direct proportion to its area. The model presumes change to be generally linear.

Despite its obvious limitations, this modeled estimate is the most plausible scenario of land use change that we possess on a global scale. Until much more detailed work is done aimed at quantifying changes in the land over time, world region by world region, we can do little more than this.

It seems to be an increasingly frequent occurrence, but it is by no means clear how frequent and how important compared to other factors driving land use.

CULTIVATION

During the past three centuries, the world's cultivated land has expanded by more than 450%. From 2.65 million square km in 1700, an area about the size of Argentina, it has grown to today's 15 million, nearly the size of South America (see Table 3.1). The rate of expansion has also increased. Over the entire period, the average net conversion of land to cropping was more than forty thousand square km per year. Between 1950 and 1980, it amounted to well over a hundred thousand per year. Farmland over the whole three centuries increased most dramatically in the once thinly settled regions of the New World colonized by Europe. In North America, it rose from thirty thousand square km in 1700 to 2 million in 1980; in Latin America, from seventy thousand to 1.5 million. In Europe, already well cultivated in 1700, the increase by 1980 amounted to only about a doubling of farmland, and the years 1950–80 saw not a rise but a 10% decline. The most rapid expansion since World War II has been in the developing world. Cropland retirement and abandonment have been more common in the developed world than the farming of new lands, and much of the land that remains in agriculture does so only because of state subsidy.

The definition of most of the world's land as unsuitable for agriculture is not simply a physical one but a techno-economic one. Crops, of course, can be grown almost anywhere. As the American geographer Isaiah Bowman wrote, we could, if we wished to do so and were willing to meet the costs, raise pineapples in greenhouses at the South Pole; we can move mountains, he observed, if we are first willing to float a bond issue. Of the technologies widely employed, irrigation has done much to expand the area that can be profitably farmed. The world's irrigated land has increased 50-fold since the end of the seventeenth century, from about fifty thousand square km to about 2.5 million (see Table 3.2). It now represents about a sixth of the total cultivated area (L'vovich and White 1990: 243; Rozanov, Targulian, and Orlov 1990: 210). The entire land area thought to be suitable for cultivation is usually estimated at about a quarter to a fifth of the total, twice the area now actively cultivated, and most of it is of low quality.

Major land-cover changes associated with cultivation include conversion – of forest, grassland, or wetland to cropland – and modification – the intensification of agricultural use. A rise in population or consumption prompts the increase of agricultural output by one of two means. More land must be cultivated at the expense of some other land cover, or more intensive use must be made of the lands already farmed, more inputs added to reap larger crops.

The least intensive form of cultivation is known as swidden, shifting, or "slash and burn." Clearance of a plot by burning sends a pulse of nutrients into the soil, which can then be farmed productively for, at most, a few rounds; then the culti-

Table 3.2. *World irrigated area since 1700*
(in thousands of square km)

Date (A.D.)	Area (10^3 km^2)
1700	50
1800	80
1900	480
1949	920
1959	1,490
1980	2,000
1981	2,130
1984	2,200

Source: Rozanov, Targulian, and Orlov 1990.

vator abandons the plot to regenerate naturally and moves elsewhere, to return after a number of years when the land cover has been replenished by regrowth. This system depends on a low pressure of population (in a subsistence economy) or of demand (in a commercial one) relative to the area in use. Most of the land must be left fallow and regrowing for most of the time. Pressure for increased output threatens soil and forest degradation unless the agricultural system is modified, for as land is left fallow for shorter and shorter periods, the natural recovery is less and less complete. If severe degradation is to be avoided, the land's nutrient resources must be supplemented with fertilizers. With this change, permanent cropping of the same field becomes a possibility, but one dependent on the continued provision of vastly greater inputs by the cultivator than swidden agriculture requires. Paddy rice cultivation, most common in the densely settled rural lands of Southeast Asia, requires little land per unit of return, but much labor to shape and maintain the land, and is typically found in areas of dense population as swidden is in sparsely populated areas.

Spreading in tandem with the extension of markets and long-distance trade, high-input commercial agriculture tends to involve local and regional specialization in crop type and output. That, in turn, spells efficiency, at least in a narrow sense; when countries produce mostly what they can best produce relative to other countries, overall output exceeds what would be produced were all countries to seek self-sufficiency. In *The Wealth of Nations* Adam Smith made much of the gains afforded by the specialization of labor. Similar gains have been reaped through the specialization of land. The division of land use, as Smith observed of the division of labor, is limited by the extent of the market; the globalization of exchange has afforded unprecedented opportunities for both.

Intensive permanent agriculture today, especially using modern high-yield crop varieties, depends heavily on the addition of synthetic fertilizers. Techno-logical innovations – pesticides, mechanization, and improved crop strains – further enhance production. At the same time, the specialization and industrialization of agriculture to serve distant consumers make producers, especially in the developing world, vulnerable in new ways to hazards of weather and plant disease and of price levels for particular commodities in the world market. Flexible multiple use of the land in the past often served to insure against risk, to limit or repair damage done to the soil, and to permit spells of natural recovery. "Local, subsistence agricultural systems are usually diverse – their human-made diversity paralleling the diversity of nature. . . . The replacement of natural and traditional cultural diversity by commercial monocultures is a way of destroying . . . resources" (Bennett and Dahlberg 1990: 79). Pollution from the fertilizers and pesticides used in high-technology agriculture adds to its environmental impact. Given contemporary and predicted future levels of population and demand, however, no serious alternative to it seems to exist today.

FORESTS

Forests can evoke widely varying reactions: from fear and hostility to sentimental affection, and most emotions in between. To some eyes, the forest is the haunt of dangerous creatures and an encumbrance to the soil, blocking cultivation or other preferred uses. To others, it is a verdant and attractive cover and a vital resource; it provides wood for building and fuel and protects the soil, the local climate, and the flow of water, while offering much else of value as well. It is sometimes a nuisance to be removed, sometimes a resource to be protected, and like many other resources, it often is highly valued only when it becomes scant.

Perhaps only water exceeds the forest in the variety of the resources that it offers to users or that it withholds from them. Forest may be cleared simply to make room for cultivation, for pasture, or for settlement. Wood serves a vital role worldwide as a fuel, as a construction material, and as an industrial raw material, and forests play important secondary roles in the maintenance of other aspects of the environment. And the state of the forest reflects not only these forces, but increasingly, as damage from pollutants rises, the state of the chemical environment as well. Indeed, "it is possible that the forests illustrate more clearly than anything else how the flows of the earth, be they migration, trade, or atmospheric circulation, interact with the face of the earth" (Williams 1990a: 197).

Change cannot be measured unless the starting and end points both are known. The difficulties of estimating past forest areas to compare with present ones are considerable. More surprising is our uncertainty about the present forest area. Some of the problems are ones of definition. When do scattered trees become a woodland? When does woodland thicken enough to become forest? Other problems are not nominal but real, gaps in knowledge rather than in the way it is stated. Estimates of forest cover in the world's major regions vary substantially. So do estimates of the rate at which it is being removed. The current wave

of tropical deforestation is a matter of much concern, but attempts to quantify it
have produced bewilderingly diverse results.

Still, the net extent of forest cleared in the major regions of the world since
preagricultural times and the approximate chronology of clearing can be
roughly calculated (see Table 3.3); rates of global deforestation in the 1980s
continued to rise (Skole 1994). The world forested area today is smaller than
that of ten thousand years ago by about 8 million square km, an area about the
size of Europe; some 15% of the preagricultural forest has been subtracted from
the world's total. The many millennia from the end of glaciation ten thousand
years ago until 1650 accounted for less than 20% of the clearance; the century
and a half from 1850 to the present has witnessed more than 50% (Kates, Turner,
and Clark 1990: 6–7). As well as net conversion, there has been substantial if ill-
documented modification, mainly the thinning of forests that have not been
entirely cleared and the replacement of unmanaged by plantation stands.

Areas and episodes of rapid clearance fall into several major types: extraction
frontiers of timbering, settlement frontiers of agricultural clearing, and widening periurban rings of fuelwood cutting. Forests have regrown, on the other
hand, in regions of agricultural and timbering abandonment and of government
reforestation and protection. Many of the frontiers of clearance of the seventeenth century are now regaining forest. The broad world trends since the beginning of the twentieth century have been two. Net clearance has changed to regeneration in much of the developed world. At the same time, clearance has
accelerated in the developing world, which has only half the forest today that it
had in 1900 (Williams 1990a: 179). What is true of each realm, though, is not
true of every country or region within it. The national and local experiences have
been quite varied. To those who regard population growth as the principal driving force of environmental change, it seems no coincidence that the developing
world, where contemporary population growth is most rapid, is at the same time
the realm where forest loss is most rapid. A closer look, however, shows matters to
be more complex. In many Third World countries, the agents of clearing are not
landless subsistence cultivators; they are small numbers of landowners or con-
tractors supplying timber, crops, or beef to the world market – sometimes with
direct or indirect state subsidy. Population growth may correlate statistically with
decline in forest without directly driving it.

Today the integration of the world economy makes the resources of almost
any place on the earth's surface available to meet the demands of distant customers, and technological innovation has magnified human ability to clear or
exploit the forest. Steam and then electricity and the internal combustion engine have powered improvements in forest cutting, wood processing, and the
transportation of products to market. Other forms of technical innovation have
less direct but still profound consequences for forest exploitation. The advent of
the railroads created demand for a host of new timber uses – railroad ties were

61

Table 3.3. *Estimated areas of forest clearance (in thousands of square km)*

Region or country		Pre-1650	1650–1749	1750–1849	1850–1978	Total high estimate	Total low estimate
North America	H	6	80	380	641	1,107	1,107
	L						
Central America	H	18	30	40	200	288	282
	L	12					
Latin America	H	18	100	170	637	925	919
	L	12					
Oceania	H	6	6	6	362	380	374
	L	2	4				
USSR	H	70	180	270	575	1,095	997
	L	42	130	250			
Europe	H	204	66	146	81	497	497
	L	176	54	186			
Asia	H	974	216	596	1,220	3,006	2,642
	L	640	176	606			
Africa	H	226	80	−16	469	759	631
	L	96	24	42			
Total highest		1,522	758	1,592	4,185	8,057	
Total lowest		986	598	1,680	4,185		7,449

Source: M. Williams 1990a.

widely blamed for forest depletion in the late nineteenth century United States (Olson 1971) – while also causing inadvertent and indirect losses – large forest fires set by sparks from locomotives, for example. The greater mobility of goods in the railway age let some regions regenerate their forests by substituting imported coal for wood as a fuel or by bringing in their food staples from outside rather than growing them on locally cleared soil. At the same time, it increased pressure on other forests by making them more accessible to external demand.

When demand for a resource rises, so does supply when markets operate smoothly. Scarcity raises prices and makes it profitable to grow new supplies or to produce substitutes. If real prices are expected to go on rising, it becomes more profitable to hold onto rather than to cut one's timber. Yet the timber supply takes time to respond to fluctuating demand. As a resource, the forest is renewable, but it is also depletable on a short time scale. What can be cut or burned quite rapidly may take many decades to recover. Extraction can even damage the soil so severely as to prevent regrowth at all. Nor does the market always account for the physical spillover effects of clearing. Wider effects of deforestation are not always clear-cut but seem often to have been significant: soil loss and sediment flow, streamflow disturbance, species loss, and climatic changes from the local to the global. Certainly, though, such effects have often been exaggerated or imagined. Successful woodland management in areas even of dense rural population (e.g., Holmgren, Masakha, and Sjöholm 1994), moreover, indicates that failures may have more to do with institutional obtacles than with any inherent qualities of the resource. And even when it has temporal or spatial spillover effects, deforestation is not necessarily in sum degradation.

Still, it has been one of the oldest and most persistent of environmental concerns. Three centuries ago, John Evelyn in England wrote at length of the need to protect and manage forests, and the French government minister Jean-Baptiste Colbert enacted a detailed ordinance governing their use (Glacken 1967). Few human activities so alarmed George Perkins Marsh as the removal of the forest. An assessment of the manifold effects of clearance formed the core of *Man and Nature.* The longest chapter by far, "The Woods," speculated on a great range of functions played by the forest in the economy of nature. Given the breadth of external benefits (especially climatic and hydrological) that he ascribed to forests, Marsh had little faith that the pursuit of private goals would best serve society's needs – "every proprietor will, as a general rule, fell his woods, unless he believes that it will be for his pecuniary interest to preserve them" (Marsh [1864] 1965: 201). He thought government ownership or direct subsidies for preservation to private landowners necessary, though he also recognized abuses to which either public or common management might lead.

Forest protection and replanting to prevent damage to soil, climate, timber supply, and streamflow had a prominent place on the agenda of the turn-of-the-century conservation movement. Even as myriad other environmental problems have emerged in recent decades, concern over deforestation has not grown less.

In part, its persistence reflects the discovery of new impacts. The role of forests in storing carbon and thereby helping to regulate the global climate was little recognized or understood by most scientists even at the time of the Princeton *Man's Role* conference in 1955. Today it drives much of the concern over global forest loss.

Prehistoric impacts on the forests were many. At the Princeton conference fire was called "the first great force employed by man" (Stewart 1956) in transforming the landscape. Its routine use by small populations of shifting cultivators, of course, does not progressively subtract from the net forested area, but employed on a wider scale it may have created and surely extended grasslands that have persisted to the present. Some other prehistoric impacts, such as the large-scale clearance of the central Maya Lowlands, were followed, when the civilization collapsed, by land abandonment and near-complete forest regrowth (Whitmore et al. 1990: 35).

Three hundred years ago, some of the most dynamic clearance frontiers were in Europe. Farmland was needed to feed unprecedented populations, and wood was required for construction and fuel. Peasant clearing in Eastern Europe "took a great leap during the sixteenth and seventeenth centuries" (Williams 1990a: 181). It continued steadily thereafter to eat away at the vast forests of the Russian Plain. Already much reduced by 1700, the forested proportion of the Plain has since fallen from more than half to less than a third. Clearing was most active before the end of the nineteenth century (Alayev, Badenkov, and Karavaeva 1990: 550). The expansion of settlement in eighteenth-century China under the Ching dynasty into the thinly peopled southern province of Hunan was a typical state-sponsored frontier of forest clearance. Government incentives – tax exemptions and assistance with farming – attracted immigrants from land-poor areas elsewhere in China. The area under cultivation in Hunan doubled between the 1680s and the 1720s and almost doubled again by 1770. Some of the consequences became apparent by the early 1800s as dense settlement erased the frontier and land grew short: "Firewood had become scarce and expensive. . . . Land clearance on the mountains had resulted in frequent, dangerous earth slides as flash floods grew more frequent and massive. Soil erosion had begun to bite into the productivity of upland fields" (Richards 1990: 170–71).

The Amerindian inhabitants of North America had cleared and thinned sizable patches of the eastern seaboard forest. The European settlers began a much larger assault on the woods – for farmland, for fuel, for buildings and fences, and for cash products such as turpentine and tannin. In the eastern United States, almost half a million square km had been cleared by the middle of the nineteenth century. The net loss there continued even after the settlement frontier had moved west onto the treeless prairie. Cropland abandonment after the Civil War, especially in New England, allowed some areas to revert to forest cover, but not enough to balance the areas being cleared and logged elsewhere. New levels of demand for timber products added to the pressure. The postbellum innovation of using wood pulp to make paper (previously manufactured from rags) is one example. The upper Great Lakes states encouraged rapid and rapacious lumbering on the assumption that farmers would settle on the cleared "cutover" land. The reality was quite different: "deserts of stumpland were created in areas with a marginal growing season and poor, glacially derived soils." Farmers shunned them, and fires completed the ruin that cutting had begun. Much the same happened in remote parts of the South and the Pacific Northwest where poor climate or soil again discouraged farmers from taking over the cleared land (Williams 1990a: 182, 185–87).

The modern clearance in the Amazon region that has attracted so much international attention had a precursor in Brazil. Earlier frontiers of clearing have by now all but erased a rainforest that once covered close to a million square km on the nation's Atlantic coast. Plantation agriculture introduced by the Portuguese colonists after 1500, widespread clearing of new soils for coffee production from the eighteenth century on, food and livestock raising to support growing local populations, and urban and industrial expansion in this economic core area of the nation have obliterated all but a few percent of the forest's original area. Only about 1% remains undisturbed (Peters and Lovejoy 1990: 364; Williams 1990a: 182–83, 187–88).

The British colonial regime in South and Southeast Asia presided over a continuing reduction in the forests of the region – some of it clearing for subsistence and cash-crop agriculture, some of it for timber exports. The imposing *kanazo* forests of lower Burma, in perhaps the most dramatic transformation, were virtually erased during in the Victorian period. Colonial authorities promoted the development of the area through inmigration, clearance, and paddy rice expansion. The forests shrank from more than 35,000 square km in the mid-nineteenth century to only a few hundred hectares in the early twentieth. Change in other parts of the region ran more slowly but steadily in the same direction.

The general world pattern today is a dual one. There is a slow regeneration of forest in the developed, largely temperate world, and there is rapid deforestation in the developing, especially the tropical, countries. But the pattern is an irregular one with many special cases. The United States regained more than a quarter-million square km of forest in several decades beginning in 1910 (Williams 1990a: 196). Since about 1960 it has been again a region of net loss because of agricultural and urban expansion (Platt 1991: 6–7), though many states still have much more forest than they did at the beginning of the century. The former Soviet Union, China, and India, surprisingly, have all gained forest since 1960, at least according to United Nations Food and Agriculture Organization statistics (Williams 1990a: 195–96). (Those for China appear to be quite unreliable [Smil 1992], and Soviet statistics likewise tended to mask severe degradation of forest

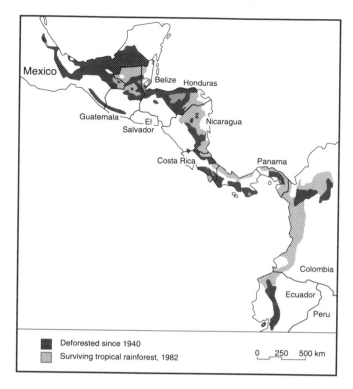

Deforested since 1940
Surviving tropical rainforest, 1982

0   250   500 km

Figure 3.1 Forest clearance in Central America, 1940–82. Redrawn from Nations and Komer 1982 for Williams 1990a.

resources [Barr and Braden 1988].) All have undertaken extensive programs of replanting. The most important element of change, in both its magnitude and its consequences, is the loss of tropical forest.

At the time of European arrival, the 550,000 square km of Central America included 500,000 square km of tropical deciduous forest – differing from tropical rainforest in being adapted to a dry season during the year. Large areas have been cleared for timber extraction, plantation agriculture, and the advent of commercial ranching (see Figure 3.1). Throughout Latin America, a prominent driving force of change has been the conversion of tropical forest to grassland for cattle pasture. The so-called hamburger connection – cheap beef raised on such grassland and exported to the United States to meet commercial demand for fast food – has achieved a notoriety exceeding its actual importance as a driving force (Browder 1988). Considerably less than half of the original Central American forest remains, and it is shrinking by some four thousand square km per year (Williams 1990a: 191–92).

The wave of colonist-based clearing in the Brazilian Amazon represents one of the most notable modern frontiers of land transformation. Government policies encouraging population resettlement and the allure of cheap land to migrants from elsewhere in Brazil have been major motives driving the influx. Home to fewer than ten thousand inhabitants in 1960, the Brazilian state of Rondônia in the late 1980s supported more than half a million, who had poured into the region along newly improved highways in search of land and jobs. The overall population of the Brazilian Amazon, a little over a million in 1910, is now around 20 million. Settlement and clearing have also been substantial in the other countries that hold portions of the basin. Mining, lumbering, and the construction of reservoirs for hydroelectric power generation have made further inroads. By the late 1980s, 6% of the Brazilian Amazon forest had been cleared, with approximately 15% significantly degraded as biotic habitat (Skole and Tucker 1993).

In many countries, especially mountain and desert ones, the present-day forest crisis is largely an energy crisis, one of fuelwood depletion to satisfy the household needs of rising populations (see Figure 3.2). Parts of the now-developed world experienced similar problems in the past. As late as 1885, the yearly growth of trees replaced little more than a third of the wood consumed annually in the Bernese Alps of Switzerland. A looming regional energy shortage was forestalled only by the introduction of coal as a fuel and of railroads to transport it and by the out-migration of much of the zone's population (Pfister and Messerli 1990: 646). Fuelwood depletion today is severe in the highlands of Bolivia, Peru, and Nepal, where clearing also contributes to steep-slope soil erosion. Arid and semi-arid countries in sub-Saharan Africa are especially vulnerable to overcutting because wood makes up 90% of the region's energy budget, a dependence unparalleled in the rest of the world. The state of Kano in northern Nigeria consumes fuelwood at five times the rate of replenishment. Much of the depletion is concentrated in expanding zones around rapidly growing cities, whose inhabitants must walk farther and farther afield to reach sources of supply. "There is virtually no wood for between 50 and 100 km around Niamey, the capital of Niger," and "around Ouagadougou, the capital of Burkina Faso, the average haul for wood is 54 km" (Williams 1990a: 194–95).

A surge has occurred in some tropical countries, notably in Southeast Asia, in exports for industrial wood processing. These regions now challenge the one-time dominance of the timber market by temperate-latitude developed countries. Some are becoming net importers even as their own forests regenerate. The United States, Japan, and Great Britain stand out among the world's principal importers. The largest amounts (in dollar values) of wood exported around the globe in the late 1980s came from the northern forests of Canada, Sweden, Finland, and Russia, but two Southeast Asian countries – Indonesia and Malaysia – contributed respectable shares of the world total, as did Brazil (Williams 1990a: 195). Industrial demand now adds to the pressure on South American rainforests, hitherto threatened mainly by land clearance.

The world's current area of forest is still about three times the area of crop-

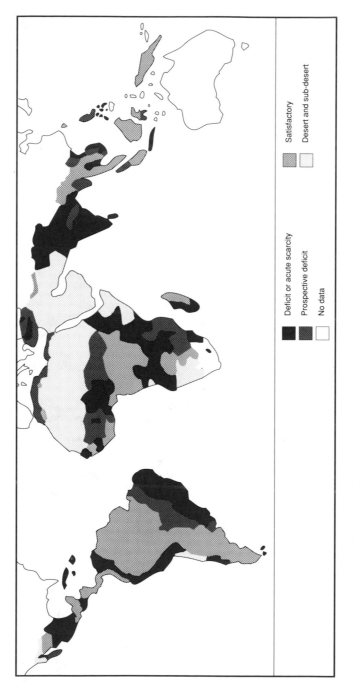

Figure 3.2 Fuelwood deficits. Source: FAO 1983; reprinted from Williams 1990a.

Deficit or acute scarcity

Prospective deficit

No data

Satisfactory

Desert and sub-desert

land. Of the forested area that existed at the dawn of civilization, there still exists more than 80%. It is not, though, entirely the same forest, either in location or in composition. Much of it is of lower quality for many uses than before. Our capacity for rapid clearance today, moreover, far exceeds the power we have ever possessed in the past, and the sources of demand on the forest are of similarly unprecedented magnitude.

GRASSLAND

The largest share of the world's land area directly used for productive activities is grassland used as rangeland or pasture. Grassland is a category of land cover; rangeland and pasture are categories of land use. Both uses primarily involve livestock grazing on the grass cover that in rangeland is sparse and unimproved and that in pasture is cultivated and often integrated with ordinary farming. Most rangeland (covering a larger area than improved pasture) lies in semi-arid and arid zones unsuited to farming, but some grassland lies in medium- and high-rainfall belts once occupied by tropical forests.

Some 68 million square km of the land surface today is grassland, using a very broad definition that includes many lands too barren for any sort of grazing. Some 68 million square km fell into the same class in 1700 (see Table 3.1). By a narrower definition, the contemporary area is 35 million square km, a quarter of the world's land (Graetz 1994: 131). Historically and today, two processes have worked at cross-purposes. In much of the world, cropland expansion (aided by irrigation) and settlement have encroached on the range. In other regions, however, tropical forest has been cleared for pasture. In Central and South America, the area of grassland/pasture has grown by 26% since 1700. Grasslands have also been modified in condition even where not converted to or from some other land cover. Most are used more intensively than ever before. Severe overgrazing of the grass cover is widespread.

Livestock raising on rangelands tends to follow one of two patterns: ranching, which is fixed in place and commercial or market-oriented; or pastoralism, which is migratory and subsistence-based. In the nineteenth century, European-financed ranching spread across many of the world's grasslands – in North and South America, in the interior of Australia, in New Zealand, in South Africa. "Ranching in general has been a frontier activity," ever displaced toward the periphery by cultivation and by intensive, mixed-farming livestock production (Richards 1990: 172–73). Pastoralism, by contrast, remains the dominant form of production over the largest class of the earth's directly exploited lands. Even so, it supports considerably less than 1% of the world's population. More even than ranching, it has suffered from the global trend toward more intensive and profitable activities. Cropland expansion in particular has cut down the area of range available for grazing, while the expansion of livestock herds has increased pressure on the vegetation cover of the area that remains.

The severest forms of grassland degradation have been described as desertification. Few terms so widely used in scientific and popular discussion today are
less standard in their meaning or so productive of confusion (Hellden 1991;
Mortimore 1989; 12–18; Rhodes 1991; Thomas and Middleton 1994). "Desertification" is most often applied to the loss of vegetation or agricultural productivity and to damage to soil, water, and land cover in grasslands or in arid or semi-
arid zones. It is used sometimes to imply a human origin, sometimes to describe
a change that may have occurred from either human or natural causes; sometimes to imply an irreversible process and sometimes not. The term and the
concept have been the topic of a "veritable sandstorm of literature" (Mortimore
1989: 15) during the past two decades.

A short detour into the history of ideas and terminology is appropriate here.
The term "desertification" seems to – but generally does not – denote simply the
creation of a "desert." "Desert" itself is a word of unstable meanings. It was once a
term of social geography denoting a deserted area, a place of few inhabitants. It
has since acquired a strictly climatic meaning: a place of low rainfall. A century
and a half ago, it was widely supposed in the Western world that most deserts – in
the modern sense of the term – were once verdant, wooded lands that had been
made unproductive wastelands by human mismanagement. The assumption per-
vades both Marsh's *Man and Nature* and the writings of his contemporaries. Religious teleology made it plausible; for what purpose would a rational Creator have
created lands as barren as the Sahara? Even the forest lands of the temperate
zone were thought vulnerable to such a fate if mismanaged severely enough. The
belief that "civilization leads to aridity" still held some currency, scientific and
popular, at the onset of the Dust Bowl in the 1930s, and lost none because of it
(Glacken 1956). Climatological advances, though, have made it clear that most
deserts owe their condition to their location in zones of meteorological stability
and consequently low rainfall, not to land-cover change. Still, earlier assumptions occasionally resurface. The geographer Andrew Goudie (1990: 53) quotes
the claim made by two prominent environmentalists in 1970 that across most of
the world, "the deserts themselves are man-made," including the Sahara, of
which assertion he remarks: "Nothing could be further from the truth. The
Sahara is many millions of years old, predates man, and is the product of the
nature of the great atmospheric circulation, occupying an area of descending
air."

But if deserts are not necessarily features of human origin, similarly unproductive landscapes can be created, extended, or further degraded by human
action – notably by the overgrazing of rangeland and the cultivation of semi-arid
regions. Such creation of desert-*like* landscapes, if not of meteorological deserts,
can reasonably be called desertification, and the term has had widespread currency ever since the United Nations Conference on Desertification convened in
1977. From the beginning, however, it has been ill defined and imprecise, more
effective in evoking vivid and inaccurate images of onrushing sand dunes than in

conveying any clear scientific meaning. One drylands researcher recalled a UN consultation that "spent at least a year discussing desertification before we got around to asking what the term meant" (quoted in Thomas and Middleton 1994: 7). Official definitions have not subsequently been lacking – indeed, in recent years they have succeeded one another with the rapidity of the later Caesars – but their very profusion and variety have been as confusing as the complete absence of a definition would have been. What the word denotes can range from vegetation and soil degradation in semi-arid and arid regions to any kind of land degradation under any conditions whatever; from degradation caused solely by human action to change produced by any agency; and from irreversible and complete destruction of the productivity of the land and land cover to change of any lesser degree and duration. The large estimates disseminated by the United Nations Environment Programme, depicting as much as a third of the earth's surface as subject to some degree of desertification, suffer so much from this haziness of definition as to have produced a scientific backlash questioning the very usefulness of the term and the concept. Adding to dissatisfaction with the official numbers have been other flaws in the research that produced them, such as a tendency to generalize findings from small study areas over much larger regions, to assume degradation to be of human rather than natural (e.g., drought) origin, and to assume it to be permanent rather than reversible (Thomas and Middleton 1994).

Yet the widespread severe degradation of grassland vegetation cover and soils is unquestionable even though much else about it remains open to debate (Graetz 1994). The high variability of rainfall in many grasslands means that water supply and vegetation cover for grazing may fall far short of the average in years or even decades of drought. When the grass cover has been overgrazed or impoverished, when the soil has been salinized by irrigation or loosened by plowing, when the subsistence needs of high human and livestock population and the pressures for production of a commercial or a command economy are added, the land may be severely degraded and the societies dependent upon it devastated. The most notable examples come from the Sahel zone south of the Sahara Desert in Africa, and particularly from the severe droughts, land decline, and episodes of famine that occurred in the region in the 1970s and 1980s. In making sense of the events of the 1970s and since, it has proven difficult to untangle the various strands of cause and consequence. Unusually severe meteorological drought cannot be ignored as an immediate factor (though some scientists have contended that that drought was itself a product of human action). Certainly its implications, and its standing as an environmental disaster rather than a mere climatic event, had much to do with changes in society, with the increase of population or of herd sizes beyond the capacity of the land, and with the breakdown of traditional systems of coping with disaster. To what degree the decline in land productivity has proven or will prove physically reversible with a shift back to more usual climatic conditions is also unclear (Tucker et al. 1991).

WETLANDS

Lands covered all or part of the year with water, but not so deeply and permanently as to be classed as water surface per se, are known as wetlands, They include a wide array of subtypes: swamps, marshes, bogs and peatlands, river margins, and so on. They overlap with several common land-cover classes, including forests, cropland, and grassland; rice paddies, for example, can be considered cultivated wetlands, and swamps wetland forests. Wetlands occur in both salt- and freshwater environments, with most of their area in the latter.

The most drastic form of wetland alteration, conversion to dry land through drainage or filling, has been a globally important form of land-cover change. Some regional numbers for its magnitude are available: some 200,000 square km have been altered by drainage in Europe and Russia and up to half a million in the United States (Richards 1986); all of the original 20,000 square km of swampland in South Australia has been lost (Williams 1974). Most of this transformation has occurred during the past century. Very rough estimates count the present world area of wetlands of all types at about 8.5 million square km and the area to date lost to drainage – mostly for agriculture – at about 1.5 million (Williams 1990b).

Conversion by drainage is undertaken both to expand the area of cultivation or construction and in quest of various fringe benefits. Wetlands have long lain mired in disrepute: as seemingly useless and unproductive territory, neither true land nor water but a treacherous impersonation of each; as the natural haunt of monsters, from the Behemoth of the Old Testament, which "lay in the covert of the reeds and in the marsh," to Hollywood's Creature from the Black Lagoon; and as the abode of smaller creatures whose banishment by drainage aroused no regrets even before some were identified as the carriers of the malaria and yellow fever widely associated with wetlands. Conversion to dry land has been seen not only as a profitable feat of environmental engineering but as a civilizing act. The grandest and most useful deed that Goethe's Faust could think of to redeem himself was the diking and draining of a vast area of coastal wetland to provide arable land for millions of settlers, crowned by the conquest of a malarial marsh on its fringe. For the inhabitants of early modern Holland, "the act of separating dry land from wet was laden with scriptural significance" (Schama 1986: 35).

As often happens, though, an activity that has served some as a yardstick of virtue has become for others the very thing to be measured and found short. If once it seemed that "the only good wetland was a drained wetland" (Daiber 1992: 164), it is now widely recognized that wetlands in their unaltered state provide important benefits. What has encouraged continued drainage is the fact that these benefits often are lost not so much by the reclaimer as by those living in a much wider area. They range from habitat and breeding ground for migratory fowl and fish to pollutant absorption to water storage that can regulate streamflow and moderate flooding. Once drained and farmed, moreover, wet-

land soils frequently deteriorate and fail to keep the promise of a sustained bo-
nanza of agricultural productivity. Medical and public health advances have diminished some of the genuine dangers that once prompted reclamation. The
very word "wetlands," H. J. Walker (1990: 277) suggests, is a modern one that
"has evolved in response to the recognition that the terms 'marsh' and 'swamp'
are not the waste lands that they were believed to be during recent history." In
much of the developed world, tightened regulation of the use of wetlands has
followed a profound change in attitudes toward them, and such regulation has
significantly slowed though it has not stopped their conversion. In the United
States, regulation has grown to the extent that "to deny that a parcel of wetland
even is really wetland is the best strategy for an owner wishing to develop it"
(Meyer 1994: 109). Reclassification has become the homage that drainage pays
to preservation; drainage itself, the transformation that dare not speak its name.

The patchwork, uncoordinated actions of many individual holders can efficiently clear vast forests; draining large wetlands has tended to require joint and
public action. Undertaken privately, it would bog down in intractable problems
of coordination. Regulating water flow in a large wetland divided into many
individual holdings requires close cooperation that runs afoul, when undertaken
in a free market, of the high costs of transactions, especially given the frequent
difficulty of the enterprise and thus the powerful incentives to back out or lag
behind. What David Hume concisely termed the "trouble and expense" of a large
drainage project can become the stuff of legend. A corps of laborers and sur-
veyors in John Bunyan's ([1678] 1960: 16) *Pilgrim's Progress* had been "for above
these sixteen hundred years" employed in trying "to make good ground" of the
miry Slough of Despond, with no results yet visible. Drained organic peat soils
are vulnerable to shrinkage and subsidence, first from desiccation and then from
decay. As well as damaging their productivity – the problems of reclamation often have only begun when the water is removed – this process can lower the land
surface and make it again prone to flooding.

Drainage, before recent years, seemed to offer positive externalities – in particular, the improvement of health throughout a wider area. For this reason, as
well as because of the difficulties of coordination, the amount of drainage undertaken by individuals for their private benefit was long thought to be much less
than the socially desirable amount. It is the mirror image of today's arguments
for preservation and offered a strong rationale for coerced reclamation as a classic public good. Unassisted private action was once thought to drain too little as
unfettered private action today is thought to drain too much. The state, unlike
the market, can direct action and apportion or absorb its costs without relying on
the consent of all concerned. It has usually proven a willing partner in reclamation ventures thought likely in the end to increase health and wealth alike.
County drainage districts with the power to take, tax, and spend formed the
indispensable engine of the American reclamation movement. Benito Mussolini
made propaganda hay out of his drainage enterprises in the malarious Pontine

Marshes as proof of what an authoritarian government could do to improve the environment. Governments have had to coerce not only would-be free riders secretly anxious to gain from drainage but the genuinely recalcitrant as well. Seventeenth-century proponents of the drainage of the English Fens promised not only to open up new land for agriculture, but as a bonus of their operations to free the inhabitants of "cloudy" air and "water putrid, and muddy, yea full of loathesome vermin" (Webb and Webb 1922: 14) Yet much of the population demurred. They saw drainage as both an impious interference with God's handiwork and an unwise interference with easy inland navigation and with the rich pastures, reeds, and "great plenty and variety of fish and fowl" that the wetlands afforded. Many joined in riots in the 1630s against the dams and sluices built by the Dutch engineers the government had brought in (Lindlay 1982). Turn-of-the-century tsarist expeditions sent to reclaim large portions of the swamps and marshes of the Ukraine and the western Russian Plain aroused fears of diminished rainfall and the damage that might be done to mills, fisheries, and navigation (French 1964). The livelihoods and cultures of the Dinka and Nuer pastoralists in the vast Sudd swampland of southern Sudan are bound to an environment that would be greatly shrunk by the proposed Jonglei Canal, a channelization project intended to increase the flow of the Nile by diminishing evaporation losses in the Sudd.

Coastal wetlands, though much smaller in area than inland ones, have come under as severe an attack. They too occur in a variety of forms – tidal flats in many parts of the world, mangrove swamps in the tropical latitudes, salt marshes in higher ones (Walker 1990: 277–78). Urban-industrial filling creates dry surface area for the expansion of ports and settlements. Agriculture also encroaches on the sea. Polders – which form a large fraction of the Netherlands and are also widespread in East Asia – are lands reclaimed from the sea that have a high but controllable water table; polderization in the Far East is often combined with rice production and fish raising. Coastal reclamation in some soils runs the same risks of subsidence and oxidation encountered inland. Being so close to the sea it is more vulnerable to renewed flooding, and especially with the prospect of sea-level rise induced by global climate change.

SETTLEMENTS

Land covers of growing importance are those associated with nonagricultural uses – settlement, industry, transportation and communication routes, reservoirs, and so on. Russian soil scientists estimate that these uses now occupy about 6% of the world's land area (Rozanov, Targulian, and Orlov 1990: 205). Human settlement is the most significant. If agricultural frontiers are fading in importance, urban ones are everywhere growing. Every urban–rural fringe zone is a miniature expanding wave of land-use/cover change where cropland that once displaced forest, wetland, or grazing is now displaced by settlement.

From less than 10% of the global population in 1700, city dwellers now account for nearly half of a much larger total (Berry 1990: 103, 115). In North America and Western Europe alike, they account for about three-quarters. Rapid urbanization in the Third World has created huge and exploding cities, their growth fueled by rural-to-urban migration. The "primate" capital cities of many Third World countries have expanded with dramatic speed, often overtaxing the built infrastructure and the resource base. Lagos, Nigeria's largest city, grew fourfold between 1963 and 1980 (Udo et al. 1990: 596). The metropolitan area of Mexico City grew by six times from 1950 to the late 1980s, reaching a total of about 18 million (Ezcurra 1990: 581). Both the number and the percentage of the world's population living in cities annually reach new heights.

Even so, densities of urban population today, at least in the developed world, do not match those of the nineteenth century and earlier. City dwellers dependent on horse and foot as the principal means of getting around lived in a congestion that automobiles and mass transportation have done much to diminish. The change has been most evident in the developed world, whose central cities have often declined in population as suburbs and exurbs have grown. The compact and crowded early modern city has in the wealthier countries now been replaced by the sprawling low-density metropolis in a process of "counter-urbanization" (Berry 1990). Even in the developing world, densities have fallen, which is to say that the land required for each new city dweller, and thus the urban pressure on the surrounding area, has grown. Mexico City is today's epitome of uncontrolled Third World megacity growth. Yet it too reached its peak population density at around 20,000 people per square km in the early twentieth century. Today, though its population is twenty times higher and its settled area vastly greater, Mexico City's overall density is less than 15,000 per square km (Ezcurra 1990: 580).

The distinctive features of urban land cover alter the environment locally and even regionally, affecting the climate, water flows, and plant and animal diversity and creating new human hazards of health and safety (Berry 1990). Cities and areas within them vary greatly, though, in the degree to which the land cover is transformed. Built-up and paved land, the most extreme case, represents a relatively small part of most cities' land area. It accounts for less of the typical developed-world metropolitan area than does tree cover (I. Douglas 1994). Besides its local effects, urban expansion strains the resources of cities' hinterlands. Urban environmental problems may be exported to the city's hinterland: physically through water and air pollution and resource extraction, economically if costs are billed to the nation as a whole. The consumption of land is the most obvious impact. The completion of the Aswan Dam on the Nile River has allowed a large acreage to be brought under irrigation, but the gain has only kept pace with the loss of farmland to the sprawling expansion of Cairo (White 1988). But the urban impacts spread in exurban waves or frontiers far beyond the area actually converted to settlement. Timber, fuel, cement, and water are also extracted from ever-widening zones around cities to meet their needs, and urban wastes – landfills, water and air pollutants – are sent out in return (I. Douglas 1994). It is around the cities of the developing world, those that today are growing most explosively, that the transformation of land to urban cover is proceeding most rapidly and with the severest consequences.

Locally, the concentration of people concentrates their impacts on the environment and their vulnerability to environmental hazards. At the same time, urbanization may have positive environmental impacts (Lewis 1992). Migration can relieve pressure on rural land cover, and the spatial concentration of population may make possible economies of scale in resource use and delivery that lessen rather than increase the net human impact on the environment.

SOIL AND SEDIMENT IMPACTS

Land-cover changes have many environmental consequences, most immediately for the land itself. Soils may be affected where they exist or they may be transported elsewhere.

SOIL ALTERATION

Various human activities, without removing soil, alter it in place. Farming without adequate inputs depletes soils of vital plant nutrients (see Chapter 6). Destructive compaction of the soil structure is the consequence of a variety of activities – such as use of farm and logging machinery, construction, and to some extent the use of artificial fertilizers – and lessens agricultural productivity. Wetland drainage in some areas, particularly in Southeast Asia, has led to severe acidification and drying and shrinkage of pyrite-containing and peat soils (Buol 1994: 219). Dehumification is the loss of humus, or soil organic matter, which is important in maintaining soil structure and productivity and in supporting the microbiotic soil community. Cultivation of new areas is usually followed by a considerable decrease in soil humus, although levels can be maintained indefinitely with proper management. Very rough global estimates of rates of humus loss from the global soil stock suggest that the average in the past 50 years is more than twice the average rate for the last 300 years, and more than 30 times the rate for the past 10,000, indicating an exponential acceleration of loss from a total stock now reduced by some 15% from its original size (Rozanov, Targulian, and Orlov 1990: 211–13).

Having destroyed Carthage at the end of the Punic Wars, the Roman victors sowed it with salt to ensure that it would never be settled again. Irrigation in many parts of the world, if slowly and inadvertently, can have much the same effect. If measures for proper drainage are not taken, the channeling of water onto the land can raise the water table. Salts are brought upward with the water into the surface layer of soil and are left behind in it when the water evaporates. Salinized ground can sometimes be reclaimed by flushing it with water, but the process can be quite difficult and expensive. Like most human impacts on the land, salinization has a long history. Archaeologists have suggested it as the cause of widespread land abandonment and agricultural crisis in Mesopotamia several millennia ago (Jacobsen and Adams 1958). George Perkins Marsh ([1864] 1965: 324) noted the tendency for irrigated soil in arid lands to be "rendered infertile by an excess of saline matter in its composition"; the process had already created areas of "sterilized ground" in Egypt and India. Matters in Egypt improved little when British colonial rule began late in the nineteenth century. The increasing control over the flow of the Nile weakened the flushing effect of its annual floods on the soil. The spread of irrigation systems designed without adequate drainage led to the failure of the Egyptian cotton crop in 1909 (Headrick 1990: 64).

Today the increase of irrigated land across the world only about matches the area lost from production due to the build-up of salt. Irrigated area is remaining about constant, not because none is being added, but because as much is being abandoned. Large areas of significant soil salinization lie in the Middle East, Pakistan, and northern India, in the regions surrounding the Mediterranean, in northern Mexico and the American Southwest, and in western China and former Soviet Central Asia (Buol 1994: 219). A team of Soviet scientists conducted the broadest quantitative assessment of global soil degradation. They estimate that a million square km – an area equal to about 6 or 7% of the entire area now under cultivation – have been rendered unproductive over human history by salinization and other impacts connected with irrigation: the productivity of another 1.1 million square km has been significantly lowered (Rozanov, Targulian, and Orlov 1990: 210).

SOIL EROSION

No impact on soil is more dramatic than its removal. Nor is any form more natural. Soil is created on site and relocated elsewhere in nature as a matter of course. Running water, wind, and waves are constantly sculpting the surface of the earth and rearranging its components. Human land use, however, often accelerates erosion, and to a rate far beyond the natural. Soil, like plant and animal species, is a renewable resource, but it too is one that can be depleted or exhausted if not managed carefully. Even in the present-day United States, after a number of decades of active government programs for soil conservation, it is estimated that erosion occurs at roughly ten or more times the rate of new formation. Elsewhere the ratio may often run into the hundreds or beyond. Difficulties arise in separating the human impact from the natural rate – a task made especially difficult by the wide fluctuations in the natural rate by setting and season. Yet the character and the rough degree of human impact are clear enough. What is not so clear is that global, regional, or local rates of loss are economically threatening or unacceptable, or that the money that would have to be invested in lowering them would be well spent.

Agriculture is the principal culprit in increased erosion rates. It is also their principal victim. The usual initial consequence of clearing for cultivation is a sharp increase in soil loss, especially where preexisting cover is removed. Overgrazing by livestock thins out protective vegetation with similar results. Crops and farming systems differ in the land covers that each substitutes for the original and in the degree of erosion that ensues. Modern population growth and agricultural commercialization in parts of the East African Highlands have led to the widespread replacement of leafy banana plants, which protect the soil relatively well, with crops such as tubers that do not (Berry, Lewis, and Williams 1990: 540). Vulnerability also depends on weather and topography. Soils on steep slopes are highly prone to erosion; so are those in tropical climates experiencing seasons of very high rainfall.

Some general indicators of the importance of human action are available. Severe water erosion has occurred widely around the globe (Buol 1994), not always becoming worse over time. Sediment records for study areas in Australia, Wisconsin, and Maryland show a common pattern reflecting similar histories of land use: high erosion rates after land clearance in the nineteenth century, lower ones after the introduction of better soil management practices in the early to middle decades of the twentieth (I. Douglas 1990). On the other hand, deforestation in much of the developing tropics is contributing at present to greatly increased soil loss. Not all of what improvement has occurred has been deliberate; human actions can unintentionally improve the environment just as they can unintentionally damage it. Forest regrowth on agricultural land abandoned for economic reasons can lessen erosion without reflecting environmental concern.

Soil loss becomes economically significant when it translates into diminished agricultural production. The 1930s saw worldwide fears of rampant erosion. The U.S. Agriculture Department's Soil Conservation Service (SCS) seized the opportunity created by popular panic over the Dust Bowl and the Depression to implement a broad program of measures protecting agricultural lands. Much of the SCS literature was inaccurate or ill founded (Crosson 1983): exaggerated in its claims of the damage done by past farming practices and the civilizations supposedly destroyed by land mismanagement, sweeping in its generalizations about land already lost and currently endangered – and quite successful in controlling a problem that truly existed even though its dimensions were overstated. Conservation measures implemented included revegetation of cleared land, contour plowing, the planting of windbreaks, and fallowing and crop rotation.

None of these techniques was new; farmer awareness of potential erosion and of measures for its control is of prehistoric vintage. Many forms of folk agricultural technology have some of their rationale in soil protection and management. Even steep slopes have been long and sustainably cultivated through terracing. But such measures, and terracing most of all, require large inputs of

labor and land that cannot always be provided when simple subsistence is difficult enough. Many of the efforts of European colonial authorities in the 1930s
and later to impose soil conservation measures of their own devising on indigenous groups failed for this reason or because the measures themselves were ill
designed, though as often as not the authorities mistook noncompliance for
ignorance, unconcern, or hidebound attachment to tradition (Grove 1990: 39–
40). Other social conditions may discourage investment in maintaining the land.
Landless farmers who cultivate others' fields as tenants may have little incentive
to improve or even to maintain their productivity. Pressure of growing demand
on a limited land base may cause farming to expand onto fragile soils. Yet it is
dense populations that may provide the labor needed to undertake the labor-
intensive measures that can protect or maintain the soil; declines, as well as
increases, in numbers can be devastating to the land for just this reason. Mutual
reinforcement of modern population growth, agricultural demand, food production, economic diversification, and land resource protection and improvement is summed up in the title of a study of a densely settled zone in Kenya: *More
People, Less Erosion* (Tiffen, Mortimore, and Gichuki 1994).

Wind erosion – also called deflation – is another natural process of sediment
removal, transfer, and deposition that human activities often worsen. Natural
forces have transported loose dust on a continental scale from such areas as the
Sahara Desert and the loess lands of northern China to deposit it many hundreds, even thousands of kilometers away. As with water erosion, most of the
human contribution is made when agriculture loosens soil that high winds may
then blow away. In severe storms, the consequences can be dramatic. On the
world's vast mid-latitude plains, wind erosion is worsened by such natural phenomena as droughts that deplete the vegetation cover and by such human ones
as plowing. The world looked at the Dust Bowl on the American Great Plains in
the 1930s and saw "deserts on the march." The Plains historian James C. Malin,
in his paper at the 1955 Princeton conference, attacked some of the wilder
claims made about the role of human disturbance in that episode. Countering
"the allegation that the dust storms of the 1930s were *caused* by 'the plow that
broke the Plains,'" he showed that such events had often occurred even before
farming had greatly disturbed the soils. Malin quoted a description of a classic
Plains dust storm: "the sun was concealed, and the darkness so great, that I could
not distinguish objects more than three or four times the length of my horse.
The dust, sand, and ashes, were so dense that one appeared in danger of suffoca-
tion." It had been written, he observed, not in 1930, at the onset of the Dust
Bowl, but in 1830, long before any substantial agricultural settlement (Malin
1956).

But if human disturbance is not a necessary condition for such events, it still
can greatly increase their severity. Cultivation often worsens – sometimes catastrophically – the dust storms that occur naturally on semi-arid plains. If the Dust
Bowl was not as fully the result of human mismanagement as has often been

claimed, neither was the human contribution to it a negligible one. Beginning in the early 1900s, agricultural development on the Plains relied on "dry farming" techniques that combined deep plowing with the systematic loosening of the surface layer. Cropland acreage in the region reached a new high just before the severe droughts and windstorms of the 1930s arrived to blow away large quantities of the loosened soil (Riebsame 1990: 569–70). Even better farming methods have not prevented high erosion losses, which – here and elsewhere – tend to occur episodically in extreme events rather than slowly and gradually. Today, "wind erosion removes 907 million t of soil a year from the United States, mainly in exceptional storms, such as that of February, 1977, which removed as much as 1,100 t/km^2 from parts of eastern Colorado" (I. Douglas 1990: 228). "Black storms" have appeared on the southern Russian Plain with the tilling of the soil: "A storm in 1960, with wind speeds up to 28 m/sec, completely blew away a 40–cm arable layer from a chernozem field not far from Donbass. . . . In the south of the Ukraine, a sandstorm moved 1.2–1.6 km^3 of solid material, which amounts to 960–1,280 million tons of fine soil" (Alayev, Badenkov, and Karavaeva 1990: 556). The current areas of most serious wind erosion are in northern China and in Africa south of the Sahara (Buol 1994: 220).

SEDIMENT TRANSFER

Meaningful global figures for human-induced sediment transfer are not easily calculated. In a large natural flow of earth materials, the human contribution is hard to sort out. Measurement is one problem, and so is deciding what to measure. Different scales of transfer pose the same question that social scientists encounter in measuring trade or migration: How short a move is too short to be counted? But figures on some forms of transfer and size of impact can be estimated and the regions of the greatest human impact separated from the others. It is clear in any case that human action, "long recognized as a major geological agent, . . . will soon account for most of the transfer of earth surface materials" (I. Douglas 1990: 230). Earth material transfer is of ancient importance at the local scale, but global totals began a rapid acceleration with the onset of the Industrial Revolution.

Some forms of sediment transfer are, at least at one stage or another, deliberate responses to human demands; there seems at the global level to be a rough equivalence in size between the intended and the inadvertent human-induced flows. The construction industry moves mountains of earth materials. In the early 1980s, the world produced almost 900 million tons of cement a year, two and a half times the output of the early 1960s and about the same as the annual sediment yield of the Amazon River. Annual world coal production was approaching three billion tons in the same period (I. Douglas 1990: 221). Canal construction, river straightening, and dredging – locally rather than globally significant – enlarge, reshape, or maintain the water surface.

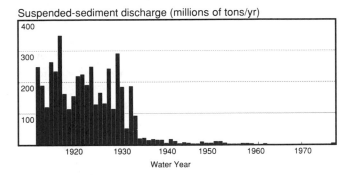

Suspended-sediment discharge (millions of tons/yr)

Figure 3.3 Historic sediment discharge of the Colorado River, in millions of tons per year. Source: Schwarz et al. 1990.

Material removed from one place must end up in another; excavations in some areas build new hills or fill depressions elsewhere. Waste in large quantities sometimes becomes a useful resource, as when landfill creates new land on coastlines for urban expansion. More often it becomes a hazard and a nuisance. Materials extraction, especially mining, can dramatically affect downstream areas by adding dislodged sediment to river channels. The nineteenth century saw local devastation of this sort in California's Sacramento and San Joaquin river basins and in the Malaysian peninsula. Metal-rich gravels (gold in California and tin in Malaysia) attracted miners employing destructive hydraulic techniques. High-pressure jets of water tore down the hillsides and released the gravel for winnowing. The incidental – though hardly hidden – consequence was the overloading of stream channels with the sediment debris. Alluvial tin mining in Malaysia supplied more than half the world's consumption in 1895, but at a considerable cost to the land: "The Perak River in the northwestern Peninsula, which 'ran clear as crystal over its sandy bed' before tin-mining began in the 1870s, was already a silt-laden eyesore" by the first decade of the twentieth century (Brookfield et al. 1990: 497). Downstream damage in both regions continued long after the mining had stopped. Sediment choked some river channels as far downstream as their ocean harbors, disrupting navigation. Unprecedentedly large floods damaged farms and towns, forcing some to abandon their sites altogether.

If mining can glut streambeds with unwanted sediment, dams starve their downstream reaches. The lost material may have been an important natural resource – for agriculture, for recreational beaches – farther down the basin, and the clear water released through the dam is likely to erode more. When Hoover Dam blocked the Colorado River in the 1930s, sediment supply to the river below ceased abruptly (see Figure 3.3). Egypt's Aswan High Dam now arrests the massive flow of sediment that built up the Nile Delta in the Mediterranean – a couple of square kilometers of the Delta's promontories slide away every year (I. Douglas 1990: 229) – and that replenished the valley's farmlands in annual floods. A

81

reservoir's effectiveness in storage is steadily reduced as the material withheld from downstream accumulates in its basin. The hydrologist Luna B. Leopold (1956: 646), writing in *Man's Role*, foresaw a time "several generations hence . . . when great lengths of major river valleys will consist of reservoirs more or less filled with sediment." Land-use management to diminish erosion in the watershed area can delay this outcome but not prevent it. China's apparent wealth of mountain hydropower potential, still only modestly developed, is much devalued by natural liabilities, especially the inescapable cascades of sediment from loess lands drained by the rivers in the north.

Fluvial sedimentation – the transport of sediment by running water – is globally the dominant form of earth-material transfer. Natural levels form a most confusing background to human impact. Rivers running through areas empty of human occupants do not necessarily run clear. Tropical mountains and weak, easily eroded bedrock furnish especially high natural sediment loads. Some river systems in high-energy, unstable zones – high mountains in low latitudes, for example, such as the Himalayas – are already loaded to or near to capacity with naturally provided sediment. For this reason, mountain deforestation, though often blamed for flooding and high sediment deposition downstream of the Himalayas, may play at most a minor role there and in similar systems (Schwarz et al. 1990: 263; Chapman and Thompson 1995).

Some numbers suggest the general magnitude of increased sedimentation in a range of situations (see Table 3.4). The dissolved content of many rivers has also been notably increased, in some cases through urban and industrial emissions, in others through the release of salt in agriculture. But sediment transport is a highly seasonal business and one that also fluctuates from year to year. Much earth-material movement occurs in short bursts rather than steadily over long periods. The current sediment load of a river, moreover, is not a reliable index to current patterns of erosion in the river's basin, because of travel delays in the system: "the sediment passing a measurement station . . . will be derived from erosion of river banks, that may contain material deposited on the valley floor during some past phase of a different climate or during a phase of brutal land clearance. . . ." Figures for total sediment transport depend very much on the spatial scale of inquiry adopted. A great deal of material may be eroded, yet most of it may be transported only a short distance. By the mid-1970s, only a third of the material eroded since 1700 within a small basin in Maryland with a varied land-use history had been removed from the basin (I. Douglas 1990: 225–28).

Coastal sediment movement is another major class of natural transfer affected by human action. The high energy and tremendous power of natural coastal processes make the zone a hazardous one for human occupance. Yet its attractions for human activities – on account of its accessibility and its richness in many resources – have encouraged a degree of occupance, investment, and exploitation out of proportion to the land area it covers (Walker 1990). Like floods in fluvial erosion, rapid and severe natural events play a more important role in

Table 3.4. *Increases of sediment yield due to human activity*

Situation	Magnitude of increase	Source
In large rivers, generally	3.5 times	Dedkov and Mozzherin 1984
In small rivers, generally	8	"
Forest clearance, Cameron Highlands, Malaysia	5	Shallow 1956
From erosion of forest roads, Idaho	200–500	Megahan 1975
Forest clearance, South Island, New Zealand	up to 100	Whitehouse 1983
Coon Creek, Wisconsin 1870–1930	10	Trimble and Lund 1982
Cultivation on forest land, Java	2	Douglas 1981
Trinidad	9	"
Ivory Coast	18	"
Tanzania	5	"
Urbanization in rainforest area, Malaysia	20	"

Source: Douglas 1990.

shaping coastlines than their rarity would suggest. Single hurricanes have cut back beach cliffs and barrier islands by as much as 30 m (I. Douglas 1990: 229). The human impact on the coastal sediment budget does not come close to matching that of nature in terms of energy expended. It operates less by matching or surpassing natural forces than by pointing them in new directions.

The shoreline is a depot for sediment arriving by river: hence any changes in the upstream output may be registered at the coast. Dams and other obstructions diminish the influx and can cause downstream riverbanks and coasts to erode; land-use change that increases erosion upstream can increase accumulation below. Once arrived at the shore, sediment drifts laterally, another process that can transmit human impacts some distance away. Engineering structures are built for a number of purposes, including navigation, harbor protection, and erosion control. Their actual results frequently differ from their intended ones. The construction of seawalls and many other shoreline structures "often enhances the erosion that they were intended to stop," by redirecting the action of the incoming waves to unforeseen effect and by blocking the lateral drift of sediment. Deliberate replenishment of beaches is the most direct response to their erosion, "a common remedy from Lagos to Zeebrugge to Santa Barbara" (I. Douglas 1990: 229). It is also a very costly and relatively unsuccessful one that as often as not simply gives the natural machinery of erosion more material to carry away.

CONCLUSION

Save for the processes of soil loss and sediment flow, most human impacts on the land are readily distinguished from natural changes, and today they far outstrip the latter in rate and degree. The land surface has been greatly altered by humankind during the past 300 years. It is being altered today more rapidly than ever. Much modern change in the most densely settled lands occurs not from a largely natural state to a human-shaped one, but from one human-shaped state to another. Much urban construction, probably most in the developed world, is redevelopment; much forest that is removed is not being cut for the first time. Rapid change in the past tended to be localized on frontiers of expansion and in and around growing urban centers. Change today remains spatially variable, but the thinly settled or little-used lands suited to primary frontiers are all but gone. Driving the intensification of land use is the worldwide drive for increased production – to feed an exploding population, to raise living standards, to compete for markets with other producers.

Land alteration is an objective fact: land degradation exists in the eye of the beholder. Many widely cited examples can be viewed from other perspectives as land improvement. That the world's lands support unprecedented numbers of people is, for some, proof enough of a net improvement; population and income growth in turn offer incentives for ever more efficient and sustainable land use. Some changes may be seen as degradation in themselves yet be considered acceptably low costs for the near-term benefits of the activities that produce them; problems that arise, it is supposed, can be dealt with by future technological innovations.

To others, it seems that the soils are being mined of their substance, and being degraded in such a way as to impair their future productivity and critically diminish the numbers that the earth can support in the long run; that soil is a fundamental resource for which no technology can substitute. Land management to sustain slowly renewable resources may not be economically sustainable under commercial pressures. Such is especially the case in periods of high inflation, when the gains from conservation are far outweighed by the gains to be had from depleting the resource and investing the profits elsewhere. And many human-induced changes in the land that tend to lower its usefulness for many activities – soil erosion and salinization are good examples – are quite persistent: they are reversible only very slowly or with enormous effort and investment, footprints less in the sands of time than in its wet concrete. This fact has gone from being an argument for transformation to an argument against it. Many, perhaps most forms of land transformation have long been viewed as a gift to posterity and not a theft from it, an investment of labor to make useful resources for future generations out of the natural wastelands one confronts today. The favorably loaded term "reclamation" has long been a synonym for irrigation and wetland drainage. "Improving" the land has long meant altering it in ways that would now, at least in much of the developed world, be thought damaging: clearing forests, plowing rangeland, filling marshes and swamps, and paving cropland. Widespread awareness is relatively recent that the persisting damage done may balance or outweigh the benefits reaped.

The immediate human impacts on the land reach a global magnitude, if they do, in a patchwork and cumulative fashion. They are, as Brookfield (1989) puts it, "changes that are local in domain, but which are widely replicated and which in sum constitute change in the whole human environment." Individually, they pose "issues of less than global domain . . . but they add up to a global effect." Yet they also connect with much longer chains of environmental consequences – detailed in later chapters – some of them reaching fluid global systems such as the climate. The variety and complexity of these further impacts greatly complicates the already difficult assessment of many land-cover changes as improvement or degradation.

4

Biota

In remodeling its home the earth, humankind has displaced many of the planet's other inhabitants. Millennia of human activities have eroded the world's diversity of plants and animals. Some species have disappeared; many more have been reduced in number and in spatial extent. Both changes began in prehistory. Both have accelerated in recent years. Rapid clearing in the species-rich tropical forest, largely a post–World War II phenomenon, alone threatens to multiply all past human-induced extinctions by several times during the twenty-first century.

Such impoverishment of the world's biota is a trend more easily asserted than felt. Nothing seems more typically modern than an ever-increasing diversity of experience. Such is the case in biological taxonomy as in everyday life; many more species are now recognized and named than ever were before. Yet the extent of variety is narrowing even though more and more of it is coming into view. In flora and fauna as in culture, the overwhelming impression of height-ened variety masks an actual decline: the widespread loss of distinctive local forms of life and their widespread replacement by a lesser number that are as cosmopolitan as the golden arches. The major agencies of human impact on plant and animal species, all tending toward the net reduction of diversity, are what Robert Peters and Thomas Lovejoy (1990: 353) term "the four horsemen of development: habitat destruction, harvesting, introduced species, and pollu-tion."

These forces, as elsewhere, act against an unsteady natural background. The history of the earth compressed into the fossil record abounds in stories of spe-cies loss and relocation. Major episodes of natural mass extinction introduce or close many of the periods of the geological time scale. Significant human-induced extinctions and transfers of species are likewise not altogether new. The late Pleistocene – the close of the last ice age in the Northern Hemisphere, ending roughly 10,000 years ago – may have witnessed the first large extinction episode in the animal kingdom in which humankind took a hand. Many large mammals (including the mastodon and the woolly mammoth) vanished from the New World. Their disappearance more or less coinciding with the widespread human in-migrations to the Western Hemisphere of that period, some scientists have attributed it to overhunting by this new predator. The case, though, remains a controversial one. It was a time not only of human migration but also of substantial and rapid global change in climate, vegetation, and water balance (Pielou 1991). These changes may have driven both the human movements and the extinctions rather than driving the latter by way of the former. The case for human impact is clearer in a number of more recent but still premodern extinctions, notably those of large island vertebrates. The Polynesian settlers of New Zealand eradicated the moa, a huge flightless bird of those islands, before the coming of European colonists. Many similar extinctions took place elsewhere.

PATTERNS OF IMPACT

A suitable first indicator of the modern human impact – though by no means a comprehensive one – would be the proportion of those species alive 300 years ago that have since become extinct as a consequence of human activity. In short, $I = L/T$, where I is the human impact, L is the number of species lost, and T is the number that originally existed.

But the values of both numerator and denominator are unknown. The denominator – the total number of species – is, in fact, a matter of wild uncertainty. About a million and a half have been classified, but the naming process is far from complete. A few million species in all would have been thought a reasonable estimate not long ago. Recent taxonomic work in the South American tropics now leads some biologists to believe that there may exist as many as 30 million or more species of insects alone (Peters and Lovejoy 1990: 356). Birds are perhaps the best monitored class; the lower invertebrates are far less well studied.

Nor can the numerator of the fraction – the number of species made extinct by human action – be calculated with precision. Extinction figures that include only documented losses are bound to be large underestimates, for it is likely that many species have been lost before ever being found. It is not always clear whether a known species has disappeared. Such is the case even when no human role is suspected, as in the case of the coelacanth. This lobe-finned bony fish, known from the fossil record, was long thought to have disappeared some 60 million years ago, until a fisherman pulled one out of the Indian Ocean in 1938. A single sighting proves a species still extant, but no number of failed attempts to locate a specimen can prove that it is gone, only increase the evidence that it is. The very notion of species extinction in Western thought is a fairly modern one. A few centuries ago, reluctance to accept it stemmed in part from religious beliefs about the inextinguishability of created forms, in part from the vastness of unexplored space in the world; fossil creatures having no known living counterparts in the European world might, it was thought, still exist somewhere else.

If the first portion of the phrase, "the number of species made extinct," is a source of trouble, the second, "by human action," is too. It is not always clear, when a species has disappeared, whether human actors are responsible. Nor is it clear whether the indictment should be for murder or merely for contributory negligence. Extinction is by no means absent from nature, as the prehuman geologic record amply demonstrates. Yet biologists venture their very rough estimate of a background rate of natural extinction only with the warning against taking that estimate as some kind of steady value across time and space. Natural rates of species loss in the geologic past as inferred from the fossil record have fluctuated enormously, periods of net gain punctuated by major extinction episodes. It is hard in analyzing modern processes to separate human and natural forces of change in a way that makes sense; they interact in complex ways. Even when a species is said to have been "hunted to extinction," what is usually meant is not that all of its representatives were killed directly, but that hunting reduced the population below a minimum level required for its survival.

All the same, it is clear that the current loss of species, too closely associated with human activities not to be their doing, is taking place at a rate far beyond natural precedent. The steady increase in human pressure on the surface of the earth is driving an "extinction spasm" that seems likely to rival or surpass in magnitude and far surpass in rate the major upheavals of the earth's past. In the period since 1600, 171 bird and 115 mammal species alone are known to have become extinct through human action (Peters and Lovejoy 1990: 357). These figures, for the known and labeled extinctions of this kind, do not count others that may have occurred unnoticed. Vertebrates, the class to which birds, fish, reptiles, amphibians, and mammals belong, represent a mere sliver of the total number of animal species on earth. If the human impact on other creatures has been approximately as severe, the losses of animal species would be several hundred times those of vertebrates. Against a natural rate of loss estimated very roughly as averaging about one species per year, some scientists now suggest that the human-induced rate is roughly one per hour.

It is estimated that about 1% of all species present in 1600 have become extinct, half of them in the century or so since 1881. Current human activity is expected to result in the loss of 20% of all species by the year 2000 (Peters and Lovejoy 1990: 353). Additional forms of impact have included and will include the considerable reduction in the numbers of many more species, which is also a loss of genetic diversity within the species and a threat to its survival, and the restriction or expansion of their geographic ranges. The transformation of the earth has made it less hospitable to many forms of life, though more inviting for a fortunate few.

Species and classes of species vary a great deal in their vulnerability to particular human impacts. Larger organisms are often at greater risk than smaller ones, because they tend to be fewer in number and to have greater requirements for subsistence. Migratory species, because they can be affected by events occurring anywhere along their annual itinerary, face more risks than do sedentary creatures. The occupants of continents have an edge over the denizens of small islands; more generally, species found across a large area are less endangered by a given degree of human intrusion and landscape conversion than those confined to a small one. In other ways, differences in vulnerability are not so clearcut. Many ecologists once assumed that complex and diverse systems are more stable and less vulnerable to stress than simpler ones; the view has given way to a recognition that, depending on other variables, either relation may hold. Tropical ecosystems are quite complex, but also quite vulnerable to some human impacts. The more the linkages, the more may be the opportunities for ripples of secondary impacts and for cascade or domino effects.

What are known as endemic species are those that exist only in a single area. Tropical species outnumber by several times those found in temperate biomes, and a high proportion of them are endemic. Also rich in endemics, because of their extreme isolation, are islands. The distinction between continental and island biota is not absolute. Australia, though a continent, is the most island-like of continents. Its long isolation from other landmasses led to the evolution of many species found nowhere else. These native fauna and flora have suffered considerably from human impact, especially from imported competitors. Britain, on the other hand, though an island, is a very continental island. As recently as the last ice age, it had a land connection to Europe, and the dispersal and exchange of species have always been quite easy across the narrow barrier of the English Channel. The native biota are, as a result, not particularly distinctive, and not particularly vulnerable.

The biota of isolated islands in the open sea are endemic and vulnerable to an extreme. The Hawaiian chain is anchored to the ocean floor some 4,000 km from any continent, and with no close island neighbors. Having, in addition. a highly varied topography and environmental zonation, it developed a distinctive flora and fauna before the first Polynesian settlers arrived. The newcomers hunted, cleared land, and introduced destructive new species – rats, dogs, and pigs. Substantial losses of native taxa occurred. More than half of the 82 known Hawaiian bird species disappeared in this time. The arrival of Captain Cook in 1778 marked the onset of European contact and a second wave of disturbance and extinction. Larger and more destructive exotics, such as cattle and goats, now made deeper inroads on the existing habitat. Twenty-three additional bird species and close to two hundred native plants have become extinct since the European arrival. Losses among associated native invertebrates, though little studied, have most likely been high as well. The coastal lowland is now largely clad in nonnative vegetation, as are even many less accessible inland areas (Peters and Lovejoy 1990: 356–57).

Extinction or thinning of one species can threaten others in what biologists refer to as a "cascade" of loss. Underlying Alexander Pope's often-quoted lines written early in the eighteenth century on the "great chain of being" – "one step broken, the great scale's destroy'd; / From Nature's chain whatever link you strike, / Tenth or ten thousandth, breaks the chain alike" – was the view, common in his time and place, that extinction was impossible because it would undo the perfect gradation and completeness of creation. Once the assumption of a guaranteed harmony is dropped, they express just as well the way ecosystems can come unraveled when a crucial thread is pulled out. The extinction three hundred years ago of the flightless dodo bird, endemic to the island of Mauritius, is a familiar story. Less well known is one of its apparent consequences. The tambalocque tree "has been unable to reproduce for the past 300 years – since the dodo became extinct – because that fruit-eating bird prepared the fruit for germination in its gizzard." Only six now remain. The aggressive Africanized honeybees introduced from Africa to Brazil, and accidentally released in the 1950s – the "killer bees" of modern folklore – quickly began to outcompete local varieties across ever-widening areas. The introduced types do not pollinate all of the same plants, and the exchange has harmed those plant species dependent on the native strains (Prance 1990: 390, 391). And the impact can work the other way as well, from floral to faunal losses, when local plant closings undermine established communities of other species.

The introduction of species to new environments, though it briefly enriches the latter, often spells impoverishment in the long term. It is not uncommon, though by no means invariable either, for a transplanted species to thrive explosively in a new habitat – where it is uncontrolled by any of the predators and competitors which which it coevolved at home – at the expense of native flora and fauna. Just as governments often enact tariffs and antitrust laws to protect a range and diversity of small producers from larger-scale, more narrowly efficient firms, they have sometimes found it desirable to maintain local variety by erecting protective barriers against a global free market in species. When it is too late to keep the newcomers out, efforts are sometimes made to contain their vigorous spread by introducing and encouraging old competitors from their native haunts. To do so, of course, is to risk further impacts from the latest arrivals.

The spread of species can sometimes be traced to particular human acts of transfer. The agents of introduction sometimes do it intentionally, often unwittingly. George Perkins Marsh ([1864] 1965: 62) remarked on the significance and some of the means of incidental transfers: "In the campaign of 1814, the Russian troops brought, in the stuffing of their saddles and by other accidental means, seeds from the banks of the Dnieper to the valley of the Rhine, and even introduced the plants of the steppes into the environs of Paris." He suspected that "man has intentionally transferred fewer plants than he has accidentally introduced into countries foreign to them," and that the same held true of small animals: "The insects and worms intentionally transplanted by man bear but a

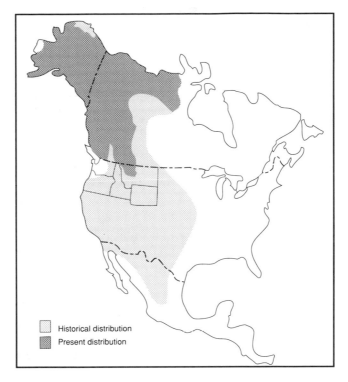

Figure 4.1 Historic and present range of grizzly bear (*Ursus Arctos horribilis*). Redrawn from Servheen 1985 for Peters and Lovejoy 1990.

small proportion to those accidentally introduced by him" (Marsh [1864] 1965: 61, 94). In other cases, humankind may be less a lead than a supporting actor, not actually transferring a species but facilitating its movements – by opening waterways between previously separate lakes and oceans, for example. Biogeographic changes have been among the results of the Suez, Panama, and Welland canals, though they played no part in their planning.

Habitat change likewise affects the diversity of an ecosystem. Even small landscape transformations can obliterate the home of an endemic species. The drainage of wetlands, the plowing of grasslands, and the clearance of forests have reduced the numbers and narrowed the range even of widely dispersed species. The coupled effects of habitat loss and hunting have greatly shrunk the range of the grizzly bear in North America (see Figure 4.1). Pollution, a special case of habitat change, represents an added form of impact, especially in highly developed and industrialized regions, though to date it is a less clear and direct contributor to many extinctions than are the other processes. Some species, of course, seize opportunities created by these transformations and flourish in the new environments. What are known as "synanthropes" benefit rather than suffer, not always or even often to the satisfaction of their unwitting human patrons. Rats, cockroaches, and pigeons in cities and crows, weeds, flies, and locusts in some disturbed rural settings are good examples.

In much of Western law, wild animals have traditionally been free-access goods, nobody's property until captured. Individuals have thus had little reason to forgo the harvesting, even – or especially – of an endangered species; one who refrains will simply allow another to harvest the more. The slaughter of the buffalo and the passenger pigeon in nineteenth-century America left one endangered and the other extinct. Each reflected a classic "tragedy of the commons," the devastation of a resource available to all because owned by no one. Not until preservation laws began to be passed did the tendency toward depletion implicit in most free-access situations begin to recede for some species. Most are more vulnerable than ever. Domestication of plants and animals – "low-tech genetic engineering" – represents a classic past and possible future answer in some cases to the problem of overharvesting of hunted and gathered biotic resources, a mechanism whereby supply can readily be made to increase to meet an increase in demand.

Preservation by habitat protection is at least as important as protection by harvesting controls. The economic argument for preservation is appealing in principle – as when one counts up, for instance, the many millions of dollars that have been made from the products of single obscure plants. It nonetheless faces many difficulties in practice. The impossibility of knowing in advance which threatened species will turn out to be useful and which will not makes preservation a lottery in which many decision makers find the prospective returns unappealingly low, especially when they may lie so far in the future as to be economically discounted to insignificance. Another problem is the difficulty one encounters whenever costs and benefits come unstuck: that of ensuring that those who bear the burden of preservation will be able to reap its rewards. Suppose a certain plant exists only in a small chain of swamps in the tropical interior of a country whose landless agricultural population is rapidly expanding outward in a wave of state-sponsored frontier clearance and drainage. In preserving the plant's habitat, the country would forgo its own gains from developing the area – gains from conversion to agriculture, say, or from construction of a hydroelectric dam that would flood the swamps. And if once found to be valuable for some productive purpose, the plant might well be transplanted and grown for profit elsewhere. The law does not recognize property rights – either national or individual – in natural genetic material (though newly bred or engineered species can now be patented in the United States).

The British adventurer Henry Wickham in the 1870s retrieved a supply of wild rubber seeds from Brazil. Transplanted, they formed the basis for the great plantations of Southeast Asia and Africa that in the early twentieth century destroyed Brazil's long-standing monopoly of the world rubber supply. Wickham liked to claim that the Brazilian government, fearful of just such an outcome, had guarded their plant from export with a rigor that had taken all his ingenuity and courage to circumvent. His yarns have been discredited by historians (Dean 1987), but they still make a good symbol, and what they symbolize is the character of biodiversity as in some ways an irrepressibly public good. Preservation imposes costs by requiring that other uses of the land be forgone, yet the benefits of preservation – access to the genetic variety thus saved – are quite difficult to confine to those bearing the costs. Let some species be proved useful, and before long a Henry Wickham will spirit away a few specimens from which vast quantities can eventually be raised. The point is not that preservation is impractical or uneconomical for humankind in general, only that arrangements for it may need to be made at the international scale if its benefits seem likely to be broadly diffused as well.

FLORA

Plants are the placid proletariat of nature's economy, the primary producers of surplus calories extracted for the needs and wants of other living things. As solar cells, they convert sunlight into biologically usable energy. As hosts to microbes, a few of them also offer workspace for the fixation of nitrogen gas from the atmosphere for the vital building blocks of protein. In weight and volume, plants form not only the wide base but most of the upper levels of the pyramid of life on earth, accounting for the great bulk of total terrestrial biomass.

It is estimated that somewhat more than a quarter of a million flowering plant species exist at present and that some 5,000 have become extinct since the year 1700. These losses experienced so far are modest compared to the ones apparently under way. About 15% of plant species are now regarded as threatened with extinction (see Table 4.1). This figure of 15%, or about 40,000 species,

> is a huge leap from the statistics of three hundred years ago or of the time of George Perkins Marsh's *Man and Nature* (1864). In 1700, there were very few extinctions of plants caused by humans; perhaps a few in the Mediterranean region and North Africa and a few oceanic islands where goats had been introduced. Almost all extinction was through natural causes. Once the industrial revolution began, however, the human factor became important and the extinction rate began to accelerate. (Prance 1990: 387)

Most plant species overall are found in the tropical rainforests of the world. So are most of those threatened with extinction; the rapid deforestation that is now sweeping those areas is the principal threat to their survival. Island species are a second class of highly vulnerable flora and perhaps the class most affected to date. Charles Darwin visited the small mid-Atlantic island of St. Helena, nearly as isolated as the Hawaiian chain – "situated so remote from any continent, in the midst of a great ocean" – in 1836. Best known for one human transplant from Western Europe, it had had many plant and animal ones who had fared better

Table 4.1. *Threatened plant species in selected countries or regions and worldwide*

Country/region	Species	Rare and threatened taxa	Extinct taxa since 1700	Endangered taxa
Australia	25,000	1,716	117	215
Europe	11,300	1,927	20	117
New Zealand	2,000	186	4	42
South Africa	23,000	2,122	39	107
USSR	21,100	653	~20	~160
United States (Continental)	20,000	2,050	90	?
Worldwide*	250,000	25,000	5,050	15,000[†]

Source: Davis et al. 1968; reprinted from Prance 1990.
* Estimated from various sources.
† Includes 4,000 species from Pacific coastal Ecuador and 3,000 from Atlantic coastal Brazil.

than Napoleon, taking firm root on the island and flourishing rather than pining away. Even at the time of Darwin's visit,

> the number of plants now found on the island is 746, and . . . out of them, fifty-two alone are native species, the rest being imported. . . . The numerous species which have been so recently introduced here can hardly have failed to have destroyed some of the native kinds. . . . It is only on the highest and steepest ridges, where the native Flora is still predominant. (Darwin [1839] 1952: 580)

Darwin's fellow evolutionist Alfred Russell Wallace paid the same island a visit later in the century. He noted how "the carelessness and improvidence of its civilised but ignorant rulers," through the introduction of competitor plants and grazing animals, had left the once verdant and varied landscape "barren and forbidding" (Wallace 1911: 294–95, 297, 309).

Severe threats are no longer limited mainly to islands, but have expanded to include the continental flora. The plants that are now most in danger of extinction may often be ones that are still peripheral in terms of their usefulness. They may even be ones not yet discovered or identified. What is lost in such species is not any current use but the potential for future ones, ignorance of which made preservation appear to be uneconomical. Many or most plants may be found on close acquaintance to possess some direct value for human use. Some figures from recent research in the Peruvian Amazon rainforest illustrate the point. Between half and all of the tree and woody vine species found on sample hectares in the territories of three native tribes were directly used in some way (Prance

94

1990: 387). Theirs, of course, is a way of life closely tied to the immediate re-sources of the local environment. Modern societies depend on genetic diversity in other ways – as a raw material for medical and agricultural innovation, for example. And many species not directly used may be important to the mainte-nance of ones that are. As check dams, they control potential cascades of loss in tightly interdependent ecosystems. The vegetation cover provides side benefits: soil protection, water regulation, and control of the microclimate; they also serve that only stand and shade.

Deforestation in the tropics in the postwar decades has seriously undermined their biotic diversity. Most clearing takes place to open up land for pasture or cultivation. Such wholesale conversion of habitat can devastate the native flora. The virtual obliteration of the Brazilian Atlantic forest has placed several thou-sand species on the threatened list. Much smaller intrusions can have horrific consequences: "A single act of agricultural clearing on the top of Centinela, an Andean foothill in western Ecuador caused the extinction of at least 38 plant species found only on this 20 km^2 ridgetop" (Peters and Lovejoy 1990: 354). Deforestation for agriculture is usually indiscriminate and aims at clearing the ground for a different use. Deforestation for logging is often focused on some trees of particular value, but the process of extraction damages many others. The flooding of lands for reservoirs likewise obliterates habitat, sometimes of species few in numbers and endemic to the project area. Many plants have undoubtedly disappeared on the advent of large impoundments. The losses of plant variety through all of these processes of land-use change are high – especially in Ama-zonia, in the timber frontier of island Southeast Asia, and in other rainforests where massive expansion of one form or another impinges on the world's most diverse ecosystems.

Deliberate collecting thins the numbers of some species, occasionally to the point of extinction. The very rarity that endangers a plant's survival can inflate its value and sharpen the hunt for the remaining specimens. For a wild species, the consequence may be depletion past the point of recovery. Some cacti in the deserts of the southwestern United States appear headed in this direction. So too do some rare orchids and insectivorous plants much favored by collectors. The sandalo tree, much prized for its scented sandalwood, grew only on Juan Fer-nandez Island in the eastern South Pacific. It disappeared by 1916 as a conse-quence of overcutting and the depredations of goats on new seedlings (Prance 1990: 390).

Such species are valued principally for aesthetic reasons. Others valuable as inputs to production can likewise be overharvested. The sorva tree of the Ama-zon Basin provides a white latex used in chewing gum. Unlike the rubber tree, it is cut down, not tapped while standing, and so, like many useful species, it is "being mined out of the forest, rather than being managed" (Prance 1990: 390). Qui-nine is extracted from the bark of the cinchona tree, native to the Andean moun-tain forests west of Amazonia; the process of peeling destroys the tree. For centuries after its discovery by the Spanish in 1638, "Peruvian bark" was the Western world's sole known treatment for malaria in an era of widespread tropical colonization. Extraction was often destructive and wasteful. The British government successfully transplanted the tree to India and Ceylon as a way of guaranteeing a supply for their malaria-plagued colonial population. The Dutch colonial government brought the cinchona to Java for the same reason. Successfully raised elsewhere, the tree "has by now been practically eradicated in Ecuador, Peru, and Bolivia" by overcutting and by other competing land uses (Salati et al. 1990: 488). Efforts to cultivate it in the Andes have not succeeded, and conversion of its habitat to cropland has prevented natural regrowth.

Domesticated animals can be fully as destructive as their owners in their assault on the flora. Grazing livestock descend on island vegetation like wolves in sheep's or goat's clothing. In such varied settings as the Galápagos Islands in the Pacific, Crete in the Mediterranean, and St. Helena in the South Atlantic, as well as in continental locales – elsewhere in the mainland Mediterranean and in rangelands in northern Africa – the vulnerable native flora has been nibbled down to varying fractions of its original extent (Prance 1990: 389). And Gresham's law has a floral corollary: inedible weeds are strongly favored against species that are eaten or harvested. Their very uselessness promotes the survival of the unfittest.

Introduced competitors include other plants as well as animals. Scarcely any has so successfully penetrated foreign markets as the water hyacinth, a tropical weed native to the inland channels of the Amazon Basin. At home, its growth is regulated by competitors. In the many rivers and lakes around the world to which it has been introduced unsupervised, it has become a serious pest. It grows so thick as to block waterways to navigation and elbows out native species in competition for nutrients, dissolved oxygen, and space. The New Orleans World's Fair of 1884–85 opened, like any Victorian-era exposition, with speeches hailing the steadily increasing connection of all countries of the globe – particularly, as the invocation put it, "the unification of North and South America." More than most such gatherings, it backed words with deeds, however unintentionally. A sample of water hyacinth exhibited by the Brazilian government in New Orleans was taken to Florida and released into the St. Johns River. It reproduced and spread with explosive speed. By the turn of the century, the plant had become a serious pest in the Gulf states, and it remains one there today. More recently, it has infested waters in tropical Africa and India. Some enterprising souls brought the prickly pear, a Latin American shrub, to the eastern Australian outback as cattle fodder and live fencing material in the late nineteenth century. It overran vast areas until brought under control in the 1920s and 1930s by the deliberate introduction of an insect predator from South America (Freeman 1992). Just such a regulatory organism is currently being sought for the mimosa plant, another South American immigrant that has conquered large portions of the antipodean landscape (Prance 1990: 391).

The very introduction of new plants, regardless of their secondary effects on others, represents a major form of human impact on the pattern of the world's flora. Introductions sometimes occur by inadvertence, sometimes by design. The globalized collage of plant species is nowhere more evident than on farmlands, the result of the deliberate, often government-sponsored transfer of domesticates from one locale to another. The famous voyage of the *Bounty* in 1789 was a relatively late essay in an established style; it had as its purpose the transfer of the breadfruit tree from Polynesia to the West Indies as a cheap source of food for plantation slaves. The crops produced by most agricultural regions make up a World's Fair or a tossed salad of geographical origins.

TERRESTRIAL FAUNA

At a rough estimate, the lands of the world hold 10 million animal species – perhaps fewer or perhaps, as already noted, several times that number. Vertebrates (amphibians, reptiles, fish, birds, and mammals) make up only about one in 500. As most of the world's species are land animals, the estimates for terrestrial faunal extinctions are little different from those for total species extinctions. Change has not been a steady upward spiral in all respects. Many restrictions now exist on the deliberate transfer of species, and measures to protect endangered animals were among the pioneering initiatives of the modern environmental movement. Documented vertebrate extinctions have slowed over the course of the past century as compared with the two or three preceding (Kates, Turner, and Clark 1990: 7). But in general, human pressure on zoodiversity continues to mount. Extinctions in one of the vertebrate classes, birds, have continued to rise sharply (see Figure 4.2).

To date, island species have suffered the most. They account for three-quarters of the documented vertebrate extinctions. Of the 171 bird species known to have disappeared since 1600, 155 are from islands. With increasing pressure on the continental lands, especially of the tropics, that share is likely to diminish, even though absolute losses of island species will continue to climb.

The high vulnerability of island biota to human impact is shared by the freshwater fish and amphibians of the continents. "Many of the freshwater ecosystems may be thought of as islands of water, whether they be lakes or isolated rivers" – and with the same tendency toward endemism – "and the fauna is analogously vulnerable" (Peters and Lovejoy 1990: 359). The threats are numerous. First, inland waters are easily harvested. The biodiversity of Amazonia is as pronounced in the fish species of the river as in the plants and animals of the rainforest around it. Fish has long been and remains the main source of protein for the growing population of Amazonia; effects of pressure from commercial demand on the most valued species, plus mounting habitat change in portions of the river basin, are becoming evident. Conservation laws setting minimum sizes for sale and restricting international trade in aquarium fish are routinely subverted

Number of bird species becoming extinct

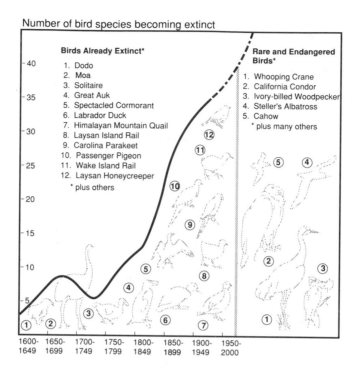

Birds Already Extinct*
1. Dodo
2. Moa
3. Solitaire
4. Great Auk
5. Spectacled Cormorant
6. Labrador Duck
7. Himalayan Mountain Quail
8. Laysan Island Rail
9. Carolina Parakeet
10. Passenger Pigeon
11. Wake Island Rail
12. Laysan Honeycreeper
  * plus others

Rare and Endangered Birds*
1. Whooping Crane
2. California Condor
3. Ivory-billed Woodpecker
4. Steller's Albatross
5. Cahow
  * plus many others

1600-1649 1650-1699 1700-1749 1750-1799 1800-1849 1850-1899 1900-1949 1950-2000

Figure 4.2 Rising rate of bird extinctions. Redrawn from Nilson 1986 for Peters and Lovejoy 1990.

(Salati et al. 1990: 491). Second, exotic competitor species are often introduced to lakes and rivers in the hope of raising yields. The U.S. Fish Commission sponsored the wide introduction of the carp to inland waters in the late nineteenth century, only to find the new species largely useless and a pest to boot. Third, common types of water management – damming, stream channelization, dredging, water withdrawal, and drainage – all transform habitats. The shrinkage of the Aral Sea in former Soviet Central Asia, owing to withdrawal of water for irrigation, has destroyed the endemic ecosystem of the basin (Micklin 1988; Kotlyakov 1991). Some 20 species native to the inland waters of the American Southwest have disappeared in this century, and more are endangered (Peters and Lovejoy 1990: 359). Finally, the close association of many human activities with bodies of freshwater, especially streams, means high pollution loads added to relatively small sinks; the confined habitat offers little room for escape. Pollutants are not limited to those released locally. Acid precipitation that kills lake fish may originate hundreds of kilometers away.

Land species of the continents are also experiencing rising levels of impact. Forest clearance in the tropics is one of the most significant threats to animals as to plants. Several centuries of clearing for agricultural and urban-industrial development have all but erased the Brazilian coastal rainforest as a unified entity

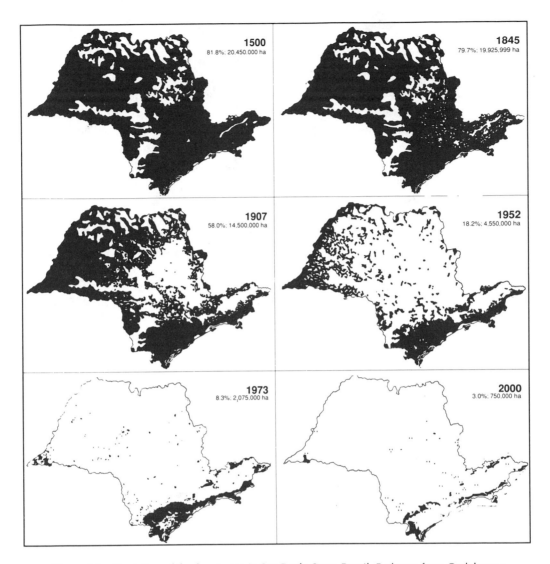

Figure 4.3 Depletion of the forest area in São Paulo State, Brazil. Redrawn from Oedekoven 1980 for Peters and Lovejoy 1990.

(see Figure 4.3). Most even of the 7% of the original forest that remains forest has been significantly altered. Once home to "a wealth of endemic species," it is now classed among the world's most endangered ecosystems (Peters and Lovejoy 1990: 364; Williams 1990a: 182–83, 187–88). Most of the primates of the area, for example, are endemic, and most are now on the endangered list; one species has been reduced from an estimated original population of 400,000 to a present-day total of 240.

The longest-settled and most densely peopled regions, those in which habitat transformation has been the most profound, are the areas of the greatest pressure on biodiversity. No part of the world is entirely unaltered, of course, and even the relatively sparsely occupied lands of recent advanced settlement show diminished variety. The United States, late settled and most of it thinly peopled compared to many other regions, has nonetheless experienced considerable and profound habitat alteration, from forest clearing to the drainage of wetlands to the plowing of prairies. Some forest, especially in the eastern states, has regenerated and some species, such as the deer and wild turkey, have returned to areas from which they vanished in the eighteenth or nineteenth centuries. Overall, however, reduction in numbers and in range of native species is the common pattern. Even official parks and reserves suffer from nearby development, from pollution, and from the pressure of use (Peters and Lovejoy 1990: 359–60).

A region of such ancient occupance as the Mediterranean has undergone "extreme degradation of natural plant and animal communities, accompanying centuries of intense human use." Most of the forest has long since been destroyed, some of it in classical times, undermining not only the biota directly but such vital aspects of its habitat as the soil, hydrology, and local climate. Spain's threatened species include 53 mammals (more than half of the native taxa), 142 birds, 20 reptiles, 18 amphibians (more than three-quarters of the total), and 12 fish (Peters and Lovejoy 1990: 362–64). The numbers for other Western European countries are of similar magnitude (see Table 4.2).

As plants can be endangered by overcollecting, so can the terrestrial fauna. Many useful species have been overharvested. Other animals have been hunted not as useful varieties to be exploited but as undesirable ones to be exterminated. Sigmund Freud wrote in 1929 that "we recognize that a country has attained a high state of civilization when we find," among a variety of landscape transformations (rivers straightened, ore deposits mined), that "wild and dangerous animals have been exterminated" (quoted in Lowenthal 1990: 123). Even before St. Patrick expelled the snakes from Ireland, part of the human impact on land animals had been a deliberate effort to reduce the numbers of the noxious and unwanted. Government bounties on rattlesnakes and wolves helped to banish these creatures from eighteenth- and early nineteenth-century New England, for example, and few regretted their departure. Often, however, the successful human impact ricochets on other human uses of the environment. Species have often not been as noxious as perceived, having some value or filling some role in the ecosystem not recognized until the depletion of their numbers makes the effects of their absence apparent. One of those effects can be the rapid increase of pests that they once controlled.

Such an explosion in numbers of unwanted species is also sometimes an outcome of the transformation of the landscape or the introduction of new species. Rabbits in Australia, house sparrows and starlings in North America, and Africanized honeybees in Brazil head the long list of cautionary tales against the too-

Table 4.2. *Threatened animal species in selected OECD countries (early 1980s)*

Country	Mammals	Birds	Reptiles	Amphibians	Fishes
Mediterranean Countries					
France	58(57)*	155(58)	19(39)	18(53)	20(27)
Italy	13(13)	60(14)	24(52)	13(46)	70(14)
Spain†	53(53)	142(37)	20(41)	18(78)	12(9)
European Non-Mediterranean Countries					
Austria	38(46)	121(60)	X‡	X	54(59)
Denmark	14(29)	41(22)	0(0)	3(21)	17(10)
Finland	21(34)	15(7)	1(20)	0(0)	4(7)
West Germany	44(47)	98(22)	9(75)	11(58)	40(23)
Hungary	14(X)	83(X)	4(X)	1(X)	2(X)
Netherlands	29(48)	85(33)	6(86)	10(67)	11(22)
Norway	10(14)	28(10)	1(20)	1(20)	X
United Kingdom	26(51)	51(26)	2(33)	2(33)	18(49)
North America					
Canada	6(6)	10(2)	2(6)	2(4)	15(2)
United States	35(8)	69(6)	25(7)	8(4)	44(2)
Oceania					
Australia	40(13)	36(5)	8(1)	6(4)	X
New Zealand	14(21)	16(6)	7(19)	X	3(0)

Source: Peters and Lovejoy 1990.

* Numbers given are total number of threatened species in each class. Numbers in parentheses are the threatened species expressed as a percentage of the total number of species known to exist in a particular country.

† Data for Spain refer to peninsular Spain and the Baleares only.

‡ Estimates not available. "Threatened" refers to the sum of the number of species in both "endangered" and "vulnerable" categories, which are roughly analogous to U.S. "endangered" and "threatened" categories, respectively.

ready transplanting of an animal to a new land. The gypsy moth was accidentally released in the town of Medford, in eastern Massachusetts, in the 1860s. It spent more than a decade entrenching itself in a single neighborhood before it exploded into the town proper, and then rapidly became a major and recurring regional problem with the ferocity of its assaults on the tree foliage. The U.S. Department of Agriculture scored an early success in the management of noxious introductions in the 1880s; it found and transplanted a beetle from Australia to control the spread of another antipodean insect, the introduced cottony cushion scale, which had begun to threaten agricultural interests in California. The episode, alas, offered a largely illusory prospect of what a bit of effort and ingenuity could do, and it inspired many failed attempts to duplicate the feat. Animals are still introduced to control new plant or animal pests as a way of recreating the controlled environment of their origin, but not without their own further effects. Australian success in controlling the prickly pear with an imported insect accustomed the public

> to the idea that miracle bugs could be found to destroy almost any introduced pest. . . . Pressure on governments to introduce new biological agents has led to some fresh disasters, like the spread of the voracious and poisonous South American cane toad (*Bufo marinus*) throughout much of northern Australia. In this case, the remedy, the toad, has proven far worse than the original pest, the cane beetle. (Freeman 1992, 428)

The very extinction of some animal species is often the result of the introduction of others. The importation of the mongoose to the West Indies in 1872 has resulted in the loss of at least half a dozen indigenous varieties of rats and birds (Watts 1987).

The mitigation of human impact has taken many other forms besides the belated introduction of competitors – restrictions on harvesting, preservation of habitat, pollution control, and prohibitions on species introductions are some of them. They are all difficult to enforce. Hunting, harvesting, and some kinds of pollution tend to be activities not easily monitored. Nor is the transplanting of many undesired species, short of expensive and intensive quarantines. This is especially true of insect pests, whose threat to agricultural interests makes them prime targets for immigration restriction. International agreements for protection of rare and high-valued animals include the bans on imports associated with the Convention on International Trade in Endangered Species (CITES) and a multitude of public and private conservation efforts directed toward the prevention of hunting and the preservation of habitat.

MARINE ANIMALS

To date, the human impact on marine animals has been registered mainly in the form of reduced numbers, not of extinguished species. The one clear case of extinction dates back several centuries. George Perkins Marsh in 1864 could already cite the sad history of the Steller's sea cow, a large marine mammal of the Bering Strait. It had been discovered by Russian explorers in 1741, whereupon "so active a chase was commenced . . . that, in the course of twenty-seven years, the sea cow, described by Steller as extremely numerous in 1741, was completely extirpated, not a single individual having been seen since the year 1768." Marsh warned that other marine mammals – seals, sea otters, walruses – "seem destined soon to follow the sea cow, unless protected by legislation stringent enough, and a police energetic enough, to repress the ardent cupidity of their pursuers" (Marsh [1864] 1965: 105). Yet this example has not been joined by others as early extinctions of terrestrial flora and fauna have been. Many other species have been diminished but none, it would seem, destroyed.

The degree of diminution is often hard to gauge because of the difficulties of census taking, and even when changes are identified the uncertainties surrounding natural fluctuations make the human role in them hard to identify. Harvesting has been easily the most important form of human impact. Its result has sometimes been "commercial extinction," where a stock is no longer exploited because it is too scarce to be worth hunting.

A few marine invertebrates highly prized for eating – lobster, crab, shellfish, abalone – have felt the pressure of demand and rank among the prime exhibits of the earth as transformed by human appetite. The effects of overharvesting along populous shorelines have been worsened by pollution and habitat destruction. The scarcity that drives up prices only rewards further harvesting, at least so long as enough remain to be conveniently harvested. And on the mammals of the sea, especially whales, human action clearly has had a profound impact. Fur seals and otters have been affected by harvesting; some seals also by marine plastics pollution.

Pressure on whale stocks dates back almost a millennium. Once twelfth- and thirteenth-century Basque fishermen in the Bay of Biscay depleted the local stocks of the right whale, they were obliged to journey out far from shore to reach new ones. Already a standard process was set that would be repeated, at wider scales, many times in the future: "discovery of a new resource or a technical innovation that makes exploitation practical, reduction of the abundance to levels that are not commercially profitable, and decline of the industry until a new stock is discovered or technology makes an unprofitable stock profitable" (Hilborn 1990: 378). The Dutch and the British overharvested the right whale in the North Atlantic by the seventeenth century. The same nations depleted the Greenland whale stocks to near-extinction by the 1850s. The rapid mining of stocks in the nineteenth century devastated the California gray, Arctic bowhead, and sperm whales. By late in the nineteenth century, the industry had pretty much collapsed. Two changes briefly rejuvenated it at the beginning of the twentieth. New technology mechanized catching and processing, and rich new grounds were discovered off Antarctica. As many whales were taken off Antarc-

Table 4.3. *Current estimates of whale population sizes (in thousands of whales and percentages of initial populations)*

Species	Southern Hemisphere	North Pacific	North Atlantic
Bowhead	Not present	1–2? (10%?)	<0.1 (1%?)
Right	3–4 (<10%)	0.3–0.4 (unknown)	<0.2? (unknown)
Gray	Not present	11–12 (~100%)	Not present
Humpback	2–3 (3%)	2 (unknown)	<1.5 (70%)
Blue	7–8 (4%)	1.5–2 (30–40%	<1 (10%)
Fin	80 (20%)	14–19 (40%)	> 31 (unknown)
Sei	50–55 (33%)	21–23 (~50%)	>2 (unknown)
Bryde's	>10 (90%)	20–30 (~100%)	Unknown
Minke	120–200 (80%)	Unknown	>10 (unknown)
Sperm (males)	128 (50%)	74 (41%)	38 of both sexes
Sperm (females)	295 (90%)	103 (82%)	(unknown)

Source: Scarff 1977, Table 2; reprinted from Hilborn 1990.

tica in the first half of the twentieth century as had been caught in all the previous history of whaling. Again the stocks were quickly depleted. Commercial whaling, after decades of conservationist pressure, is now under an international moratorium, and even scientific whale catching is strictly regulated. Yet in many whale stocks, the damage done has persisted into the present. The Arctic bowhead whale, a prime commercial target in the second half of the nineteenth century, has not been hunted for many decades, yet its present-day population of some 3,000 is still only a tenth of the pre-whaling size of 30,000. Some other populations have been reduced more dramatically yet and show few signs of recovering (Hilborn 1990) (see Table 4.3).

The anadromous fishes – salmon, sturgeon, shad, and others – are the second major group of marine biota considerably affected by human impact. That they lay their eggs in fresh water, though spending part of their lifetime in the oceans, brings them into a close connection with human activity that makes them especially vulnerable. (So does the fact that most spend time in several different national or in free-access international waters.) The best-known anadromous fishes, the salmon, illustrate many of the forms of impact and management. The direct-drive waterpower that turned the spindles of the early Industrial Revolution required the damming of rivers along the coasts of Western Europe and New England; the dams blocked Atlantic salmon and other anadromous fishes from their upstream spawning grounds. Further industrial and urban growth polluted the same streams; salmon, once common in the Thames, disappeared from the river after 1833 (Hilborn 1990: 373; Schwarz et al. 1990: 261). Though steam soon replaced the waterwheel as a source of energy, hydroelectricity followed. Hydropower projects have obstructed further lengths of salmon grounds in the twentieth century, most notably in the Columbia River system in the Pacific Northwest. Another technological change, mechanized canning, arrived in the late 1800s. It touched off a wave of exploitation of the vast but previously neglected salmon runs of the North Pacific – many times the size of the Atlantic ones. Concerns about their overexploitation were voiced as early as the turn of the century. International arrangements–restricting catches and supplementing numbers with cultivated hatchery introductions – now maintain yields.

It is far less easy to trace the human impact on those species that spend their whole lives in the oceans. Marine fish supply 10% of the world's protein consumption; the share, of course, differs by location and is far higher in some regions (Hilborn 1990: 371). The species exploited range widely in size, value, and abundance, from such familiar large food fish as tuna, to the smaller and more abundant herring, anchovy, and sardines, to the highly abundant but little-exploited microfauna such as plankton. Some populations are highly localized, most near coasts or on the continental shelf. Others migrate widely through the open oceans. Harvesting pressure has increased explosively in a short span of human history. During most of the nineteenth century, the annual world fish catch was at most a few million tons. It exceeded 10 million in the first decades of the twentieth, and today it is not far short of 100 million (see Figure 4.4).

To what degree has this increased harvesting led to changes in population sizes? The problem is the familiar one of "equifinality" – the pattern of impact might have been produced by any of several processes. Most observed declines in fish populations could be the result of natural factors, human impact, or the two in combination. It is now clear that even in the absence of human interference, marine fish stocks fluctuate enormously in size. Long-term booms and busts in population can be estimated from the changing abundance of fish-scale debris in dated anaerobic bottom mud layers. The Santa Barbara basin (off the California coast) over the past 2,000 years shows patterns of significant and irregular natural change in species numbers long before human impact could have been a factor (see Figure 4.5). Early ecologists supposed that undisturbed fish stocks would fluctuate around some stable equilibrium level, and that a certain calculable level of "sustainable yield" could be safely extracted. That view has been more or less abandoned. Instead, fish stocks are classed as following several distinct patterns of growth and decline denoted as steady-state, cyclical, irregular, and spasmodic. In many realms of the environment, the natural processes, at least over a time scale of a few centuries, are understood well enough for the human contribution to be assessed. Such is not the case with fish populations. Though the different patterns of fish population change are well documented empirically, their causes are not understood well enough to make these changes predictable. (Climatic factors are thought to be important.) It adds to the complexity that individual fish stocks sometimes cannot be studied adequately in isolation, for the same reasons that govern cascade effects in terrestrial ecosys-

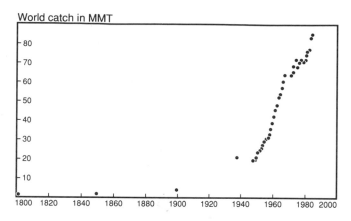

Figure 4.4 Historic trends in the catch from the sea, in millions of tons. Source: Hilborn 1990.

tems. Ecosystem-level changes may also occur in the marine realm. The natural or human-induced depletion of one species may change the abundance of others with which it is associated (Hilborn 1990).

So the contribution of human actions to the decline of marine fish stocks remains scientifically controversial; there are fewer cases than once thought where they have played a clearly dominant role compared to natural fluctuations. To note that a decline might have been produced naturally, though, is not to prove that it was, it is merely to require other evidence for a convincing demonstration of human responsibility. Did populations fall "naturally," or were they pushed by overharvesting – or were they perhaps pushed, or did they fall, from a position made precarious by some other process? Examples of overharvesting do exist, and it is beyond doubt that excessive fishing pressure can lead to severe population declines. But few cases are so simple. The collapse by 1950 of the highly productive California sardine fishery "used to be considered a classic example of severe overfishing." Yet in light of the long-term natural swings in its abundance recorded in fish-scale layers, "it is possible that fishing has had no detectable effect" on this stock. The Peruvian anchoveta, during the 1960s the world's largest fishery, collapsed in 1972 in association with a severe natural El Niño event (see Figure 4.6), but years of heavy harvesting pressure had made the population quite vulnerable to any such shock (Hilborn 1990).

The problems of management, and many of the problems causing degradation in the first place, in this realm of the biosphere are the classic ones of situations where free access by multiple users is either permitted or difficult to prevent. The oceans were once important mainly for navigation. Other uses, notably fishing, rarely before recent times grew so demanding as to lessen noticeably the supply of the resource being exploited. As a result, the ocean ac-

106

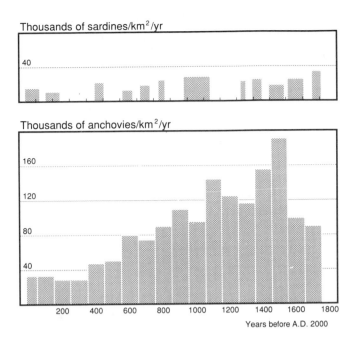

Figure 4.5 Estimates, based on fish-scale debris in dated bottom mud layers, of numbers of major fish species in the Santa Barbara basin off California for the past 1,700 years. Redrawn from Soutar and Isaacs 1969 for Hilborn 1990.

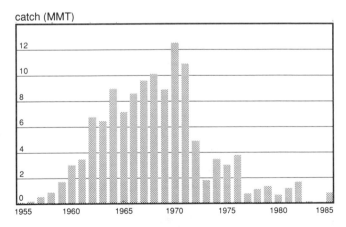

Figure 4.6 Catch history of the Peruvian anchoveta, 1955–85, in millions of tons. Source: Hilborn 1990.

107

quired a deeply entrenched legal status as a realm of free access. That status has proved quite ill suited to the ocean's new importance as a site of intensive resource extraction. Innumerable international disputes have risen over rights to nearshore fishing grounds, sometimes settled by treaty and in other cases continuing to fester. Since World War II, the area under exclusive national control, once 3, then 12 miles offshore, has spread far out over the continental shelf and beyond with the widespread establishment of 200-mile (320-km) "exclusive economic zones" (EEZs). These zones are open to all for nonextractive purposes such as navigation, but only the nation in control has the right to extract their resources. The open ocean basins beyond, larger but far poorer, remain an area of free access with the failure in the 1980s of the United Nations Law of the Sea conference to gain international consent to a regime of common world ownership and management.

In 1883, the eminent British biologist T. H. Huxley described the ocean's resources as inexhaustible (Cushing 1975). So they long seemed. Nations quarreled and parleyed over access to favored harvesting grounds long before the mid-twentieth century. But they were – with some exceptions – arguing not so much over how a limited resource would be divided up, as over how and by whom a limited demand for it would be met. Poacher fleets posed a commercial more than an ecological threat, less to deplete the physical supply than to drive down prices by flooding the market. Whales and some inshore mollusks and crustaceans were some of the exceptions evidently threatened by overharvesting. The fur seals of the Bering Strait occasioned the most controversy. Their management strained the relations of the United States, Canada and Great Britain, Japan, and Russia at the turn of the century. The seals numbered a couple of million in the 1870s. They were at first harvested mainly on the Pribilof Islands – owned after 1867 by the United States – by commercial sealers who purchased the right from the government. Restrictions on the harvest ensured the maintenance of the herds. But the seals also spent time at sea in the Bering Strait, international free-access waters in the days before 200-mile EEZs were claimed. There Canadian, Russian, and Japanese sealers caught them in added numbers sufficient to threaten their survival. Threatened though they all were with the utter destruction of the resource, none of the nations would stop sealing altogether, leaving the entire catch to its competitors. Not until 1911 – with the herd down to a few hundred thousand – did the four nations sign a treaty that set terms of harvesting for each (Tomasevich 1943).

Today depletion is not a marginal but a core issue in the management of most fisheries. The days are gone when only a few nations could compete for the riches of any one fishing ground. Technologies of transportation, of harvesting, and of storage have greatly increased the range and the power of fishing fleets, and few need fear that they will catch more than they can sell. At the same time, though, the area open to them has shrunk drastically. The territorial seas and EEZs of the closest countries now cover most of the richest fishing areas, lessening the free-access problems and making management easier. Migratory fish that spend portions of the year in different jurisdictions remain a problem, as does the regulation by a country of access within its population. A nation's assertion of sovereignty over a resource will not solve, but merely circumscribe, the free-access problem if its citizens are still permitted – by law, custom, or failure of enforcement – to harvest the resource without restraint.

As with other species, if numbers could be increased with an increase in demand, scarcity would not raise price and price scarcity in a vicious spiral. Aquaculture and mariculture – the artificial raising of fish in, respectively, fresh water and seawater – play a modest but growing role in meeting demand, especially in East Asia. The species suited to such cultivation are relatively few. Shrimp and mollusks are good examples, and assorted fish can be raised in inland freshwater ponds. Maricultured species must be raised in fenced portions of the coast or in cages floating in the water to avoid their escape or their loss by poaching in open waters, and competition from other uses and damage from pollution along the coastline can be added obstacles. But although the range is restricted, intensive cultivation can be made extremely productive, and it becomes more profitable as pressure increases on the resources of the open waters.

PATHOGENS

The least visible but in some ways the most immediately significant human-induced changes in the distribution of species have been in species too small to see – in the pathogenic microorganisms responsible for infectious disease. In few realms of the biosphere have such immense consequences been set in motion by human activity long before science achieved an adequate understanding of their cause.

The link between human ill-being and the actions of organisms invisible to the unaided eye long escaped detection. Ascriptions of some illnesses instead to the direct action of the environment, especially the air, go back to antiquity; *On Airs, Waters, and Places*, a treatise from the fifth century B.C. ascribed to Hippocrates, is a classic of this school. Balancing the apparent connection of diseases with an impure atmosphere throughout the history of medical thought, though, was their apparent tendency to be spread by contagion, from person to person or from place to place. These two insights coalesced a few centuries ago as the opposed schools of "anticontagionism" and "contagionism."

Anticontagionism, asserting the direct atmospheric causation of many kinds of epidemics, made steady headway in the eighteenth and early nineteenth centuries against a version of contagionism that suffered from an important and crippling difference from today's. Contagion, most assumed, must occur directly from person to person. The recognition late in the nineteenth century of indirect pathways of transmission between individuals – of malaria and yellow fever by way of mosquitoes, for example, or of cholera and typhoid through water –

was a belated and crucial advance. Contagionism ebbed and began to advance again after mid-century. The research of Louis Pasteur, Robert Koch, and others added disease after disease to the list of those demonstrably contagious in origin, cholera, typhoid, and tuberculosis among the more notable. George Perkins Marsh in 1864 had taken anticontagionism more or less for granted. Revising his volume in the early 1880s, however, he noted that "the whole subject of ani-malcular, or rather minute organic, life has assumed a new and startling impor-tance from the recent researches of Pasteur and other naturalists and physiolo-gists into the agency of such life, vegetable or animal, in exciting and communicating malignant and contagious diseases." Marsh now thought it "ex-tremely probable" that such microscopic organisms "are the true seeds of infec-tion and death" in many illnesses that had been ascribed to other causes (1885: 147n). The identification at the turn of the century of the mosquito-borne pathogens causing malaria and yellow fever replaced what still remained of anti-contagionism with germ theories as medical orthodoxy.

Some of the most dramatic global impacts of the human-induced spread of the microbiota were registered prior to 1700. The population of the Basin of Mexico, well over a million when the Spanish conquistadors arrived in 1519, had fallen to less than a hundred thousand a century later, a drop of more than 90% owing largely to such introduced diseases as smallpox (Whitmore 1992). The Mexican collapse is the supreme case in point, but it had parallels in massive deaths among other Amerindian (and later, Pacific) peoples whose long isola-tion from the Old World had left them bereft of immunity even to some illnesses regarded as relatively mild in Europe. The transfer may not all have been in one direction. Scholars still debate the possibility that the epidemic outbreak of syph-ilis in Europe at the end of the fifteenth century represented a return current of disease carried from the New to the Old World through Columbus's crew (Baker and Armelagos 1988). Devastating epidemics would continue to occur through the wider occurrence of some infection spread through the increasingly inte-grated world system. The global influenza epidemic at the close of World War I cost 20 million or more lives (McNeill 1976: 288–89).

Pathogenic organisms are not confined to the animal kingdom. Plant dis-eases, especially fungi, ravage crops and other floral resources. Once Ireland's rural population had become dependent on the potato as a staple food, it be-came vulnerable to devastation by the potato blight in the 1840s. Eight million at the onset of the disease, the island's population fell below six million as a result of famine and induced emigration (and has never since recovered to its earlier level). The chestnut blight circled the world in the early twentieth century, and the Dutch elm disease of more recent decades is another such global plague. One of the principal vulnerabilities of monocultural cultivation is the risk of infections destroying an entire crop; modern agriculture depends heavily both on the constant breeding of new varieties to keep a step or two ahead and on the application of chemical fungicides along with the pesticides aimed at insects.

Pathogens have been affected by human action in the same general ways as other species. The transfer of diseases from place to place by trading and communication links has "globalized" many diseases as it has globalized other forms of life. Habitat alteration has often inadvertently made areas more inviting habitats for particular pathogens. Medieval and Renaissance cities harbored plague-bearing rats. Victorian-era urbanization provided a hospitable setting for cholera and other diseases. Reservoirs and irrigation projects, especially in the tropics, invite the mosquitoes that carry malaria and the vectors of such parasitic diseases as river blindness and sleeping sickness. When undertaken deliberately, through the eradication of the habitat of affiliated and carrier organisms, landscape transformation is an effective tool of public health. Here the close interconnections of species are turned to human advantage rather than loss. The lever that dislodges one species can also loosen the grip of its unwanted microscopic companion. Wetland conversion, whatever damage it does to the soil, to hydrology, and to fish, waterfowl, and other animals, has lessened the incidence of mosquito-borne yellow fever and malaria. Protection of reservoirs from contamination breaks the chain transmitting waterborne diseases such as cholera and typhoid and has nearly banished them from many parts of the world. Antibiotics play the role of introduced "predators" or competitors. Yet their introduction, as an experiment of sorts in natural selection, has unintended consequences as well as direct ones. Just as insect control campaigns promote the survival of resistant varieties, so the survival of chance variations lets new disease strains develop in a transformed microbiological environment.

Management in these aspects of the environment has led to some of the clearest transformations of the earth for the better of its human inhabitants – in the modern eradication of smallpox, for example. Again, the overall trend, in both improvement and deterioration, has been toward the unifying and simplifying of the globe, if also toward a diversification of conditions within many locales. Contacts between regional populations involve far less risk today than they did several centuries ago. No longer possible are the staggering epidemic-induced population collapses that could once accompany the incorporation of a peripheral society into the Europe-centered world system. A biological unification in terms of disease resistance – inoculation at the societal level – has been more or less completed. But the other side of this increased security is an increased scale of vulnerability. Precisely because the world is more unified, the entire human population may be more endangered by novel pathogens from which no regions or subpopulations are insulated or immune. The rapid spread of AIDS suggests something of what might occur.

CONCLUSION

The paradox of a world growing at once bigger and smaller is a familiar one. In its biotic composition, as in much else, a world that seems more diverse because we know more about it is in fact becoming steadily less so. Human activities in the past few centuries – mainly land-cover changes and harvesting – have led to the loss of some 2% of the terrestrial plant species and perhaps 1% of the terrestrial land ones. They have significantly reduced the numbers and the genetic diversity of many more. Harvesting has caused large if hard-to-calculate declines in some marine animal populations and fish stocks. Once largely a matter of island and freshwater species loss, extinction has become a serious threat to the land flora and fauna of the continents as well. Human-induced changes in the spatial distribution of species have been important both in contributing to loss in diversity and as alterations in their own right. No changes in distribution have reacted on the human population more rapidly and sometimes catastrophically than the redrawing of the disease map of the world.

The changes to date, though significant, are modest compared to the ones apparently under way, particularly through habitat loss as a result of today's rapid deforestation in the species-rich tropics. Global climatic change to which deforestation (along with fossil fuel combustion and other emissions) contributes would be the most far-reaching form of habitat alteration. Many species would need to migrate to find a suitable habitat and would not necessarily find one available. Just as the rate of species loss through human action now greatly exceeds that of past natural extinctions, so human-induced greenhouse warming might outpace past natural fluctuations in climate. In particular, many plant and tree species, which migrate (by seed dispersal) far more slowly than animals, might well fall behind in the race to keep up with the climatic conditions that they require.

Arguments for action to slow the erosion of biodiversity mingle preservationist, conservationist, and environmentalist themes. Around few topics have preservationists aroused support more successfully. Public interest in species protection is sometimes criticized for superficiality, for a focus on "cute, exotic creatures" that smacks of "vertebrate chauvinism" (Lowenthal 1990: 128). But the point may rather be that such images are dramatically effective in making the abstract concrete. Moral, spiritual, and emotional considerations play and have long played a significant role in appeals for species preservation, raising questions about the human place in the world and obligations to other beings. Writers such as H. G. Wells late in the nineteenth century played effectively and disturbingly with the implications that denying rights to lesser species – and also, at the height of Victorian imperialism, of "lesser races" – would have were the tables turned – were humankind ever visited from afar by creatures as much advanced beyond it as it is beyond the earth's flora and fauna.

From the perspective of resource conservation, the loss of species is the irretrievable loss of any uses that the species might have been found to have. The heavy reliance on the biological resource base that has so far characterized research in such fields as agriculture and medicine suggests that high rates of loss may be cause for much concern in this regard. Like the destruction or degrada-

112

tion of soils, the destruction of genetic diversity has significant temporal spillover effects; the unknown costs of present-day gains are charged to later times, when a resource that can be exploited renewably is instead permanently exhausted. And from an environmentalist perspective, the secondary effects of biodiversity loss are worrisome even if – and to some extent because – they are hard to foresee or calculate. How long can single threads be frayed or pulled from the fabric of life before it disastrously unravels?

Environmentalists have been fond in the past two decades of quoting the Amerindian Chief Seattle from the 1850s to the effect that "if all the beasts were gone, man would die from a great loneliness of spirit. For whatever happens to the beasts soon happens to man. All things are connected." Quoted thus, alas, in the *Earth Transformed* volume, these words were in fact penned by an American movie scriptwriter in the early 1970s. They have been mistaken for an authentic statement from an idealized past precisely because of the way in which they speak to concerns far more common. and more widely relevant, today.

5

Water

Writing in mid-eighteenth century Britain, the philosopher David Hume could liken water to air as being, "though the most valuable of external objects," substances so naturally abundant as to escape competition or ownership. "Where there is such a plenty of anything as satisfies all the desires of men . . . ," wrote Hume, "the association of property is entirely lost" (Hume [1739–40] 1985: 546). To put the idea in modern jargon, the abundance of each resource had made it logically a free-access good rather than a private or a common-property one. As no one argued more persuasively than Hume himself, though, ideas come from experience. His own assumptions about water were distinctively those of a dweller in the rainy temperate latitudes before the full onset of the Industrial Revolution. Even then, there were places where water had fallen short of demand and had been put under either public or private control. The passage of time has added others.

Water's very usefulness is part of the problem. Even where nature provides it in abundance, a resource so versatile invites so many demands as to make it a thing of value and an object of rivalry. Conservationists have long warned of the exhaustion of water supply, preservationists the fouling of aquatic environments, and environmentalists the effects of water pollution. Water's versatility in harm as well as in good heightens the chances of friction over management. Some human uses of water, such as flood control works and wetland drainage to banish disease, do not exploit water as a resource but defend against it as a threat.

Water's physical properties distinguish it in other ways from other resources. Though water is fluid, human impacts on it tend not to spread far. Timber, oil, foodstuffs, and other staple resources of the world economy are transported around the globe from source to consumer. Fresh water is not. The large volumes and weights needed for most human uses cannot cheaply be moved over long distances, and water steadily evaporates when exposed to the open air. It is still very much a local or regional resource, and so are problems of its shortage or pollution. The earth's surface is almost as readily divided into distinct water units as its political map is into sovereign states, and the boundaries of the former have changed much less over time. Surface water flows remain largely confined to separate basins that discharge their contents into the ocean or an enclosed inland sea drained only by the atmosphere. Such basins can be as vast as the 5.5 million square km of Amazonia, a third of South America. They can be as small as the catchment area of a coastal rivulet. The human impact on water is only the sum of the separate human impacts on the various drainage basins and groundwater aquifers.

The same global totals for human demand or for waste emissions could spell anything from a crisis of scarcity to comfortable plenty, depending on their distribution among these unevenly endowed units. Global trends are more an artifact of aggregation than a meaningful reality. What happens to flows and quality in one surface or groundwater system has no immediate physical consequences for another system; even within one river system, pollution or withdrawal at one locale affects only locations downstream. Transporting water from one basin to another is a theoretical possibility and in some areas a reality, but not on such a scale as to alter much the existing pattern. Action by one country is likely at most to affect a neighboring land lying in the same basin. To the degree that the effects of waste and mismanagement do not spread, that is good news; to the degree that improvement cannot be shared, it is less so.

THE RESOURCE

Fresh water (water that is free of ocean salt, not necessarily of other impurities) exists in a variety of reservoirs (Schwarz et al. 1990: 254). Two of the global accounts are quite small and turn over rapidly. The plants and animals of the world hold 1,100 cubic km of water and the atmosphere some 13,000 cubic km. The principal deposits are the land surface (including soil moisture and saline lakes and inland seas), which stores between 300,000 and 400,000 cubic km; the subterranean realm (8.2 million cubic km of groundwater, held in the pore spaces of sediment and bedrock); and glaciers and the polar ice (27.5 million). Most of the groundwater and the polar ice is unavailable for most uses; most readily tapped are the surface holdings of freshwater lakes, ponds, and streams. Lakes account for most of this total, and just a few of them – Lake Baikal in Russia, the Great Lakes of North America, and the lakes of the East African highlands – for a very large portion of it. Streams hold little more water than the biota, some 1,700 cubic km. But all of these amounts are less the property of the terrestrial realm than a rotating collection on loan from the far vaster holdings of the oceans, on varying schedules of length and renewability. The yearly flows of water through these compartments and the ocean add up to half a million cubic km per year evaporated and the same amount falling as precipitation.

Evaporation and runoff from the land restore to the oceans and atmosphere what was received as rain and snow.

One of the central facts about water in the global system is the natural variation in its availability. All lands are not watered equally. One easily can map gross world patterns of surplus and deficit, the former those lands where income from precipitation exceeds potential loss through evapotranspiration on a yearly basis. Yet even that measure omits some important sources of difference. Individual locations that seem well supplied in terms of annual and long-term average rainfall are still not guaranteed against either recurrent seasonal shortfalls or less predictable episodes of drought (or inundation). Annual rainfall is far more dependable in some areas than in others. Monsoon lands that would not be considered water-deficient on the basis of their annual averages still have dry seasons in which the supply may fall near or below a minimum required. Even in reliably well-watered places, the demand may press hard against the supply, while too great a plenty carries with it its own set of problems for many human uses.

Natural fluctuation in the faces and flows of water can serve as a gauge of the relative significance of human-induced change. It can also be of direct human concern. Natural changes over earth history have been immense. The past ups and downs, owing to climatic wobbles, of the water levels of the Caspian and Aral seas in central Eurasia dwarf the recent, though more rapid, human-induced changes in level that are now of grave concern along their shores. On the geologist's time scale, lakes are ephemeral puddles left by climatic storms moving over the landscape like high and low pressure fronts. Rivers constantly shift their courses even within the timespan of human observation. Volumes of flow are erratic too. While climatic change is reflected rather quickly in the surface waters, though, the snows of yesteryear have left substantial remnant resources in now-arid lands in the fossil form of groundwater aquifers. The hydrologic cycle today is no more immune than ever to shorter-term natural shocks. Perhaps the most striking fluctuations are those in the South and central Pacific, from the desert coasts of Peru and Chile to the rainforests of Borneo, associated with the ENSO (El Niño Surface Oscillation) events. These periodic and sometimes catastrophic reversals of ocean current and weather patterns can generate torrential rains in usually rainless areas matched by drought and forest fire in ones usually well watered.

Another central fact is the human powerlessness even now to effect a truly global rearrangement of the map and calendar of supply. The prospect of fundamental change exists only on the distant horizon and perhaps as a mirage at that. Desalination is still prohibitively expensive except under the most unusual circumstances of high demand and/or cheap energy. The laborious building of aqueducts and channels permits only limited transfers across the divides of neighboring basins. Our fumbling and inadvertent experiments with the climate system have yet to yield any clear results beyond the local scale. Broadly speaking, water availability has shaped population patterns more than it has been shaped by them (the world's two largest rivers, the Amazon and the Congo, are exceptional, flowing through areas still relatively bare of population and industry). Deserts remain areas of sparse occupance, and lakes, rivers, and plentiful rainfall, other things being equal, remain magnets for settlement. We still depend on the solar-powered desalination machine to smelt water free of the impurities with which it is mixed in the seas. Yet distribution at the local and regional scales is no longer entirely beyond human control. Water within most basins now flows more evenly in space and time than before. The ever-expanding ability of management to smooth the ups and downs that most deter settlement has permitted population and activity to expand, though riskily, into areas not naturally capable of meeting all their demands.

Human action affects the quantity of water available at a locale at any time by changing either the total volume that exists there or the aspects of quality that restrict or devalue it for a particular use. Sharply rising withdrawals have neither depleted nor increased the absolute quantity in the global system. We have reconstructed the global waterworks not by obtaining new sources of supply, but by rearranging the pipes, valves, and tanks and changing the secondary ingredients, in ways as deliberate as fluoridation or filtering (change in quality is by no means always for the worse) and as inadvertent as agricultural or industrial waste pollution.

Measuring human impact on surface water patterns can be easier than tracing changes in land use. Maps often do not detail the conversion of forest to pasture or pasture to cropland; they usually do distinguish land from water, however inaccurately. A series for a given area often records the creation of reservoirs, the drainage of lakes and wetlands, the cutting of canals, and the reshaping of river channels. Measuring human impact on the flows of water, even today's, is much harder. Direct withdrawals for particular purposes can be metered with some accuracy. Far harder to gauge are the secondary impacts on streamflow of such land-use changes as farming, forest clearance, and urbanization, especially as natural variation in flow is considerable. Small and carefully tended watersheds have for some time been used in controlled experimental studies of land-use impacts. The results, though, are difficult to extrapolate convincingly to other scales and settings. Other opportunities to separate the natural and human elements in change occur in enclosed basins, more inviting for such study now than when most were thought to drain out to the sea through underground channels. Larger systems of this sort include those of the Caspian Sea and of the Aral Sea in central Eurasia, of Lake Chad in Africa, of the Dead Sea between Israel and Jordan, and of the Great Salt Lake in the United States. Whereas the flow of most rivers is swallowed up in the ocean, in such landlocked systems reductions or increases due to human action may sometimes be readily seen in a change in the level of the receiving body of water. But even here the variables cannot be controlled like those of a laboratory experiment. Fluctuations in weather and climate often submerge the consequences of any human interference. Predicting the rise and fall even of enclosed lakes is still no easy task. Recent rises in the levels of the Caspian Sea and the Great Salt Lake, reversing earlier trends, and apparently of climatic genesis, have surprised professional managers and lay residents alike. Recent experience of stability or of steady decline had led them to expect more of the same (Kosarev and Makarova 1988; Leont'yev 1988; Morrisette 1988).

The best available estimates of global water resources and the volumes withdrawn over time for various purposes come from a monumental study directed by M. I. L'vovich, then of the USSR Academy of Sciences, in the 1970s, and revised, through international cooperation and further research, for the *Earth Transformed* volume a decade later (L'vovich and White 1990). These estimates will be drawn upon extensively throughout the chapter. As any global assessments today must be, they are far from perfect. Yet they do indicate the rough dimensions of global change. Where water is concerned, though, global and continental totals must be supplemented by tales of particular basins or hydrological units, both to underline the spatial confinement of water impacts and to illustrate the highly varied physical details and social processes and consequences of transformation.

THE HUMAN FRAMEWORK

Water management has been helped by the growth of scientific hydrology within the past few centuries (Biswas 1970). Medieval and Renaissance scientists thought rainfall too scanty to account for the volume flowing in streams, and they could explain springs that issued from hilltops only by according processes deep inside the earth a major role in the circulation of water. The hydrologic cycle as they envisioned it ran from the oceans through submarine outlets into underground caverns. There evaporation purified water and sent it rising to the mountain crests, from which it emerged into the open air and flowed downhill. A picture much like today's emerged only in the late seventeenth century with the work of Pierre Perrault (1611–80) in France. Perrault showed that rainfall in the Paris Basin was indeed sufficient to account for the flow of the local streams and springs, and that large subterranean reservoirs need not be invoked. Marsh's *Man and Nature* dealt at length with the influence of forests on floods and on precipitation, and also with the drainage of marshes and swamps and with the possible consequences of several large projected river diversions. The primary modern advance in scope has come in the greatly increased knowledge of the role of soil moisture and groundwater in affecting surface flow. Research in all areas has effected "a lively expansion of knowledge" since the 1950s (L'vovich and White 1990: 249). Much uncertainty remains, however, about the character and magnitude of human impact on a resource that behaves erratically even when left to its own devices.

Fully as important as the history of ideas among the water specialists has been the evolution of related disciplines whose progress and concerns in one way or another affected what was thought desirable or feasible. Changing medical theories of the origins of disease have dictated changing strategies of water quality management. And engineering has blended at innumerable points with the main currents of water management over the past three hundred years. Influence, like a tidal creek, has flowed in both directions. Water problems have stimulated technical innovation – the makers of the first practicable steam engines in Great Britain were seeking a source of power capable of draining deep coal mines of the accumulated seepage in the shafts that rendered them unworkable (Wilkinson 1973) – that has then become an independent variable in water management. Once invented and refined, the steam engine, to say nothing of the coal reserves that it liberated for use, became available to run new machines of drainage, dredging, and pumping. It also represented the onset of industrial energy sources that today demand vast quantities of water to wash away the waste heat and other effluents that they produce.

Some related technical fields have by now been partly dissolved, along with hydrologic science, in a broader profession of water resources management. Beyond it, outside the pale of accredited science, lies a separate realm of popular and folk belief, as it does in every environmental realm. An aversion persists in many modern countries to the use for drinking purposes of "reused" or "reclaimed" water, filtered and purified from previous use, despite scientific assurances as to its safety (Kasperson and Kasperson 1977). Different theories of disease have obstructed attempts to transfer some medical measures to non-Western settings. In cultures where illness is understood as a matter of an imbalance of "hot" and "cold" in the body, not as one of transmission by germs, the boiling of drinking water has been resisted as not only useless but positively harmful (Rogers 1962: 7–12). Belowground exists the most room for divergence between science and the public. The belief that groundwater typically occurs, not in pore spaces, but in subsurface "lakes" and "rivers," was a common one in classical and medieval times, closely tied to notions of subterranean flows in the water cycle. Historians of science usher it firmly out of their pages with the triumph of the modern view in the seventeenth and eighteenth centuries. Yet while the notion has largely disappeared from the cities and suburbs of Western academic science, it has continued to flourish in the poorly charted wilds around. Even throughout this century, intellectual explorers in the developed and developing worlds alike have reported sightings of it too numerous to be discounted (Meyer 1987). On balance, the popular view offers a much rosier picture than the revised standard version, depicting a resource renewed so rapidly as to escape the exhaustion or contamination that are very real threats to groundwater as it actually exists. But it is not simply a form of denial, for it can also open a window on some kinds of human impact that have gone wholly unnoticed by experts. On a train journey several years ago I overheard a passenger explain to his seatmates that dangerously rising levels in the Great Lakes – then a subject of much attention in the news – were caused by the dumping into the basins of urban waste. This garbage had "clogged" the subterranean channels, "like veins in your body," through which much of the water ordinarily flowed out.

Social institutions governing water resources take several forms. Water's indispensability as a resource has provided a strong argument, even on the grounds of economic efficiency, against purely private ownership. So has the near-public character of many of its benefits, such as navigation, scenery, and habitat, as well as of such costs as flooding and disease. Effects of use often spill over between private holdings and between political units because the boundaries were not often drawn with water units in mind. Governments, national or regional, have often retained control of water or have obtained it as an incident to assorted public works. In many countries, water remains public property under the management of the state, which allocates rights of use by permit. This system can have the advantage of facilitating the rapid and flexible reallocation of supply to higher or more equitable uses by managerial fiat. It can also have the defect of subsidizing inefficient and wasteful but popular uses to which the market, left in control, would signal a halt.

In Anglo-American law, private surface rights to water are granted, depending on the jurisdiction, under variants of the two positions known as the riparian and the appropriation doctrines. Under the former, a landowner along a stream may use its water, but may not significantly lessen its volume or worsen its quality for downstream users. Under the appropriation doctrine, priority of land ownership brings the right of abstraction even for consumptive uses, like irrigation, that lessen downstream flow. The shapers of Anglo-American water rights chose in the nineteenth century to regard groundwater in a different light, as akin to wild animals, belonging to no one until "captured" by actual extraction. Capture of groundwater, given the laws of trespass, could occur only from property lying atop an aquifer, but the water that could be captured from such a property unit was not confined to the water lying beneath its boundary lines. Withdrawal by any one owner abstracted from the common pool and not from a well-defined individual unit. The practical effect was to hand over aquifers underlying multiple property units to the richer owners, those able to sink deeper wells or use more powerful pumps than their neighbors. It was also to encourage the mining of the supply. In such a classic common-pool resource, similar to an oil pool or an ocean fishery, when use mounts under a realm of free or dispersed access, a competitive frenzy of depletion – Hardin's "tragedy of the commons" – is a possible outcome in the absence of managerial restraint. The lowering of the Great Plains Ogallala Aquifer has prompted the abandonment of a purely private (and effectively free-access for landowners) regime for groundwater in a number of states in favor of varying degrees of regulation intended to prolong the life of the resource (Schwarz et al. 1990: 267).

Water conflict includes not only competition over scarce supplies for the same uses but competition among different uses. Conflict is not inevitable in multiple exploitation. Some uses are entirely compatible with each other: navigation and many kinds of waste disposal, for example. Some uses are even symbiotic; damming for power generation, water supply, or flood control creates lakes that can also be used for recreation. But some uses generate ripples within their basin violent enough to swamp others nearby, and any degree of coexistence requires a careful balancing of rights. Navigation seems a classically undemanding, non-rival use. Yet it restricts the level to which a channel can be drawn down for the supply of other needs and may conflict with plans that would involve obstruction by dams and other control structures. When reservoirs are built for multiple tasks it may turn out that they can do none of them well.

AGRICULTURE, LAND USE, AND WATER

Agriculture represents a long-standing and still by far the world's foremost source of impact on water resources. Water may be withdrawn from surface or aquifer to irrigate crops where rainfall and soil moisture are inadequate; return water flowing downstream from cultivated fields may be polluted with sediment. salt, fertilizer, and pesticides; and such land-cover changes as plowing and forest clearance that accompany rural land use affect the rate and volume of surface flows.

IRRIGATION

Most of the water tapped annually from the global hydrologic cycle, perhaps three-quarters, is used for irrigation (L'vovich and White 1990: 242–43). The figure has risen more than 25-fold in three centuries, from close to 100 cubic km in the late seventeenth century to 2,700 cubic km today, over a period when the world's population has grown only about sevenfold (see Figure 5.1). The world area of artificially watered farmland has increased 50-fold in the same period, from about fifty thousand square km to about 2.5 million.

Irrigation, in contrast to some other uses, is highly consumptive. Because of evapotranspiration and seepage losses, little water returns after use to the system of flow. Of the current withdrawal for irrigation, some 2,300 cubic km, or 85%, is consumed. The ratio in particular basins varies by the natural setting and the crops and technologies involved.

Irrigation's importance in the water budget is spatially quite uneven. Two-thirds of the withdrawal occurs in Asia, a continent where it represents well over 90% of total water demand (see Figure 5.1). Neither proportion has changed much from earlier times. On other continents, irrigation is far less important; irrigators withdraw less water in both Europe and North America than do industry and power generation. In many individual countries and hydrologic basins, irrigation represents little or none of the total withdrawal.

That civilizations, early or modern, created deserts was long a common belief.

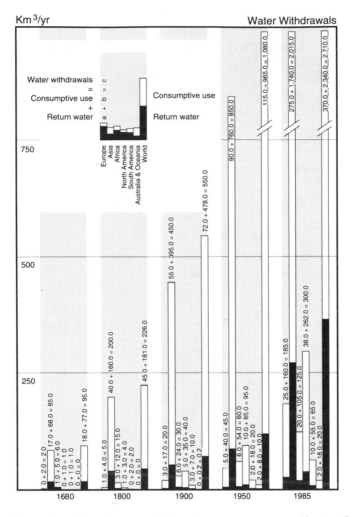

Figure 5.1 Estimated world total water withdrawal, consumptive use, and return flow for irrigation, 1680–1985, in cubic km per year. Source: L'vovich and White 1990.

To explain the same apparent link between the dawn of societies and an arid environment, others have reversed the cause and effect by supposing that deserts created civilization, that they encouraged and indeed required cooperation in the collective transformation of a challenging environment. For water cannot readily be impounded, withdrawn, and channeled across the land from source to crops in quantity merely through the independent acts or agreements of individuals. As with drainage, such actions require the joint effort or at least consent of large numbers, which only state intervention can guarantee. Irrigation works, ancient and modern, have thus been ascribed a tendency to invite repressive and

122

corrupt government management. A rosier view that diverges sharply in finding community and equality the natural fruit of arid environments and large-scale irrigation has not lacked for defenders at least since Jean-Jacques Rousseau (Moran and Gode 1966: 41–45). Theorizing in the latter vein burst even the bounds of the earth in the American astronomer Percival Lowell's turn-of-the-century theory that a planetary-scale system channeled scarce water from Mars's seasonally melting polar ice caps to irrigate farmland in the desiccated middle and lower latitudes. Lowell (1908: 377) saw in the surface of Mars as transformed by Martian action a sign of the utopian harmony of the planet, a reflection of "the necessarily intelligent and non-bellicose character of the community which could act as a unit throughout its globe."

The earliest uses of irrigation are lost in antiquity, but large and advanced systems developed with the growth of civilization in the Tigris-Euphrates lowlands of Mesopotamia after about 4000 B.C. Even several thousand years ago, they began to leave a mark in the form of land made unproductive by salinization and silting. Many impressive networks of irrigation in the Old and New Worlds had risen, flourished, and crumbled by the end of the seventeenth century; others in Asia continued uninterrupted for millennia. Of the area artificially watered in 1680, most, as today, lay in Asia, with some small but sophisticated systems in operation elsewhere.

During the eighteenth and nineteenth centuries, the world land area under irrigation grew steadily but slowly – by not more than about 2% per year (L'vovich and White 1990: 242). British colonial engineers in the Nile Valley and in India were among the foremost agents of its nineteenth-century expansion. They replaced simple forms of basin irrigation in Egypt, tied to the annual flooding of the Nile, with ever-larger impoundments and distributing works that made possible the large-scale growing of cotton for the world market. Work in India began with the restoration of decayed irrigation works from the Mogul period and proceeded to new construction (Schwarz et al. 1990: 262–64). The Ganges Canal, finished in 1854, irrigated half a million hectares, the single largest system in the world at that time. The restoration and extension of much of the vast ruined tank irrigation system in the Dry Zone of northern Ceylon opened up land for a century of peasant colonization. Demand for irrigation water in India was greatly spurred by a disastrous series of droughts in the mid-1890s that triggered large crop failures and famines. By the time of independence in 1947, some 60 million acres in India were irrigated. Expansion and intensification have continued, despite rising problems of salinization. Compare today's annual hydrograph for the Ganges River with ones estimated for 1850 and 1900, and the effects on streamflow of withdrawal for irrigation also become apparent (see Figure 5.2).

Continental expansion led nineteenth-century Russians and Americans alike into new environments, vast plains of rich soil but unreliable rain. Irrigation on the Russian Plain, begun in earnest in the nineteenth century, has grown from

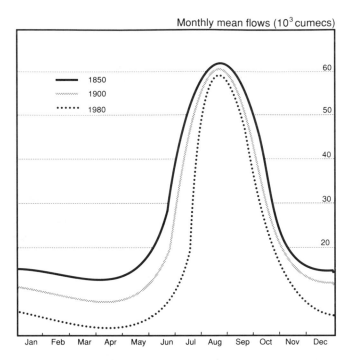

Monthly mean flows (10^3 cumecs)

Figure 5.2 Mean monthly hydrograph of the Ganges River and reconstructed hydrographs for 1850, 1900, and 1980, in thousands of cubic m per second. Source: Schwarz et al. 1990.

one million hectares at the turn of the century to five million in 1980 (Alayev, Badenkov, and Karavaeva 1990: 553). Russian Central Asia had boasted large and sophisticated irrigation systems before the Christian era, largely destroyed or abandoned after Mongol invasions. Tsarist programs to restore and expand the systems were enthusiastically continued by the Soviet regime. The federal Bureau of Reclamation supervised a considerable expansion of irrigation in the western United States beginning in the late nineteenth century. The area irrigated in the region, 15,000 square km in 1890, doubled by 1900, doubled again by 1930, and reached 180,000 square km in the late 1970s (Richards 1986: 64). No less remarkable a spurt in growth has occurred worldwide in the second half of the twentieth century in the global totals of irrigated area and of water withdrawn. Development in Africa, though, remains relatively modest compared to the other world regions, save in the Nile Valley of Egypt and Sudan and along the Mediterranean coast.

The very word "irrigation" evokes images of human-made oases, sparkling water channeled into thirsty lands, deserts made to blossom green in an almost magical transformation of the landscape. The term "reclamation," a common synonym for either irrigation or drainage, implies the restoration of damaged places to some better state from the past. Irrigation would not have spread so far and fast if it did not do all that it is credited with. It has made possible a massive expansion of agricultural settlement and production; at least a sixth of the world's cropland is irrigated, and it produces more than a sixth of the world's food.

These benefits are plain enough. The adverse impacts are less obvious, but some of them have long been the object of comment. George Perkins Marsh was of two minds on the subject of irrigation. Acknowledging its usefulness, he cited among its environmental costs the danger of soil salinization and among its social costs a tendency to concentrate land in the hands of a few. His wariness became downright hostility toward the growing of rice in flooded fields. This form of agriculture Marsh ([1864] 1965: 323n) found "productive of very prejudicial climatic effects"; the emission of malarial gases was "so prejudicial to health everywhere that nothing but the necessities of a dense population can justify the sacrifice of life it costs in countries where it is pursued." The medical objection was widely advanced against irrigation. In an updated form, stressing disease carriers such as mosquitoes and parasites rather than miasma, it still is. The expansion of the system in Egypt and British India produced a sharp rise in malaria in many of the canal districts in the late nineteenth century (Klein 1973: 645–48), although the authorities redesigned a number of the irrigation systems in order to alleviate the problem (Schwarz et al. 1990: 264). Even today, the habitat created by irrigation remains a significant hazard to health – not only through malaria but through many other diseases.

Being highly consumptive, irrigation diminishes the flow of water downstream. The volume of the Colorado River in the southwestern United States and Mexico has shrunk steadily as irrigation and municipal withdrawal have increased. Lake levels drop when the streams that feed them are thus depleted. Irrigation demand has reduced a number of lakes in the western United States in area and volume. Such great enclosed saline seas as the Caspian and the Aral in central Eurasia have been depleted by irrigation withdrawal from their tributary rivers. In a classic collision of incompatible uses, cropland expansion has been achieved in each region at the expense of other livelihoods and values. The Caspian, a behemoth inland salt sea with the surface area of Montana, dropped some four meters in the earlier portion of this century (Kosarev and Makarova 1988; Leonty'ev 1988). Natural climatic change contributed, but in the last several decades human withdrawals may have been the more important factor. In consequence, the sea's fishery was damaged in both quantity and quality. The inward retreat of the coastline forced the abandonment of many shore facilities. Only frequent dredging kept others in operation. The surprising sequel was a yet-unexplained rise of about a meter in the level of the sea during the 1980s.

The Aral, the smaller sea, has suffered much more dramatic and damaging change (Micklin 1988; Kotlyakov 1991). During the first half of the twentieth century, its level fluctuated within a range of a meter or so. In less than three

Table 5.1. *Hydrologic parameters of the Aral Sea from 1960 to 1989*

Year	Sea level (meters)	Sea area (thousand sq. kilometers)	Sea volume (cubic kilometers)	Mineral content (grams per liter)	Total river run-off into sea (cubic kilometers)
1960	53.3	67.9	1,090	10.0	40
1965	52.5	63.9	1,030	10.5	31
1970	51.6	60.4	970	11.1	33
1975	49.4	57.2	840	13.7	11
1980	46.2	52.4	670	16.5	0
1985	42.0	44.4	470	23.5	0
1989	39.0	37.0	340	28.0	5

Source: Kotlyakov 1991.

decades, from 1960 to 1989, it dropped by more than a dozen meters; the sea lost 60% of its original surface area of 68,000 square km and two-thirds of its volume (see Table 5.1). It broke apart into two separate bodies of water in the late 1980s when the shallow ridge separating its two deeper basins emerged into the open air. Such changes in the sea's dimensions are far from unprecedented over the long term. The Aral's level fluctuated considerably in prehistoric and even recorded time for reasons having nothing to do with human activity. But the current rapid desiccation, the most severe in this millennium, clearly reflects the rising demands of irrigation. Before 1960, withdrawal, though large, was nearly balanced by diminished loss through evaporation in the sea's reclaimed wetland fringe. Increasing water use since, to support the level of cotton growing decreed as the region's function by Soviet central planners, led directly to losses in surface area and volume. The sea may well disappear altogether if trends in withdrawal continue under the Kazakh and Uzbek successors to the Soviet authorities. Further consequences already apparent have included the increased salinity and pollution of the sea – more pesticides, fertilizers, and wastes have gone into the water just as there has been less water to dilute them – reflected in rising illness rates and infant mortality. The fishery has been destroyed and ports have been left high and dry. Agriculture has been damaged for many kilometers around by dust and salt storms from the dried seabed. The regional climate has deteriorated, with less rainfall and heightened extremes of temperature. Cotton output has fallen even with greater inputs. Plans were advanced for many years for a massive engineering solution: the diversion southward into the Caspian and Aral of several large rivers that now flow north into the Arctic Ocean. Such plans were approved in the early 1980s, then abandoned shortly thereafter, although the mounting crisis led to calls for reconsideration. The breakup of the Soviet

126

Union, and the continued dependence of the region on irrigated production, leaves a solution apparently farther away than ever.

So too have some vast underground "seas" been depleted (though, *pace* Jules Verne and Edgar Rice Burroughs, with no impacts that we know of on their shorelines, navigability, or fisheries). The dependence of many farming lands on such exhaustible reserves of groundwater foreshadows a crisis. The best-known groundwater reservoir in the United States is the Ogallala or High Plains Aquifer. It underlies portions of eight Great Plains states and now supports a fifth of the nation's irrigated cropland. Early Plains settlers used wind-driven pumps to draw up the "underground rain." Cheap and plentiful energy to run more powerful pumps arrived in the region around the end of World War II. Major increases followed in extraction rates and in the area of irrigated land, and drastic declines quickly ensued in the aquifer level. The aridity of the climate means a minimal amount of natural recharge. The Ogallala is a fossil resource like coal or oil. It is replenished more rapidly than they are, but not enough to matter on the social scale of time. Barring unforeseeably profound climatic change on the Plains – and global warming is thought more likely to lessen the region's rainfall than to increase it – "there can be no future but one of exhaustion" (Schwarz et al. 1990: 267). The management and regulation measures that have been introduced in modern decades can delay that outcome but not prevent it.

Return water from irrigated fields, moreover, carries pollutants into streams: salt, pesticide, and fertilizer runoff. Irrigation is most environmentally benign when it is completely consumptive. Salinity in the Colorado River, naturally high in any case, has been approximately doubled by the human use of the basin (Schwarz et al. 1990: 259). Direct withdrawal of water, mainly for agricultural use, and evaporation from reservoirs have increased the relative salinity of the river, while return water from irrigation has raised the absolute content and added other undesirable substances. As the Caspian and Aral Seas have shrunk, not only has their natural salinity risen, but the sewage and chemical pollutants also added to them have been correspondingly more concentrated.

LAND USE AND STREAMFLOW

Running water shapes the landscape, but in the short term the influence tends to run the other way, water being affected by the character of the land surface over which it flows. In particular, the clearing of forests and the plowing of grasslands have long been thought to alter the rates of streamflow and of infiltration into the soil.

Two insights, both correct, have long clashed in the interpretation of floods. One is the realization, a matter of common sense to our ancestors but not so obvious today, that extreme high flows do occur under purely "natural" conditions. Hence not all such events today can be blamed on human disruption of the land surface; some result from weather conditions that are unusual but by no means unknown. On the other hand, it has long been recognized, again correctly, that land-use change can affect the surface flows of water, and that the most common changes bring heightened extremes and reduced stable rates of flow. The rationale for the belief that flooding increases after forest clearing is easy to accept: that forest cover acts as a kind of sponge delaying the immediate runoff of all precipitation into the streams. But the belief is hard to verify to any skeptic's satisfaction because of the problems of adequately controlling the variables that may be of importance. Floods, like dust storms or coastal erosion, can be both natural and human-worsened. In any of these processes, charges are readily leveled at careless land users and indictments handed down, yet convictions beyond a reasonable doubt are far more difficult to reach.

Governments in many places have not waited for proof; much state investment in forestry grew out of the notion that tree cover moderated or even prevented floods, as well as decreasing soil erosion, protecting the climate, and maintaining timber resources. The forest–flood relationship is a major theme in Marsh's *Man and Nature* that was already an axiom of geographical literacy before the book's appearance. In mid-nineteenth century Switzerland, a series of devastating floods coming down to the lowlands from the Alps was popularly ascribed to mountain deforestation. The central government was given powers to intervene, and a program of replanting the denuded slopes was undertaken – though modern research has tended to bolster the conclusions expressed by a scientific report of that time, that these floods were the result of the chance occurrence of extreme weather events, not of land clearance (Pfister and Messerli 1990: 642, 650). At the beginning of the twentieth century, the United States established forest reserves in the Appalachians expressly to help control streamflow in the coastal lowlands – even though the best scientific studies available at the time suggested that their effect would be minimal (Dodds 1969). Modern flooding and sedimentation in the Ganges and Brahmaputra basins in India and Bangladesh have been blamed on deforestation in the rivers' sources in the Himalayas. Yet recent studies have pointed out that the high natural instability of these river systems, reflecting the climate and topography, produces such a pattern of variation and of extreme events that any human role is difficult to identify, but probably not substantial (Ives and Messerli 1990: 130–44). The claim was made in the 1970s that deforestation in the Amazon Basin was raising flood heights downstream. That claim has likewise been challenged by careful analyses of the evidence. Hydrologists now ascribe by far the largest share of responsibility for floods to precipitation and to the configuration of the drainage basin. Neither is under the close control of humankind, and forest cover, which is, seems to play a minor role (Richey, Nobre, and Deser 1989; Sternberg 1987).

The point is not that there is no relation between forest cover and streamflow. The connections are well established by experimental watershed studies. Annual flow in a forested basin is typically somewhat less than in a denuded one, because of consumption of water by the forest. It is also more regular and uniform than in a comparable basin cleared of its trees. Catastrophic floods in most hydrologic systems are largely the result of the weather; they are the impacts for which land-cover change is least likely to be responsible. Rural landscape changes more subtle than deforestation also affect streamflow, but again the impacts are difficult to study and may depend heavily on the local context. Draining wetlands does often sharpen extremes of flow, the regulating effect of their storage capacity being lost. Most studies find that plowing of grasslands affects the local water flow, though they disagree as to how. Some find increased, others reduced surface flow. Both are probably correct in different circumstances. Overall, "the impact of nonirrigated agriculture and forest management has been studied insufficiently to permit global generalization, although it is clearly of major importance in some drainage areas" (L'vovich and White 1990: 248).

INDUSTRIAL WATER USE

Industry uses water mainly as a medium of waste disposal. At one time, direct-drive power from water was important, and the Industrial Revolution broke out on the banks of streams that turned its wheels and turbines. Even as steam and later electric power have freed manufacturing to wander away from waterfalls, running streams have remained useful and even essential to carry away the wastes of production. Among these wastes is excess heat, much of it produced by those new energy sources themselves. If irrigation still leads all sources of withdrawal across the globe, industry runs a (distant) second at some 700 cubic km per year. Irrigation demand is heavily concentrated in Asia; industry is the foremost consumer in several other world regions, Europe and North America among them (see Figure 5.3).

Industrial uses are far less directly consumptive than is irrigation. Half of the industrial withdrawal is for cooling, and most of it is returned. The requirements of quality are somewhat less stringent than for some other water uses, and there is flexibility as to quantity as well. Industrial demands tend to be sensitive to price, and many could be lowered significantly through economy, reuse, and recycling if hidden subsidies were removed and the price rose to reflect more accurately the real cost of provision. Such rationalization seems likely to progress in the countries of the developed world, where industrial water demand is still concentrated, though demand is likely to increase in the near future in the developing countries.

Waste heat dissipates quite rapidly, though before doing so it can have locally severe effects. The industrial water pollutants of most significance are persistent chemicals. Possibly toxic substances created or released in large quantity into the waters are the newest cause for concern over water and health. Many more substances are now emitted than can be assessed with confidence for their medical

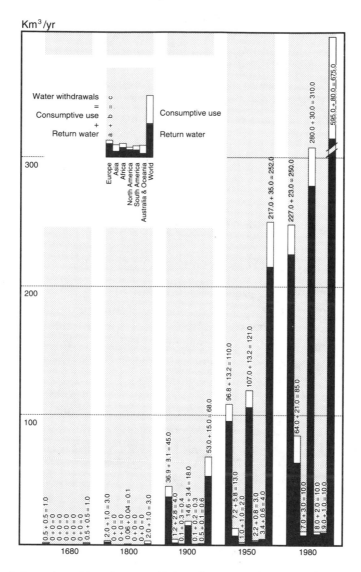

Figure 5.3 Estimated world total water withdrawal, consumptive use, and return water for industrial and power production, 1680–1980, in cubic km per year. Source: L'vovich and White 1990.

implications, especially their possible effects at low concentrations over the long term. Groundwater contamination is especially worrisome because of the slowness with which aquifers are rid of pollutants. Even in surface flows, contaminants may not be washed rapidly out of the basin to the sea, but may accumulate in the channel sediments and be reawakened when disturbed by dredging.

CITIES AND WATER

The urban impacts on water roughly mimic the rural and agricultural ones. Farmers irrigate crops; cities channel water to their otherwise parched and rain-less residences. Return flows from both activities pollute water downstream. Ur-banizing the land surface affects the flow of water more sharply than does culti-vating or deforesting it, though in different ways and to some extent deliberately, whereas the rural changes are largely inadvertent. These effects are quite modest as a share of the net global water flows, but in individual basins they can be considerable.

More significant is the dependence of the health of a population, urban or rural, on the supply and disposal of water. Both city and country dwellers, of course, withdraw water for direct personal use. Urban areas, though, differ from rural ones in the concentration and magnitude of such demand. More problems of water quality deterioration arise in cities; so do more opportunities, through economies of scale and density, to provide good water efficiently and to treat wastes. Where these opportunities are taken, the city can achieve an unusually high level of health, cleanliness, and development – though at a price, some of which can be passed on to others up- or downstream. If the opportunities are neglected, the likely outcome is an unusually low one.

URBAN WATER SUPPLY

City populations have long relied on private enterprise, often in the primitive form of individual water carriers, to meet their needs. That reliance was still the near-universal rule a century and a half ago. Such a delivery system was ill adapted to satisfying large demands or to realizing economies of scale; to provide one more unit of water by hand-carried bucket from a river cost about as much as to provide the first. The similarity of the water supply systems of the major world regions in this period is reflected in the statistics for domestic-municipal water withdrawal (L'vovich and White 1990: 244). In 1800, over half, some 4.5 cubic km, occurred in Asia, where some 65% of the world's population was found. Europe and North America together accounted for only a third of the world domestic-municipal consumption, a pattern that persisted through the middle of the nineteenth century. (Most of this withdrawal, of course, was rural, as was most of the population.) Among the characteristics of these supply systems a suscep-tibility to waterborne diseases ranked high. Sources convenient for domestic sup-ply were no less convenient for the disposal of germ-contaminated wastes. The transmission of diseases – cholera, typhoid, and others – by waterborne germs was little understood until the latter decades of the century. So long as filth and odor were accorded the principal role in epidemics, public health measures oc-curred for the wrong reasons even when, as was sometimes the case, they repre-sented genuine improvements. Philadelphia, with an ample and unusually well-

131

protected water supply, suffered little from the great cholera epidemic of 1832, yet its deliverance was ascribed not to the cleanliness of the drinking water but to its use in abundance to wash the streets clean of decaying and miasma-generating wastes (Blake 1956).

The mid-nineteenth century saw a transformation in urban supply in Europe and North America. One aspect was government control or at least involvement, which made sense for a variety of reasons. New or traditional public responsibilities and public goods – protecting health, cleaning the public streets, and fighting fires – all required a suitable supply of water. That supply, in turn, could, with the advent of steam power for pumping, be most cheaply provided through systems of pipes that required rights-of-way impossible to assemble by private action. It sometimes also required larger sources of supply – such as lakes and reservoirs – unusable without the power of eminent domain. The result was a classic natural monopoly suited to state operation or control. Decision makers could consult John Stuart Mill's ([1852] 1967): 434) observation that in this business, unlike food supply, there existed "virtually no competition" because of the crushing size of the infrastructural outlays that would be required of a new entrant into the market, and particularly note Mill's comparison of water supply to "the making of roads and bridges, the paving, lighting, and cleansing of streets," and protection from fire and epidemic as having an essentially public character.

These new sources, institutions, and technologies of transfer, in the service of ever-increasing demand, developed so rapidly in the Western world that by the early twentieth century, Europe and North America, still with less than a quarter of the world's population, consumed two-thirds of the global withdrawal for urban uses, some 16.5 cubic km, and Asia, still with more than half of the total population, withdrew only about 7 cubic km. The public health consequences of the new systems were revolutionary. The water-related diseases that had ravaged the world cities of the Victorian era – cholera, typhoid, yellow fever – dropped rapidly in incidence in Europe and North America as water supplies became purer, treatment (filtration and chlorination) was introduced, and urban drainage systems became more efficient. What has occurred at the same time as the increase in urban supply and use is a widening of the gap across much of the world, the developing as well as the developed, between urban and rural populations in access to safe and plentiful water. The public assumption of responsibility for urban (and often industrial) water supply, moreover, has tended to make it a subsidized good, with costs hidden from the consumer and paid through other means – typically a recipe for excessive and inefficient use.

Groundwater, a key early source of municipal supply, remains an important one despite its decline in quality in many places. In some locales in humid climates, natural recharge is adequate to maintain levels for future supply or is enhanced by management; elsewhere, though, urban demand can deplete aquifers just as irrigation can. Several meters of land surface drop in and around such cities as Beijing, Osaka, Tokyo, Mexico City, and Houston testify to such depletion (Walker 1990: 289). Coastal aquifers already lie in an uneasy balance with ocean waters. That balance can be upset, and saline intrusion can occur, as a consequence of urbanization. Both the withdrawal of groundwater to meet increased demands, and the land-surface changes of city sprawl, making for less permeability, reduce freshwater recharge.

URBAN EFFLUENT

Three hundred years ago, "the volume of all municipal waste water was minute and was significant chiefly in a few cities (London, Moscow, Paris, and Rome)" (L'vovich and White 1990: 244). Systematic disposal was limited to a few regions such as East Asia, densely populated and intensively cultivated, where municipal waste made a highly valued fertilizer for periurban farmers. Little changed, save for a gradual expansion of effluent volume, for a century and a half. In the world cities of the Victorian era, though, growth in population and activity and in the water supply available for waste carriage overtaxed the existing means of sewage removal, precipitating a widespread sanitary crisis and a search for solutions. Fortunately, in most cases ready channels for waste disposal existed close at hand. The Providential wisdom that, as an old joke had it, had caused rivers to flow near large towns provided them with a means of easy sanitation. Paris as rebuilt at mid-century by Napoleon III's city planner, Baron Georges-Eugène Haussmann, included a large network of sewers to remove street wastes promptly to the Seine, replacing the decrepit, jerry-built system depicted by Victor Hugo. London saw the rapid spread in the 1840s and 1850s, accelerated by sanitary laws, of water closets connected to the Thames River, replacing cesspools and cellar vaults that had been manually emptied. The quality of the river deteriorated with alarming speed (Schwarz et al. 1990: 260–61). Most large cities had similar experiences. Sewage treatment rarely kept pace with the increasing pressure of expanding populations and the mounting load of effluent added through growing sewer systems. Responses more often than not took the form of more efficient ways to transfer the offense given by the river pollution downstream to the nostrils of a smaller audience. Its complaints about this new nuisance rarely prevailed against the greater weight of the urban interest.

Victorian improvements in the quality of the Thames gave way under increasing pressures of use. New forms of pollution, such as synthetic detergents and waste heat from power plants, supplemented the more traditional forms. As dissolved oxygen nearly disappeared from the water along a long stretch of the Thames around and below London, so did fish, and those living above the river's surface found it almost as unbearable. A commission set up in 1951 prescribed standards for river quality. Improved sewage treatment and limits on industrial discharges have effectively implemented its recommendations. Fish reappeared, hesitantly at first, as dissolved oxygen content now consistently reaches the mini-

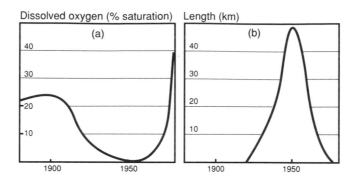

Figure 5.4 (a) Average autumn dissolved oxygen concentrations in the tidal Thames River. (b) Length of the tidal Thames River with dissolved oxygen concentrations below 5% of saturation. Redrawn from Wood 1982.

mum level that the commission prescribed (Schwarz et al. 1990: 261–62). A graph of the ups and downs in dissolved oxygen traces the course of the deterioration of the Thames and its restoration by management (see Figure 5.4). Similar stories can be told of other rivers in the developed world. The nadir of quality in the Hudson River, for example, seems to have been reached after a long and steady decline in the early 1960s. A rapid expansion of sewage treatment then produced rapid improvement (Tarr and Ayres 1990: 628–32). Yet in many other countries, quality continues to decline. Many rivers in the Second and Third Worlds are severely degraded by the pressure of urban agglomerations and unregulated industrial centers on their banks. Intranational river pollution has wider impacts. Much of the gross sewage pollution that befouls rivers in Poland, for example, flows downstream to foul the international waters of the Baltic Sea as well.

CITIES AND STREAMFLOW

The transformation of the urban land surface by paving and construction creates a set of hydrologic effects clearer and more uniform than those produced by rural land-cover change (Berry 1990: 113–14). Urbanization produces more rapid runoff and greater peak flow downstream. Floods become higher and more frequent. These effects are not of much importance in the global water budget, but they can be considerable in the downstream basin. Where rural land-use impacts on flows are essentially inadvertent, the urban ones are at least in part the result of deliberate construction – of sewer systems, aimed at removing storm waters as rapidly as possible from the streets to prevent flooding, and of paving and other surfaces also intended to hasten runoff and keep streets from becoming the morasses into which heavy rains transformed earlier thorough-fares.

IMPOUNDMENT

Modern water demand – agricultural, industrial, and urban – can no longer be consistently satisfied by tapping either the surface flow that runs past the would-be users or the reserves of groundwater that lie below them. Water is increasingly impounded in open-air reservoirs to guarantee a more reliable supply than nature provides, by retaining for use in the dry periods at least a portion of what would run off as waste during the rainy spells, or for use in the day what would be lost at night. The creation of reservoirs is not confined to humankind. Geologic forces impound water in lakes through both sudden twitches and gradual up-heavals. Beavers build dams and other hydro-engineering works, sometimes with locally annoying consequences for neighbors. Yet modern human activity in this realm remains altogether distinctive in terms of the size and rate of the change it produces.

Most of the human-induced changes are a product of the present century. A fragmented inland Atlantis some 400,000 square km in area, about the size of France, has sunk beneath the rising waters of large reservoirs in the past 300 years. Only the very fringe of its coastline had foundered before the twentieth century. In 1900, the world had 41 large reservoirs, defined as those with volumes of more than 100 million cubic m (0.1 cubic km), containing less than 15 cubic km of water in all. By 1950, the 539 such reservoirs held a little more than 500 cubic km, and in 1985, 1,777 large reservoirs impounded a volume of nearly 5,000 cubic km: in short, practically all of this storage was achieved in less than a hundred years (see Figure 5.5). The average volume held behind all those 1,777 dams, to be sure, could be emptied several times over into the basin of the single largest natural lake in the world and still leave its shores high and dry, and it accounts for only a small fraction of the surface fresh water. Still, it took thousands of years to create most of those lakes and less than a century to impound these reservoirs.

Nor do reservoirs transform only the faces of water; they also affect flows significantly. The regulation of streams evens out the seasonal extremes of river discharge. It has produced an estimated increase in stable runoff of about 30% at the global level, though differing by continent. The greatest increase, well in excess of 50%, has been calculated as occurring in North America and the former Soviet Union; the smallest, and also the most recent, in South America (L'vovich and White 1990: 239).

Part of the reason for the modernity of a transformation that in smaller forms is of great antiquity lies in the history of the technologies that made it possible. Engineering research into the strengths of materials and the stresses of im-

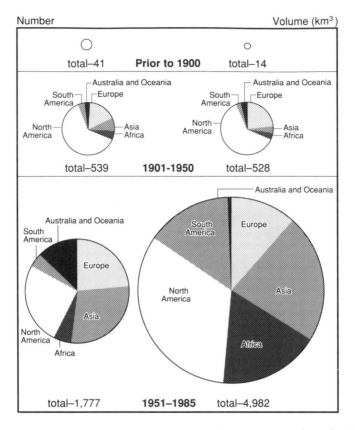

Figure 5.5 Number and volume (in cubic km) of large reservoirs through 1985. Source: L'vovich and White 1990.

poundment has made ever higher and wider dams feasible. A dam, once built, can provide many more services than it once could. The development in the late nineteenth century of hydroelectricity and its long-distance transmission funded multipurpose dam projects also offering programs of flood control, recreation, irrigation, and water supply in the way that commercials support television shows, by sharing their medium in a division of resources beneficial to all. Hydropower now represents about a quarter of the world's electric generating capacity. Close to 20% of the potential world hydropower capacity, measured purely in physical terms and neglecting economic constraints, has now been harnessed (L'vovich and White 1990: 240–41). International aid donors have enthusiastically supported such projects as a stimulus to development. The prestige that they bring is a motive that is, if by nothing else, demonstrated by the frequency with which heads of state attach their names to them. Today's map displays Lakes

Nasser, Mobutu, and Assad; Boulder Dam on the Colorado River did not become Hoover Dam until after the presidency of Hoover's adversary Franklin Roosevelt.

In some parts of the world today a politician might prefer to name such schemes for adversaries. If the public – save perhaps the populations flooded out – once accepted great dams as great improvements, more recently such projects have become tarnished by criticism in the developed and developing worlds alike. Their social and environmental costs belong mainly to this century, but earlier cases foreshadowed many of them. One might fix the beginning of the era of large impoundments and the controversies that they arouse at the turn-of-the-century closing of the Nile River by the original Aswan Dam. Proposed in the mid-1890s by British colonial engineers, largely to furnish water for irrigation, the dam was scaled down in order to save the ancient temples on the island of Philae after plans for one high enough to flood them had caused a "furious controversy" in Europe. The engineers and administrators involved in the project found the outcry bemusing. One suggested that if "the London County Council had discovered a cheap and easily executed plan for clearing the Thames of sewage, annihilating London fogs, and at the same time solving the great problem of agricultural depression throughout the country," yet Americans protested because of the flooding thereby of "some picturesquely situated ruins" that they had been accustomed to visit, the English would surely take it amiss. Foes of the dam touched on many of the issues of central modern concern: the drowning of much potentially productive land, "the ruthless expatriation of the inhabitants of all this district" to be flooded, and the likelihood that the river, "cleared of its deposit by standing in large reservoirs," would "lose a large part of its fertilising qualities" (Baker 1894; Dillon 1894). The dam, at its more modest scale, was completed in 1902. Within a decade or so, it was raised twice, leaving Philae submerged after all, except during periods of low water. The construction of the Aswan High Dam, which raised similar controversy in the 1960s by drowning the site of the temple at Abu Simbel, at the same time restored Philae to the open air, though much damaged by its long submersion.

The most direct impact is the loss of land to flooding. Brazilian Amazonia (Salati et al. 1990: 481, 487) and Switzerland (Pfister and Messerli 1990: 647) represent two very different cases. Brazil, like many developing countries, has sought to reduce a costly foreign dependence on foreign energy by developing internal sources. Many hydropower projects have been developed or planned in recent decades on the Brazilian Amazon and its tributaries, their number and dispersion made necessary by a subdued regional topography – the river falls only 107 m in the final 2,400 km of its course from Iquitos, Peru, to the sea. Very sizable areas must be sacrificed for reservoirs large enough to generate substantial amounts of energy: the Tucuruí Dam on the Tocantins River, for example, has flooded more than 2,000 square km of rainforest to produce 4,000 megawatts of power. Another dam under construction in the late 1980s was to flood almost an equal expanse for a much smaller output. In steep mountain areas, on the other hand, hydropower offers a far better return for the area invested, though it sacrifices scarce valley lands that are of particular value. In Switzerland, rich in relatively few other resources, exploitation of mechanical hydropower began early, and the adoption of hydroelectricity was rapid. A more than fivefold expansion since World War II has now brought into use virtually all of the nation's usable capacity – more than 10,000 megawatts, generated from a surface area of artificial lakes of only 120 square km.

Impoundments of all sorts, in trapping water as they were designed to do, also capture silt that would ordinarily have been carried downstream. Consequently their useful lifetimes are measured, as by an hourglass, by the time it takes for the reservoir basin to fill up with sediment, and their capacity and hence their usefulness decline steadily during the process. Filling with sediment promises eventually to restore any reservoir basin to dry land, but during the lengthy interim its human population is displaced, usually to inferior and almost always to unfamiliar lands. Large impoundment projects begin with tens of thousands of eviction notices. Nigeria's Kainji Dam, built in 1968 for hydroelectric generation and secondarily for irrigation, displaced more than 40,000 inhabitants from the 1,300 square km that it flooded. Ghana's Volta River dam, also completed in the 1960s, entailed nearly twice that number of relocations. The mammoth Three Gorges project under way on China's Yangtze River will flood the homes of over a million people.

The human inhabitants at least are resettled; valued biotic resources, even whole species, may be lost in the flooding of their habitats. It is a particular hazard in tropical forests rich in endemic varieties. Other creatures move in, of course; the creation of reservoir fisheries is often cited as a gain from impoundment, though more as a chance side effect than as a primary purpose. Small fish ponds have been constructed in large numbers around the world, but rarely are large impoundments promoted for mainly this reason. The windfall catch typical of early years does not usually last; yields drop rapidly. Indiscriminately hospitable, reservoirs attract other species that the human population finds less welcome. The diseases promoted by large water projects vary by climate and place. They are especially numerous and troublesome in the tropics. Mosquitoes carrying malaria and yellow fever flourish in anthropogenic wetlands. So does the tsetse fly, which spreads sleeping sickness. Impoundment also creates a new hazard of flooding from dam failure, whether because of an earthquake, heavy rains, or poor construction. The major floods that can be clearly traced to human action are those resulting from this cause.

Impoundments increase the net supply of water available for use but not without some costs. Evaporation imposes a tax on the hoarding of water that rises to almost confiscatory levels in the arid subtropics. An extreme example is Lake Nasser, behind the Aswan High Dam, which loses a tenth of its volume per year to the atmosphere (White 1988). Such loss is a frequent result, but it is not an invariable one. Some reservoirs in the Caucasus region, for instance, have displaced vegetation so demanding of water that loss by evapotranspiration is now less than it was before (Badenkov et al. 1990).

Impoundment, whatever its motive, regulates surface flow to some extent; impoundment for flood control is a purposeful attempt to transform it. The same goal is also sometimes sought by the confinement of the river channel itself within levees: impounding it laterally rather than head on. This practice in particular and large-scale water management in general have their longest continuous history in China. As Needham (1971: 212) writes, "the Chinese are outstanding among the nations of the world in their control and use of water." With rainfall highly variable within and among years, with vast areas in the north requiring irrigation for agriculture, water channels have been profoundly transformed over several millennia to serve multiple purposes of supply, flood control, and navigation. A "Confucian" view prescribed the imprisonment of a river within high embankments to contain its overflow, thereby accelerating the current and scouring the channel. It won out in the formation of policy over an opposite perspective of Taoist provenance that held that nature should be allowed a freer rein lest sediment deposition in a confined course build up the riverbed and force the banks to be raised ever higher until catastrophic flooding occurred (Needham 1971: 222–37). The victory of the former approach was inscribed in the landscape in the form of riverbeds that did indeed gradually elevate themselves above the countryside. Today the Huang He stands an average of 3 to 5 m above its plain, and along one segment it rises 11 m above (Zuo and Zhang 1990: 475, 476). In what the historian William H. McNeill (1989: 1–2, 7) cites as an instance of "the conservation of catastrophe," frequent smaller floods have been contained at the price, inevitable sooner or later, of infrequent but disastrous levee breaches inundating huge areas. Deforestation and wetland drainage upstream may have added to the flood heights. In 1855, after a period of government neglect, the Huang He put an elbow through its much tattered straitjacket and shifted its channel to a new outlet to the sea hundreds of kilometers north of its old. In 1938, the Guomintang government deliberately opened the Huang He's banks as a defensive measure against the invading Japanese army, flooding more than 50,000 square kilometers and causing close to a million deaths (Zuo and Zhang 1990: 475).

Success in regulating flood flows is not always an unmixed blessing; periods of high and low water are not in themselves bad. It would be surprising indeed if floodplain dwellers had over the centuries reacted irrationally to each deluge by promptly resuming vulnerable land-use practices that had just been devastated, only to be surprised again the next flood season. Sometimes the adjustment to flooding has been undertaken for them; American policies of subsidizing flood insurance for high-risk areas had the inadvertent if predictable consequence of encouraging speculative expansion by shifting the costs of failure to taxpayers in general. In other cases, means devised over long periods to transform seasonal high water into a usable asset rather than a hazard run afoul of new policies for streamflow regulation. Agricultural systems known as *fadama* cultivation, basic to subsistence in much of tropical Africa, exploit the rainy-season inundation and dry-season exposure of lands along the major rivers. The smoothing out of flow by dams, constructed and operated largely to generate a steady current of hydro-electric power for urban industry, robs such forms of cultivation of their basis.

CONCLUSION

The annual human withdrawal of water from the hydrologic cycle has increased from about 100 cubic km three centuries ago to more than 3,600 cubic km at present (see Figure 5.6). While a large part of this growth reflects the increase in the world population in that period, much is due to increases in use of water per capita, which has risen fourfold as the range of uses has widened. Especially rapid increases in both population and its requirements have been phenomena of recent times. Net demand was only about 1,400 cubic km in 1950; the rise to the current totals, with the global spread of new forms of use, exceeded in a mere three and a half decades the growth registered in all the previous portion of the 300 years under study. The increase manifested itself earliest in the developed world but has rippled outward around the globe. It is not ubiquitous, though; water use in the United States dropped between 1980 and 1985 (Solley et al. 1988).

These figures for withdrawal do no more than hint at other important ways in which the world's water resources have been transformed, especially the pollution of surface and underground supplies and its consequences for health. Changes in streamflow quality have been no less marked than those in withdrawal. Human impacts on groundwater, not readily estimated at a global scale, are perhaps the most serious, for many are persistent and even permanent.

Schwarz and colleagues (1990: 254) class past human interventions in the flow and quality of water into four stages – not necessarily occurring in sequence or progressing invariably forward. They are:

1. the use of water "without regard to health or ecological effects, which were considered inconsequential";
2. "Health effects, property damage, and social impacts were clearly visible, but accepted as unavoidable or escaped by those who could through position or wealth";
3. the use of water management technology to abate the harmful effects, "but often with spotty results and sometimes unanticipated consequences";
4. "In this final stage, human knowledge is applied to anticipate effects and to avoid, or at least mitigate, possible deleterious effects before their occurrence."

140

Km³/yr (thousands)

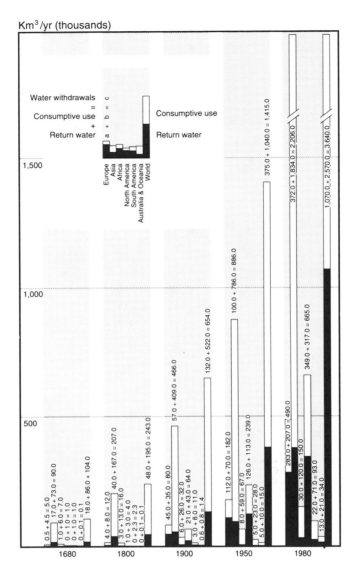

Figure 5.6 Estimated world total water withdrawal, consumptive use, and return flow for all purposes, 1680–1980, in cubic km per year. Source: L'vovich and White 1990.

Table 5.2 shows the rough history of human intervention in these terms in the major areas of the world.

To the extent that there is a world water crisis brought on by the acceleration in withdrawal and pollution, it is the sum of a set of basin and subbasin crises. Problems of shortage that are very severe in a region usually have, at most, minor

141

Table 5.2. *Stages of human intervention in the waters of the world*

Continent	Eighteenth century	Nineteenth century	Twentieth century
Africa	No impacts on regional scale	First stage – probably only minor local impacts	Second stage in some major basins
Asia	First and second stages – concentration of local population and irrigation	Second stage – large impacts from locally dense population and irrigation	Second stage continuing
Australia	No effects	First stage – probably only local impacts	Third and probably fourth stage, with planning for compatible development
Europe	Second stage – health effects are the major impacts	Mostly second stage, due to increasing population and the Industrial Revolution. Third-stage improvements near the end of the century	Third stage throughout the periods around the world wars; fourth stage strongly indicated
North America	First stage – limited local impacts	Second stage – population and industrial growth – little recovery in the last years	Third stage throughout; fourth stage initiated in many areas
South America	No significant impacts on a regional scale	Second stage in some areas, no impacts in others	Second stage in many large areas; some third stage near urban centers

Source: Schwarz et al. 1990.

physical consequences outside of it. A true water crisis exists around the Aral Sea, and appears to be in the making in much of northern China (Smil 1992), but not in some other basins, nor do these crises directly affect conditions elsewhere. Global changes in freshwater resources are not systemic in the manner of the greenhouse effect but patchwork and additive in the way that soil degradation is. Management is thus made easier and the number of parties to any conflict is restricted. Impacts are not only confined to basins but constrained even within them by the direction of flow; downstream uses can do little to harm those up-stream. Withdrawal of water for consumptive uses such as irrigation lessens the amount available farther down. Return water from irrigation or urban and indus-trial wastes may reduce the quality of flow and thus the amount available for certain uses. Changes in land use also may send blurred repercussions in flow levels downward through the basin system. Only transbasin water diversion spreads physical impacts more widely. Such diversion is not uncommon on a small scale, especially for municipal supply. While vast projects for interregional transfer across thousands of kilometers have been proposed or even begun in China, North America, and the former Soviet Union, the few seriously under-taken remain of marginal overall importance. A more recent reaction against such schemes, moreover, has led several to be halted or officially rejected, includ-ing ones to replenish the Aral Sea.

International rivers include both "successive" ones that flow from one country into another and "concurrent" ones that form a boundary for some distance. In the management of such rivers, routine forms of national sovereignty encounter problems and issues with which they have developed little competence to deal. Legal conflicts over international rivers did not begin with strictly environmental ones. Landlocked Country A, linked to the sea only by a river that runs through maritime Country B downstream, is likely to have spent centuries arguing – with meager success – that the "law of nations" gives it a right to free navigation of the channel. Such issues of access, not ones of environmental damage, planted the seeds of international water law. But today it is issues of pollution and lessened flow that most sharply point up the conflict between a nation's absolute national sovereignty over resources within its territory and an international version of the doctrine of riparian rights. In our hypothetical case, it is A's lavish consumptive withdrawal for irrigation and the salt and chemicals added like insult to injury to the unreliable, sediment-choked trickle that now crosses the border, that are likely today to roil relations between the two countries. Country B's diplomats and legal scholars now speak of duties and responsibilities between neighbors and resist the claim that a nation possesses absolute sovereignty of activity in its portion of a shared waterway. The flow of a river offers a tempting means for upstream generators of waste to extract benefits and export costs downstream. Such conditions provide opportunities and causes of friction between countries, though they may impose the need for cooperation. The latter may be the more likely case in rivers that form boundaries, where neither country is immune to

143

damage that it inflicts. The former may typify the case of successive rivers that flow across national boundaries; here the costs of damage and the benefits of abatement are not shared between states but simply transferred from one nation to another. Chronic water shortage and strained political relations in the Middle East merge to create the potential for severe conflict or unwonted cooperation over the management of international rivers and aquifers. The political map of the world is largely beyond redrafting in the short term, but these and other cross-national environmental issues promise to alter radically the meanings of boundaries in coming years.

Even in the face of rapid demographic and economic growth, the world's water resources, properly managed, may not prove inadequate to the demands made on it (L'vovich and White 1990). Scarcity is likely to stimulate an increased efficiency of use in all of the major classes of withdrawal. Much current water withdrawal and water pollution is directly or indirectly subsidized in a way that obscures or transfers real costs, discourages simple conservation, and distorts the tendency of water use to seek its appropriate level. Stricter management could – on some optimistic assumptions – produce a global trajectory of great improvement in water use. If the localized nature of water impacts detracts from the meaningfulness of global estimates of use, so does the failure of the estimates to identify uses that are large merely because water happens to be cheap or plentiful.

Global climatic change induced by greenhouse gas accumulation in the atmosphere could substantially alter the distribution of rainfall and evaporation across the earth's surface. There is yet no accurate forecasting of the results, should such change indeed occur. The climate models used to forecast a greenhouse warming are still of doubtful validity even globally, and much more so at lower scales. They are hardly more useful in predicting the water balance in store for a specific locality than a world map would be for finding a downtown street address. Climatic change does not proceed neatly poleward or equatorward in parallel zones; patchiness and variability are its typical patterns of manifestation. Water managers are well accustomed to dealing with excesses and shortfalls in supply, but climate change might go beyond the range within which they have so far been able to cope. Some regions now short of water would certainly gain in supply by any change, though not necessarily to the entire benefit of their ecosystems. A place just getting by on its current allotment, on the other hand, might see it further reduced and face a resource crisis.

6

Chemical Flows

In publishing *The Coal Question* in 1865 to urge his country to manage carefully an exhaustible resource so crucial to its future, the British economist William Stanley Jevons exemplified one form of concern over the relationship of nature and society. His was a conservationist emphasis focused on the efficient use of a key natural resource. A newer form of concern today accompanies and in some quarters overshadows the older. It is better classed as environmentalism than as conservationism. It is concerned with the effects of resource use not on the supply of the resource, but on the environment or surroundings of the use, with the earth's limited capacity to absorb the wastes of resource use as well as its limited capacity to provide the resources being used.

If Jevons's essay is one of the classics of conservationism, Rachel Carson's *Silent Spring* (1962) is perhaps the basic text of the later movement. Focusing on the environmental persistence and side effects of the synthetic pesticide DDT, the book remains, as David Lowenthal (1990: 129) writes, "irresistibly polemical. . . . Nothing did more to awaken the world to the consequences of meddling with nature." But many subsequent, well-publicized events have kept the world from falling back asleep: other postwar episodes of poisoning and contamination of air, water, and soil – by industrial mercury emissions at Minamata, Japan; by radiation at Chernobyl and elsewhere; by oil tanker accidents through the *Exxon Valdez* disaster of 1989; and by atmospheric smog locally, acid rain across regions, and carbon dioxide accumulation globally.

The exhaustibility of coal troubled Jevons and other conservationists. From an environmental point of view, it now seems more a blessing than a curse. The day when all of the coal will have been used up now looks more remote than it did in the nineteenth century, even though demands on it have proliferated. Yet physical (or economic) exhaustion, for all the problems that it would cause, would alleviate others. Not coal exhaustion, but coal emissions today occupy the center

145

of concern. Combustion not only consumes the fuel and hence depletes the resource, it emits chemical compounds to the atmosphere, causing or threatening consequences from global climatic change to transcontinental flows of acid rain to local smoke and smog pollution. If we had an unlimited supply of coal at hand, we would sooner or later have to find ways to stop using it. We will surely have to find ways not to use all that is available.

Coal provides but one convenient illustration of how human activities, as well as deliberately drawing together raw and finished materials as useful inputs, inadvertently release wastes. Some are generated in the extraction and production processes. Some are generated in the consumption or the discarding of the product, for elements are not destroyed when they are "consumed," merely scattered. Conservationism and environmentalism usually are complementary, not conflicting perspectives, focused on different aspects of the same process. Conservationists have long warned of the exhaustion of usable metal ores and the need to use such resources efficiently; environmentalists now stress the damage done by metals when released into the air, water, and soil. "The biosphere," Robert Ayres (1989: 23) observes, "is very nearly a perfect system for recycling materials." It makes the output of one process – the wastes released in the production or consumption of one good – the resource input for another. The goal for the social production system, in Ayres's words, should be "an industrial metabolism" – analogous to biological and biospheric metabolism – "that results in reduced extraction of virgin materials, reduced loss of waste materials, and increased recycling of useful ones" (Ayres 1989: 39). Save in traditional (and low-yield) agriculture, it is a goal that has not come close to being achieved. As one consequence, resources have been depleted. As a second, wastes have been emitted beyond what the environment can handle.

The masses of many elements set in motion through the biosphere by human activities have now begun to match or rival at the global scale the amounts circulated by natural processes. The human output of a number of heavy metals exceeds the natural manyfold. The human output of sulfur approximately equals the natural, and in the case of carbon, nitrogen, and phosphorus has become a significant fraction of it. The creation of some synthetic organic chemicals that do not exist in nature has initiated flows entirely novel in the biosphere. All of these impacts are relatively recent. Half of all human carbon releases to the atmosphere, the product of deforestation and fossil-fuel burning, have occurred since the end of World War I; half of all human releases of lead to the environment, since the end of World War II (Kates, Turner, and Clark 1990: 6–7).

By itself, an increased human input to any biospheric cycle or initiation of a new one is not undesirable. It does, though, mean change – the creation of an additional source of possible harm. To the familiar hazards of the natural environment are added the novel hazards of the transformed. The latter are more threatening in some ways because it is only with the former that humankind has had experience and has proven able, to live and to cope. Unwittingly, in the pursuit of immediate and narrow goals, we have created "a 'techno-sphere,' super-imposed upon the geo- and biospheres," that "temporarily draws an immense number of elements into its orbit, until they are sent back again, as a rule at many more localities than they came from" (Hägerstrand and Lohm 1990: 617).

Various activities, of course, have long transformed natural flows in small areas and minor ways. Local damage and even devastation have ensued. But to local changes, themselves become more frequent and severe, is now added a more widespread if less acute human alteration, global or continental in its sources, reach, and effects. As Clark and Mathews (1990: 140) note: "Once, locally severe disturbances in the chemical balance – around smelters, downstream of cities, in smoky industrial districts – were swamped by natural flows in the global aggregate. Now, the human input to the basic chemical flows of the biosphere is a significant fraction of, or even overshadows, the natural." As the dominant concerns over most chemical flows have shifted from the conservationist to the environmentalist, the environmentalist concerns, once local, have risen to the global scale. Our distant ancestors learned the dangers of many substances by trial and error; occupational medicine has cataloged chemical hazards of the workplace for centuries. More recently, we have seen the emergence of less concentrated but much wider increases in chemical levels, with effects less easy to specify but hardly less worrisome.

Century after century from classical times onward, people have discovered and rediscovered the hazards of acute and chronic local lead poisoning from water pipes, from storage and drinking vessels, from paint, and from manufacturing processes; since the 1920s, the addition of lead to gasoline has produced a global mobilization of the element, far lower in overall concentration but far vaster in scope. Copper smelters devastated nearby pasture and farmland in the nineteenth century and even earlier by releasing toxic metals and sulfur dioxide gas; sulfur dioxide emissions from fossil-fuel burning are now a major source of acid precipitation that crosses continents from source to destination. Methane (CH_4) first gained attention as the odorless, highly explosive gas "firedamp": its build-up in the air of coal mines touched off disastrous explosions, prompting early nineteenth-century scientists to devise reliable ways of detecting its presence. In a few centuries, the concentration of methane, a powerful "greenhouse gas," in the global atmosphere has doubled, owing to such varied human sources as rice paddies, landfills, and livestock. It threatens today to contribute substantially to global climatic change. Most change, as well as most concern, has ascended this historical trajectory from local to regional and/or global scales, even while remaining significant – though more easily controlled or mitigated – in their local manifestations.

THE MAJOR BIOGEOCHEMICAL FLOWS

The half-dozen key elements of life – hydrogen, oxygen, carbon, sulfur, nitrogen, and phosphorus – cycled in vast quantities through the biosphere long before human intervention or indeed human existence. We have had little significant impact on the first two elements (save on a rare form of oxygen in the atmosphere, the triatomic molecule ozone, to be discussed in the next chapter). The natural flows of the remaining four have been changed substantially. In each case, human action has increased the flow of the element, spreading it more widely, with important secondary consequences. Of these elements, the big four of biogeochemospheric change, carbon is the one that possesses a truly global reach. Its key flows operate at a world scale in a way not quite true of the rest. Phosphorus is the most limited in its mobility. It is largely confined to soil and water, without the atmospheric phases that are important in the flows of the others.

Human actions create no new quantities of these elements, any more than intervention in the hydrologic cycle involves the creation of water; rather, contents are transferred among accounts, drained from some reservoirs to irrigate others. The changes in these cycles have been essentially ones of degree and not of kind. Their effects are more predictable than those of more scarce or novel components of the biosphere. As we know from long experience what they already do, we can guess what greater quantities are likely to do, though new effects can always emerge if thresholds of concentration are passed.

CARBON IN THE GLOBAL SYSTEM

Life "is basically a matter of carbonaceous compounds in wet tissues" (Smil 1990: 423). There is no sharper distinction between the organic and the inorganic realm than carbon's role in each. It accounts for only 0.25% of the mass of the earth's crust, but close to 50% of the dry-weight mass of living matter. It also has an importance in the atmosphere quite out of proportion to the size of its presence. The climatic effects that may result from changes in two carbon-containing gases, CO_2 and methane, give the element its principal claim on modern environmentalists' attention.

Concerns over imbalances in the carbon cycle go back at least a couple of centuries – but the concerns have not remained the same. When the localized build-up of carbon dioxide gas prompted worry in the nineteenth century, it was not, as today, because of its expected climatic effects, but because of the asphyxiating powers with which the gas had been associated ever since its discovery by the chemists Joseph Priestley and Antoine-Laurent Lavoisier. Victorian scientists monitored the levels of "carbonic acid" in cities and buildings and calculated the relative contributions of breathing and coal combustion. Urban reformers promoted trees and parks as the "lungs of the city" to absorb the suffocating CO_2 given off by a crowded population. The quite different modern concerns about carbon flows date only about as far back as the 1950s as a sustained and widespread issue for research. Various individuals had anticipated many of these concerns earlier in the century, but with little or no sense of urgency; indeed, pre–

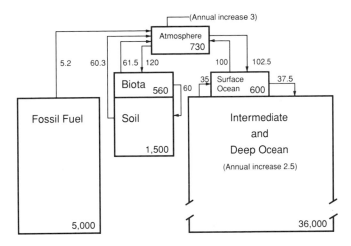

Figure 6.1 The major reservoirs of carbon for the globe, ca. 1980, in Pg (one Pg = 10^{15} grams). Source: Houghton and Skole 1990.

World War II predictions of a global warming from CO_2 increase typically treated it as an improvement (e.g., Callendar 1938: 236). Measurements begun in 1957 demonstrated a steady, year-by-year rise in the carbon dioxide content of the atmosphere. Theoretical advances likewise discredited older assumptions that the oceans would promptly soak up any excess released by human action, and climatologists began to warn of the effects on global temperature and precipitation of these accumulating gases.

Most of the carbon cycle on the land and in the atmosphere is a shuttling up and down a two-rung ladder of energy content, between the element's two most biologically important forms: (1) the reduced, high-energy state of organic matter ($C_6H_{12}O_6$), including components of fossil fuels, and (2) the oxidized, low-energy forms of inorganic carbon dioxide gas (CO_2) in the atmosphere and the bicarbonate ion (HCO_3^-) found in large quantities in the oceans. The change from the reduced to the oxidized form, either by respiration or by combustion, releases energy for use. The opposite reaction, through the process of photosynthesis, stores energy, that of the sun, which is captured and converted into a form in which it is available for use by organisms.

The biosphere's readily available stock of carbon sits in several distinct reservoirs highly unequal in size (see Figure 6.1). The most naturally secluded is that of the fossil fuels of coal, oil, and natural gas in the earth's crust. Marine carbon – apart from the carbon held in ocean-floor sediments – exists largely in the form of the bicarbonate ion; the oceanic flora holds very little. On the land surface, by contrast, carbon occurs largely in its organic forms. The carbon in vegetation, which accounts for practically all of the mass of the element in living matter, is about equal to that in the atmosphere. Forests hold three-quarters of it. The world's soils store about two to three times the biotic amount. The atmospheric reservoir consists largely of oxidized carbon in the form of CO_2, mixed with a few other substances, notably methane. By far the smallest of the global subtotals, it is roughly a third of the amount stored in terrestrial ecosystems, only a tenth of the fossil-fuel carbon, and only a fiftieth of the marine.

These reservoirs have fluctuated a good deal over the long term. Ice cores and other indicators show that during past glacial periods, atmospheric CO_2 fell as low as 180 parts per million, two-thirds of the preindustrial background level of 275 parts per million with which we began three centuries ago. The amounts stored in the terrestrial biota have undulated with the long-term ups and downs of the global vegetation cover. Twenty million years ago, a plant cover far more dense than today's held twice the carbon that the global flora held at the onset of human impact. Yet ordinary transactions kept the reservoirs in equilibrium in the geological short term, certainly on the time scale of human history. Carbon's biotic importance means a high natural turnover. Natural flows of carbon amount to an annual atmospheric exchange of 90–120 billion tons with terrestrial ecosystems, and about the same between the atmosphere and the ocean. Terrestrial photosynthesis withdraws about 100 billion tons and marine photosynthesis 50 billion, and there is an exchange of some 30 to 40 billion between the surface and the intermediate and deep layers of the ocean.

Humankind affects the carbon cycle through industry and through land-cover change. The rising demand for energy, now met principally from fossil fuels, has tapped the lithospheric carbon reservoir and funneled part of its contents – about 4% to date – into the other realms. The longer-running human assault on the forests and soils of the globe has diminished their net holdings of carbon and thereby enriched the other reservoirs.

Forests hold more carbon than does any form of vegetation with which human intervention is likely to replace them. The thinning of forest or its conversion to crop, pasture, scrub, or entirely cleared land releases carbon to the atmosphere, whereas reforestation absorbs it. The forests of the tropics (though not their soils) hold much more carbon per unit area than do those of higher latitudes. Thus the current pattern of biotic-cover change, with a net loss of wooded area in the tropics and a gain in temperate lands, adds up to a net release of carbon to the atmosphere. During the past 6,000 years, the total biotic storage of carbon has been reduced by 240 billion tons or by 30% as a result of human activity; over the past three centuries, it has fallen to 560 billion tons from 700 billion in the year 1700.

The earth's fossil-fuel carbon reservoir holds more than twice the carbon of the biota and soils combined. Current fossil-fuel releases are more than twice those produced by land-cover change. The biomass of the Brazilian Amazon, including ground litter and belowground material, contains about 60 billion tons of carbon (Salati et al. 1990: 484). Yet even this vast reservoir, if drained into the atmosphere by the complete and permanent clearance of the region's vege-

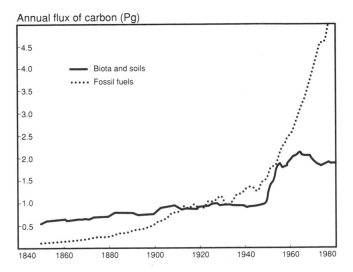

Annual flux of carbon (Pg)

— Biota and soils
····· Fossil fuels

Figure 6.2 The annual net releases of carbon from changes in land cover (solid line) and the annual emissions of carbon from combustion of fossil fuels (dotted line) between 1850 and 1980, in Pg (one Pg = 10^{15} grams). Source: Houghton and Skole 1990.

tation cover – an impossible prospect in the short or medium term – is little more than a decade's worth of fossil-fuel emissions at current rates, and less than that as the rates continue to climb. The world draws most of its energy from fossil fuels. The choices and tradeoffs for managing growth in world energy use and in atmospheric CO_2 content are narrowly circumscribed, not unlike those of a government seeking to regulate inflation and unemployment at the same time. Different policy options offer varying combinations of making do with less energy, increasing the role of noncarbon energy sources, trying through such means as massive reforestation to absorb the carbon back out of the atmosphere, or accepting the increase and its likely climatic consequences and seeking ways to adapt.

Industry and land-cover change have released about equal amounts of carbon over the long history of human impact, their shares changing over time. As late as the beginning of the twentieth century, land-cover change was the dominant human source of carbon emissions. Between about 1910 and 1950, the two processes maintained a rough parity (see Figure 6.2). Since 1950, fossil-fuel combustion has come to dominate, even though land-use emissions have remained high in absolute magnitude. In 1980, human action caused the release of a total of 7 billion tons of carbon to the atmosphere. More than 5 billion tons came from fossil fuels.

The global graph of modern fossil-fuel carbon emissions presents a visual impression of modern world economic history. It records a steady upward trend of

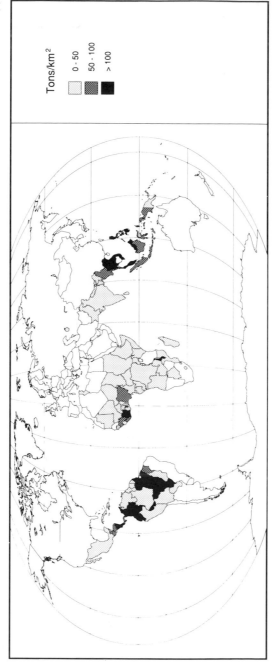

(a)

Tons/km²

☐ 0 - 50
▨ 50 - 100
■ > 100

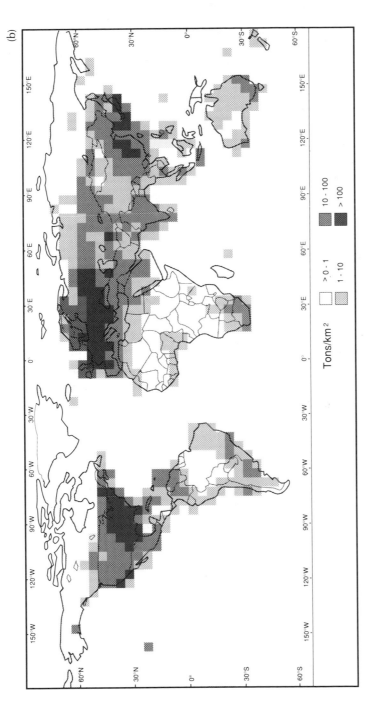

Figure 6.3 Releases of carbon from (a) land use and (b) fossil-fuel combustion, 1980, in tons per square km. Source: Houghton and Skole 1990.

development in the twentieth century followed by a postwar explosion, the curve serrated by interruptions of global depression, world war, and oil price shock. A series of maps of shifts in these physical emissions would make a historical atlas of world economic geography. The distribution of land-use and fossil-fuel releases for 1980 (see Figure 6.3) differentiates the developed industrial world from the developing nations, though much less sharply than for earlier periods. In 1925, the United States, Western Europe, Australia, and Japan together accounted for 88% of fossil-fuel emissions. With the dispersion of production they now produce less than half, but their releases have grown in absolute terms and their per capita contributions remain by far the world's highest.

So small is the atmospheric reservoir that the addition of a given mass that would be little noticed elsewhere can greatly expand or contract its bounds. Such an addition could hardly occur if carbon made its journey through the biosphere's compartments – from land to air to ocean – instantaneously, or nearly so. But the system contains a bottleneck, and it lies between the ocean surface and the deeper waters. In the long run, diffusion across this boundary, aided by marine photosynthesis, will absorb into the oceans the vast bulk of the carbon added to the atmosphere. Exchange does not occur between the entire volume of the oceans and the atmosphere, however; it is only possible where their surface layers meet. The marine waters, though fluid, are much less so, and mix much less rapidly, than the atmosphere. The absorption of carbon is timed by the interval required for the saturated ocean surface layers to be replaced by ones capable of further uptake. Only in two relatively high-latitude sinks, one in the North Atlantic and one near Antarctica, is express service available to transport surface water to the deep basins at the rapid rate of a few years. These avenues aside, the ocean is the Tahiti of chemical realms, offering its merely superficial explorers an idealized image of fluidity and free mixing quite alien to the rigid stratification and barriers to mobility that actually pervade it. The slowness of transfer prevents an excess of atmospheric carbon dioxide from being promptly removed. Of the 7 billion tons of carbon released in 1980, only about half was taken up by the ocean waters. The earth has been raining carbon into the atmosphere for centuries, and the drains are badly backed up. The level of CO_2 in the atmosphere, 275 parts per million three centuries ago, is now more than 350, and rose during the late 1980s at about 2.5 parts per million per year, though in the early 1990s the rise abruptly gave way, if only momentarily, to a still-not-understood trend of slower increase.

Though by far the commonest form of atmospheric carbon, CO_2 is not the only important one. Methane is produced by the bacteria that haunt the dark oxygen-deprived back alleys of the biosphere, from the intestines of ruminant livestock to decaying matter in landfills to wetlands of both natural and anthropogenic origin (notably rice paddies). Human action has expanded and enriched their habitats considerably in the past three centuries, leading to heightened methane emissions and to a doubling of atmospheric methane concentrations to the current level of about 1.6 parts per million. Peat bogs, of which large, nearly untouched areas exist in the high latitudes of Canada and of Russian Siberia, might also be sources of large emissions of methane. Direct exploitation of the peat as a fuel could release methane from these deposits into the atmosphere; so could decay hastened by global warming.

The human contribution to the annual global flux of carbon appears fairly modest when stated in proportional terms. It is still less than 10% of the annual natural flows involved in photosynthesis and respiration, or of the annual natural ocean–atmosphere exchange. Only the atmospheric carbon stock has been changed in size by more than a few percent. Yet with only a small drop in level in the other reservoirs drawn upon, the atmospheric pool has experienced severe flooding because of the inadequacy of its drainage channels.

SULFUR, NITROGEN, AND PHOSPHORUS: RESERVOIRS AND FLOWS

The flows of the other major biogeochemical elements – sulfur, nitrogen, and phosphorus – are shorter in range than carbon dioxide's is. Their flows largely involve reactive compounds, which are more rapidly broken down or washed out of the air and water than a stable gas such as CO_2 is removed. The principal forms of sulfur released stay in the air for only several days. This lifetime gives them, as carried by the prevailing winds, a spatial range on the order of a thousand kilometers, or roughly a subcontinental reach. Nitrogen compounds range from the very transient to the very long-lived. The most important – apart from nitrous oxide, a long-lived greenhouse gas – cluster near the short-lived end of the scale. Phosphorus compounds, though fairly stable, are essentially restricted to waterborne transportation, a medium of transport over the land surface that is physically confined and fairly rapid. As accomplices in some biospheric process of growing importance – most notably acid precipitation, the depletion or enhancement of soil fertility, and the eutrophication of fresh waters – these elements are appropriately examined as a group.

SULFUR. In classical times, sulfur was known to accumulate in its pure form around volcanoes and geysers. It burned with a smoky blue flame and a pungent odor that made it a prized fumigating agent; Homer praised its "pest-averting" qualities. The Middle Ages knew it as "brimstone," an essential ingredient, along with saltpeter (sodium nitrate) and charcoal, in the making of gunpowder, the staple of advanced warfare until the close of the Victorian era. By that time, it had diversified its activities into a range of compounds. Sulfuric acid in particular became a vital ingredient in many industrial processes. Sicily's exploitation of its near-monopoly of the world's sulfur supply through the early nineteenth century prompted an intensive and successful search for new deposits elsewhere. As a source of input into the environment, though, mined sulfur has long since yielded first place to inadvertent release through the extraction and burning of fossil fuels.

Sulfur is more unevenly distributed among its compartments than carbon. The lithosphere contains by far the greatest share, mainly as metal sulfides and sulfates. Most of the ocean reservoir, a distant second (about 5% of the size of the lithospheric reservoir), is inorganic sulfate. The soils and the biota hold far smaller stocks; the atmosphere holds the smallest, about 5 million tons, most of it in the highly stable, evenly dispersed gas carbonyl sulfide (COS). The atmosphere is important in the cycle, like the rivers and fresh waters, less as a major compartment than a channel through which the element is rapidly transported from one compartment to another.

Several natural processes turn sulfur loose into circulation: the weathering of rock, the decomposition of soil and organic matter, and the occasional volcanic eruption. These natural sources are no more spatially uniform than the human ones. The natural sulfur content of rivers varies widely across the globe, with high levels typical of such large islands as those of Japan, Indonesia, New Guinea, and New Zealand. Many human activities magnify these flows. Fossil-fuel combustion and metal smelting (many important ores are sulfides) emit sulfur compounds to the atmosphere. Crop and timber harvesting and forest fires (which also occur in nature) remove a significant quantity from the soil, to some degree countered by its addition through fertilizer. The element is mined directly for industrial uses, and drainage from coal and ore mines increases sulfur runoff into rivers. Fossil-fuel combustion is globally the dominant human source, and has been for more than a century.

The totals of sulfur added to the atmosphere by the major human activities have been calculated for the last century (see Figure 6.4). A steady increase in use over the entire period rose to a particular explosion in the decades following World War II. An approximate leveling off has taken place since the mid-1970s at a rate something in excess of a net natural output from weathering and biogenic emissions of close to 120 million tons per year (the natural flux is assumed, for the sake of convenience, to be constant). This stabilization clearly reflected the rises beginning in the early 1970s in world oil prices.

These trends are the global ones, but sulfur, as noted, tends to be a pollutant of less than global range (though it may affect the global climate by reflecting away solar radiation: see Chapter 7). The net emissions of carbon, wherever they occur, can ultimately affect all regions because of the worldwide mixing of greenhouse gases, but even the atmospheric component of sulfur output must be studied with a constant focus on the regional scale. Freshwater sulfur runoff is even more closely confined in its range, to the narrow channels of river basins. While many regions contribute in their different ways to the carbon budget, moreover, sulfur output is much more highly concentrated. A global map of modern densities of emission to the atmosphere, broken down only by continents (see Figure 6.5), shows a highly uneven pattern of plateaus and lowlands in

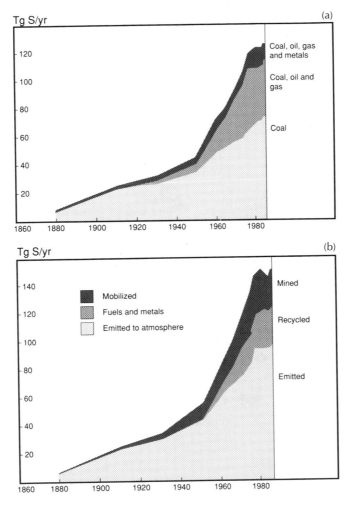

Figure 6.4 (a) Sulfur flow from fuels and smelting and (b) world industrial sulfur mobilization, in Tg (one Tg = 10^{12} grams) per year. Source: Husar and Husar 1990.

sulfur output and hence in impact. Emissions occur disproportionately in the industrial zones of the world. Europe, with its concentrated industry and high density of population, by far dominates. Elsewhere the average release per unit area is much lower; vast regions of low emissions offset industrialized cores of high. Within every continent there is a much finer topography of peaks, valleys, and ridges that a broad brush fails to capture. A map of North American atmospheric emissions during the late 1970s (see Figure 6.6) shows densities in the Ohio Valley, with its high level of fossil-fuel combustion, exceeding by many times the continental average (and about twice even the European), and it shows values over a wide expanse in the west, north, and south far below the average.

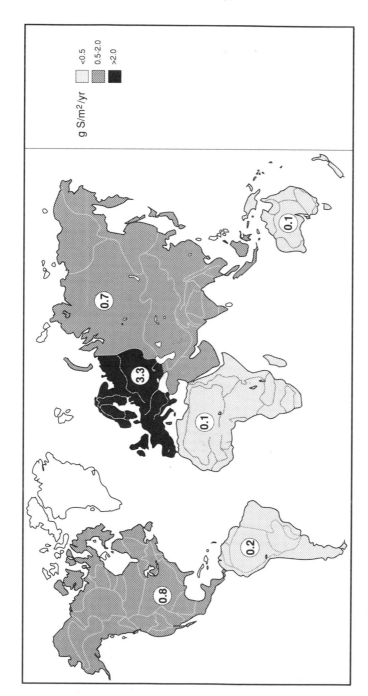

Figure 6.5 Sulfur emission density of the continents, in grams per square m per year. Source: Husar and Husar 1990.

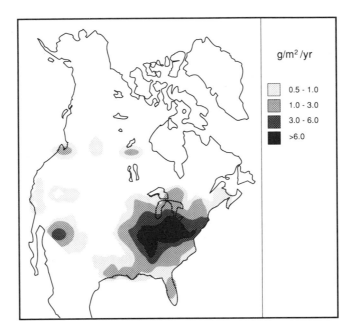

Figure 6.6 Sulfur emission density for North America, 1977–78, in grams per square m per year. Source: Husar and Husar 1990.

Even across a metropolitan area the patterns of sulfur density show a similar unevenness. The temporal trends across the globe roughly mimic those of fossil-fuel emissions of carbon, with a modern dispersion of output as industry grows in the developing world.

NITROGEN. This is a much more vital element for the chemistry of life than its subdued presence in organic matter – less than 1% of dry biomass in plants by weight, a couple of percent in animals – would suggest. Carbon abounds in living matter but comprises a tiny fraction of the atmosphere, less than 0.04% even with the human contribution. Nitrogen in its gaseous form (N_2) dominates the air, but no biospheric element at once so abundant and so essential plays harder to get in the organic realm. Nitrogen is difficult for practically all living creatures, humankind included, to obtain in a biologically usable form – the "fixated" forms of nitrates and ammonia. We stand immersed in the overwhelming abundance of nitrogen gas like sailors thirsting on a ship in the middle of the ocean. Seawater is unusable because it is mixed with other components; N_2 is unusable because it is not.

Igneous rocks hold, by varying estimates, between 14 and 57 million billion tons of the element; most of it is well beyond reach. The atmosphere is the largest of the nitrogen pools directly interacting with the biosphere, containing

159

almost 4 million billion tons. All but a couple of billion is in the form of N_2 gas. The oceans hold 23,000 billion tons, the soils contain somewhere on the order of a few hundred billion, and terrestrial and marine biomass holds perhaps 10 million.

Some of the key strategies of life are means for coping with one failure of evolution: to provide more than a relative handful of plants with the ability to host bacteria with nitrogen-fixing powers. Only the set of crops known as legumes are exceptions. The major pathway of reactions in the biospheric nitrogen cycle runs from atmospheric N_2, converted through fixation, usually by bacteria, to biologically usable forms of nitrates/ammonia, followed by denitrification, the reduction of nitrates to nitrogen oxides, and then back to gaseous N_2. The considerable uncertainty in the data, especially over rates of bacterial fixation, makes global estimates of natural flows and human additions based on knowledge of those processes rather shaky. While not so greatly increased as sulfur in terms of percentages, the human inputs of nitrogen appear to have risen by two orders of magnitude to become significant fractions of the natural flows.

Human input comes from a triple set of sources. The first is the biological, represented mainly by sewage wastes and by biomass burning. The second is fossil-fuel combustion, both by industry and by dispersed consumption (by automobiles, for example), releasing nitrogen oxides that contribute to smog and acid rain. The third set of human impacts comes from agriculture. It includes both the direct fixation of nitrogen into fertilizers for crop production, and the indirect promotion of the natural process – through cultivation of legumes and application of wastes/natural fertilizers, and through the removal of nitrogen compounds from the soil by harvesting. The world's annual output of synthetic fertilizer amounts to 75 million tons of nitrogen annually, as against a net removal of 45 million from the soil through crops. But the appearance of a healthy surplus in this budget is deceptive, for besides harvesting, such processes as denitrification, runoff, leaching, and volatilization continually subtract from the soil reservoir. Fossil-fuel combustion releases close to 30 million tons, and biomass burning some 5 million.

Nitrogen releases occur in a range of different forms representing different kinds and scales of problems. At one end is the fairly stable gas nitrous oxide (N_2O), released through denitrification in fertilized soils and also to some extent from combustion, which can have global consequences. A "greenhouse gas," it also contributes to stratospheric ozone-layer damage. Other atmospheric releases are in the form of nitric oxide (NO) and nitrogen dioxide (NO_2), collectively referred to as NO_x. These much shorter-lived compounds, stemming largely from fossil-fuel burning, have their principal impact at the regional and local scales – in creating acid precipitation and in catalyzing the formation of ozone smog in urban areas. During the present century, worldwide emissions of NO_x have risen at an exponential rate, interrupted by global malaise and warfare from 1930 to

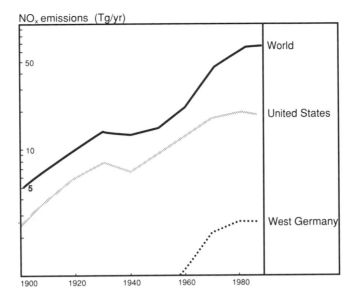

Figure 6.7 Historical rates of NO$_x$ emissions, in Tg (one Tg = 10^{12} grams) per year. Source: Smil 1990.

1950. Only in very recent years have they shown signs of leveling off, partly as a result of controls in the developed world on their largest source, automobile emissions. The world curve is approximately duplicated in lower case by one estimated for the United States (see Figure 6.7). Finally, waterborne nitrogen from fertilizers and organic wastes largely takes the form of nitrates (NO$_3^-$).

PHOSPHORUS. Because phosphorus is far less mobile than are carbon, sulfur, and nitrogen, its global cycle is simpler. It is essentially confined to biota, rock, and soil; in its human release, to fertilizers and organic wastes, rather than fossil-fuel and biomass combustion; and in its transportation, to water as a medium rather than having atmospheric pathways as well. The problem so typical of the others, of massive human input overloading a small atmospheric reservoir, is not encountered in this cycle. Unlike nitrogen, phosphorus is not even a component of protein. Even so, it is biologically indispensable in several ways. At the cellular level, it is an element of ADP and ATP, which catalyze the vital processes of protein and complex-sugar synthesis. It is also a major structural element of vertebrate skeletons. More than three kilograms of the average human body is phosphorus.

The oceans contain about 100 billion tons, with roughly 15 million more transported there in a one-way flow from the lands each year through losses from soil erosion. The sum of global reserves, or the deposits available for profitable

161

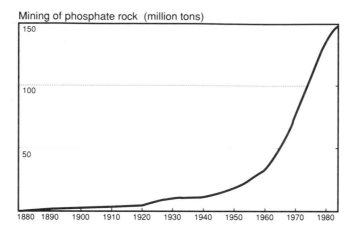

Figure 6.8   Global mining of phosphate rock. Source: Smil 1990.

exploitation under current conditions of economy and technology, ranges according to different estimates from 20 to 70 billion tons; resources, or the entire supply, from 110 to 300 billion tons. Far smaller are the reservoirs in plant (about 1–3 billion tons) and especially animal mass (25 million tons, one-tenth of it in the human population). Currently the main sources of phosphorus mined for fertilizer are marine sedimentary carbonate ores and apatites. The extraction of phosphate rock has undergone an exponential increase (see Figure 6.8). Organic wastes, though, remain the main direct source of phosphorus emissions in densely populated watersheds.

CONNECTIONS: DEPLETED SOILS, DEGRADED STREAMS

The human input into the flows of nitrogen and phosphorus, of long standing, is also now of unprecedented magnitude. It involves both deliberate and incidental releases. Of the former, Smil (1990: 434) remarks that "modern agriculture is . . . inextricably dependent on a steady flux of synthetic fertilizers," and that such "massive intervention" in the nitrogen and phosphorus cycles "through fertilizing has no practical alternatives in a world of growing populations and expanding meat production."

By the late seventeenth century, millennia of folk experience offered sufficient testimony that one could not grow crops indefinitely on the same soil without a rapid progression from diminishing yields to near-complete sterility. Trial, error, and chance also identified a handful of crop types that seemed to revitalize the soil, and suggested moreover that the impoverishment produced by growing the others could usually be reversed by the addition of certain substances. The nature of the problem was not clear. It might have been one of pollution or poisoning by undesirable crop additions that only with the lapse of time were removed by physical, chemical, or biological processes. One theory still credible in early nineteenth-century Europe advanced this view of the matter, and saw irrigation as washing out these toxins left by previous crops faster than they would be removed naturally, and fertilizers as neutralizing them. Understanding of manures, fallowing, and crop rotation in other cultures rested on folk rationales about "letting the earth rest" after the labor of production or building up its strength; innovations gained currency on a local basis of trial and error. What is known as the agricultural revolution in Western Europe – a mix of innovations that made possible a leap in production – preceded a scientific understanding of its workings. Key advances affecting soil fertility involved the planting of the legume clover, with its seemingly magical power to restore productivity, in fallow fields and the systematic collection and use of manure for fertilizer.

With the advent in the early and mid-nineteenth century of chemically informed agricultural science, a more general understanding of the process of growth emerged. Planting legumes as a grassroots approach to alleviating soil poverty was superseded by the direct and large-scale infusion of outside aid. Developments in soil chemistry began to specify the substances needed and the ones unnecessary for successful cultivation. The first to be struck off the list was carbon. The "humus theory," dominant in Western Europe until about 1840, had identified the organic carbon of plant debris in the soil as the main essential nutrient. The work of the eminent German chemist Baron Justus von Liebig, along with such other researchers as J.-B. Boussingault in France and J. B. Lawes and J. H. Gilbert in England, thoroughly discredited it. With the carbon dioxide in the atmosphere recognized as the source of plant carbon, humus was relegated to a useful but decidedly secondary role: as provider of high levels of CO_2 to the roots of the plant, as host to useful soil bacteria, and as a maintainer of soil structure. But the change in thought was revolutionary in its implications; the mass of living matter was capable of almost unlimited increase. The humus theory had depicted a zero-sum game in which the world's stock of humus was fixed though recyclable. The newer perspective dispelled this imagined limit to growth. It flung open the door to as boundless an expansion in food production and in the population dependent upon it as artificial nutrients for its subsistence could be mobilized.

But along with this revolution in thought came a principle restoring a sense of proportion. Not only were several soil nutrients necessary – nitrogen, phosphorus, potassium, and other elements in chemically suitable forms, plus some metals in trace amounts – but no plenty of one sufficed to offset a deficit in another. If a soil held too little fixed nitrogen to sustain a certain level of plant growth, adding all the phosphorus and potassium in the world would improve matters not at all. This insight, or what came to be known as "Liebig's law" or "the law of the minimum," has since been recognized as a structural principle undergirding a much wider set of processes in the biosphere. Liebig himself invoked the image, perhaps not yet a cliché at that time, of the strength of the chain being defined by its weakest link to suggest that the productivity of a cultivated field was defined by its content of the nutrient least plentiful relative to plant demand. In other contexts, as we shall see in regard to eutrophication, it has appeared in a new light, not as a prison cell unfortunately confining production but as a straitjacket preventing it from doing still more damage than it actually does. And optimists have occasionally suggested that rising levels of atmospheric CO_2 carry within them the seeds of their own solution; that the world's vegetation cover could act as a rough global thermostat or safety valve. An increase in a trace gas essential to plant growth, perhaps accompanied by the higher temperatures of a CO_2-induced warming, might stimulate such an exuberant boom in plant growth as would mop up all or much of the surplus and in any case be a benefit in its own right. Yet it is phosphorus, rather than atmospheric carbon, fixed nitrogen, or any other major nutrient, that seems usually to be the key element limiting plant growth. By Liebig's rule, no amount of addition of an element already present in relative excess can raise the level of production. It may be that the increased loading of the environment with phosphorus and nitrogen will make possible just such an acceleration in growth, but it is certainly the case that to date the global vegetation cover has not nearly succeeded in absorbing out of the atmosphere the rise in CO_2 that has occurred since preindustrial times.

With the basic requirements established, the search for supplies began. Phosphorus was relatively easy to find in quantity; usable nitrogen compounds, less so. Guano, accumulated bird excrement, was found in abundance on several arid Peruvian islands along South America's Pacific coastline. Rich in ammonia, it impressively raised crop yields (a purpose for which the Incas had put it to use much earlier) and became a lucrative commodity on the world market. Early to mid-nineteenth-century exploration then revealed vast deposits of nitrates in the nearby Atacama Desert, stretching along the same coastline to the south. A rainless region so hostile and seemingly worthless that neighboring nations had not bothered to clarify their boundaries or put themselves to the expense of establishing an effective presence – the Sahara of the Western Hemisphere – suddenly became a lucrative resource frontier and a bone of violent contention. Chile finally won full control over the Atacama by defeating Bolivia and Peru in the "Nitrate War" of 1879–84. In a modest fashion it became the OPEC of its time, reaping wealth from its control of a globally essential resource. Just as closely as the OPEC nations did, it tied its fortunes to those, good or ill, of its product.

Other sources of usable nitrogen existed closer at hand in most countries. In the Victorian-era problems of urban sewage pollution and rural soil impoverishment, there existed an apparently providential match between a supply and a demand, a way to solve one problem of resource conservation and another of environmental quality. A number of European cities – Berlin, Paris, Edinburgh, and others – took the hint and established municipal sewage farms irrigated and fertilized by their wastes. Such agricultural application had for many centuries been routine in the densely settled lands of East Asia. Around Tokyo, the value of the wastes to suburban farmers made their removal "a seller's market" even through the early twentieth century (Seidensticker 1983: 83). Yet hampering the adoption of this approach in Europe and North America was the dominant nineteenth-century filth theory of disease, which identified noxious gases as the sources of epidemics; the advent of germ theories carried with it a new fear, that applying sewage to farmland might transmit disease through the food supply. Nor were such farms popular neighbors; the possible overloading of their absorptive capacities raised the horrific prospect of "sewage swamps" ravaging health for miles around. By and large the domestic supply of soil nutrients was largely neglected, and imported supplies became a mainstay for many countries. Yet at the end of the nineteenth century, mined fertilizers still did little to offset the losses from the soil, both in the global totals and in most localities. The annual world use of nitrogen fertilizer did not exceed 60,000 tons; the extraction of phosphorus rock, a couple of million (Smil 1990).

The physicist Sir William Crookes delivered the most influential turn-of-the-century warning about the cumulative effects of global soil impoverishment in his 1898 presidential address to the British Association for the Advancement of Science. He spoke in the conservationist spirit of Jevons posing *The Coal Question* three decades earlier, and he cited his predecessor only to declare his own concern – the exhaustibility of the mineral nitrates on which world food production must come to rest, and the consequent need to develop some new source of supply – "a matter of far greater importance." Crookes pointed to a significant problem on the horizon. He also pointed with considerable prescience to the likely solution: "the fixation of atmospheric nitrogen" by more energy-efficient processes than were yet available (Crookes 1898: 443). In 1913, the German chemist Fritz Haber developed just such a process for making ammonia under high pressure from atmospheric nitrogen. Delayed by World War I, production of fertilizer by the Haber process spread rapidly thereafter, and even more rapidly after World War II (see Figure 6.9). Its incidental consequences included the collapse of the Chilean nitrate economy.

The history of the human food supply has thus been that of the progressive abandonment of a hunter-gatherer policy of laissez-faire in the biosphere's economy for a Keynesian one of deliberately stimulated expansion in the gross natural product. As a result, we find ourselves confronted with the familiar problems of ill-controlled growth: a range of unsightly and undesirable side effects. As with coal combustion, conservationist fears have given way to environmentalist ones. Fertilizers applied to the land release nitrous oxide – a greenhouse gas and a stratospheric ozone depleter – in substantial quantity. And lakes, rivers, and

Synthesis of fertilizer N (million tons)

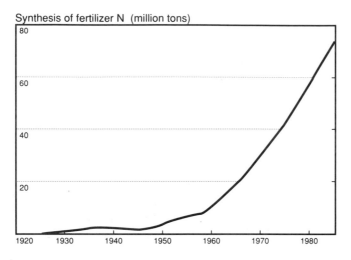

Figure 6.9 Global synthesis of nitrogenous fertilizer, 1920–85. Source: Smil 1990.

groundwater have been affected just as the economies of Chile and Peru were disrupted and debauched in their boom periods by the rapid and unbalanced growth stimulated by the global influx of fertilizer money.

Eutrophication of water bodies is not an "unnatural" process. Its root meaning signifies feeding or nutrition or enrichment, which hardly even sounds like a form of damage. But damage does occur when the enrichment of the water with organic compounds promotes explosive biotic growth that depletes dissolved oxygen and releases poisonous hydrogen sulfide. Both processes degrade the conditions of life for the valuable species. Lakes and reservoirs fill naturally with sediment, but land-use changes can speed the process; in eutrophication, too, the problem is not the occurrence of a process that will occur anyway, but its acceleration by human action. Degrees and rates of impact, under similar levels of waste input, depend greatly on the size and character of the basin affected. Rivers and streams run less risk than do ponds, lakes, and estuaries, because of the speed with which the wastes are washed out.

Phosphorus is usually the controlling element in eutrophication, the one whose absence in the necessary share according to Liebig's law prevents the process from going on, even though the characteristic recipe for algal growth stipulates only the rather lopsided ratio of 106 parts of carbon to 16 of nitrogen and 1 of phosphorus (Smil 1990: 432). Fortunately, phosphorus is also the most easily controlled of these elements. In populous basins, it enters largely as urban waste. In the 1960s and 1970s, cities accounted for more than two-thirds of the input to the Potomac, the Hudson, Lake Erie, and the Chesapeake. For a couple of decades after World War II, technological innovation added to the burden of population, as new phosphate-rich detergents supplemented human wastes in the

166

developed world. They contributed perhaps a third of phosphorus emissions in American cities, and they magnified nutrient loadings in the Thames and elsewhere, until growing concern over pollution led to restrictions or bans on their use. Phosphorus levels are further controlled through sewage treatment. Aquatic nitrogen pollution, "one of the greatest environmental concerns of the late 1960s and early 1970s," is less of a problem than was once thought. Phosphorus availability, as mentioned, is the principal control of eutrophication. Monitoring of nitrate levels in American streams, moreover, has shown "no dramatic increases" since World War II, despite waste emissions from growing urban populations and increased fertilizer use (Smil 1990: 428).

CONNECTIONS: ACIDIFICATION AND FOREST DECLINE

Not the atmospheric impacts of combustion but the mining of sulfur-rich coal brought about the initial recognition of the element's knack for acidifying the environment. The basic processes that produce what we now call acid rain were described by R. A. Smith in the mid-nineteenth century from a close observation of the effects of coal smoke on the London atmosphere. The inhabitants of some regions had learned much earlier that the water draining from coal or sulfur-ore mines and mine debris was often "acidulated" to a dangerous degree. It killed fish downstream and made the water unusable for industrial purposes, irrigation, or drinking. The problem still afflicts districts where high-sulfur coal and ores are extracted.

When they entered the air, freed from the bonds that constrain the flows of surface water, such pollutants began to pose new sets of problems. Sulfuric acid, formed in the atmosphere by sulfur dioxide (SO_2) emitted from coal, was joined by the acids formed from the emission of some nitrogen compounds. As we have seen, SO_2 is a major (though not a global) export of the world's industrial core regions, with emissions much higher than the world averages. Combustion releases of NO_x and ammonia from fossil fuels, though relatively small, are of growing importance in some places, mainly in the Northern Hemisphere temperate latitudes. They have, like SO_2, a spatial range of a few hundred kilometers downwind of their source. The spatial scale of the processes is of central importance; through it, acid substances and impacts are transferred long distances from the place of origin to the place of impact. New England and eastern Canada receive acid deposition from the burning of coal in the Midwest; Scandinavia, from Western Europe.

Much of the impact depends on the characteristics of the downwind receiving site. The waters in limestone regions are well buffered and can neutralize considerable amounts of deposited acid; those on top of igneous bedrock are more sensitive. Acid deposition harms biota, especially fish and vegetation, not so much directly – though such is the case with some species – as through the chemical changes it induces, especially the mobilization in the soil and water of such toxic metals as magnesium and aluminum. Forests in Europe and North America have been buffeted by multiple blows from several directions, probably including ones of both natural and human origin. What in Europe is called *Waldsterben* is known in English as "forest death" or "forest decline." This phenomenon does not appear to be the result of acid deposition only or perhaps even primarily; it is thought to reflect emissions of other atmospheric pollutants, probably including ozone, heavy metals, and fertilizing compounds. Half of the forest area in West Germany was reportedly affected by the mid-1980s, and "*Waldsterben* could be as great a threat to the continued existence of the forests of the temperate, developed world as land clearing and fuelwood extraction are to the forests of the tropical developing world" (Williams 1990a: 197). At the same time, accelerated tree growth reflecting nutrient enrichment has been reported from some areas. In Sweden,

> never in history has there been such a large annual growth of forest as at present. This is due in part to the higher density of spruce . . . but the increased flow of nitrogen – quite apart from its role in the acidification process – probably also acts as a fertilizer. Some trees may indeed be forced to grow to death because other necessary nutrients are no longer available to match the intake of nitrogen. (Hägerstrand and Lohm 1990: 620)

TRACE POLLUTANTS

The term "trace pollutants" has several meanings. Sometimes it refers to those substances that can be shown to be present in a sample but at levels too small to specify. Here, more broadly, it designates undesired substances that are present at relatively small concentrations in the chemical environment, at most a few parts per million (Brown et al. 1990: 437). Trace pollutants of importance in the global environment are mainly metals and radionuclides, which have natural sources as well as human ones, and organic chemicals, which often do not. Like the major biospheric elements, these trace substances act over a range of space and time scales, depending on the chemical forms in which they occur.

The principal natural biogeochemical flows can boast of annual volumes on the order of a hundred billion tons (carbon) and hundreds of millions (nitrogen). The annual natural releases into the environment of 19,000 tons of lead and 160 tons of mercury are minute by comparison, even when vastly increased by human action to, for example, some half a million tons of lead and two thousand of mercury. A synthetic organic chemical like carbon tetrachloride has no natural flows to speak of, only its annual industrial production of 830,000 tons (Brown et al. 1990: 439, 447). Yet trace pollutants, like small quantities of poisons in the body, can do serious environmental damage even in small amounts.

168

METALS

The rapid modern rise in global industrial capacity has meant an explosion in both the numbers and the quantities of metals extracted from the earth and put to use. The relationship of humankind to metals is one of the enduring interests of conservationism; fears of resource scarcity lead to projections of shortage and to efforts to restrict use, to unearth new supplies, or to develop substitutes. The world's high-grade copper ores, for example, have been substantially depleted, and extraction now focuses on the common but much lower-grade ores that remain. But just as concern over biodiversity loss had to await the development of a biology and a natural history that accepted the possibility of extinctions, so concern over mineral resource depletion required a foundation in a metallurgy that was slow to develop. Even 300 years ago, some reason still existed for the belief that metal ore deposits were renewable resources akin to forests or game. The "growth" of ores into progressively more valuable metals was thought to be governed by the intensity of the sun, and the occurrence of gold thus restricted to tropical latitudes. Alchemical experimenters in their transmutation only sought ways to accelerate changes believed to be routine in nature.

Some of the environmental impacts of metal use accompany the extraction process. Metal mining scars the landscape and swells the flow of sediment – most severely, as we have seen, in the use of hydraulic techniques to loosen gold- and tin-laden gravel. It often consumes timber for construction and for fuel to smelt ores. A severe and growing environmental problem among the many that are transforming Brazil's Amazonia is the use of mercury by thousands of small operators as an agent to precipitate gold from riverbank gravels; several hundred tons of mercury are believed to be released annually. In addition to posing immediate health risks for the miners themselves, the highly toxic metal accumulates in the river's sediments and its fish, the latter a prime source of food for the region's inhabitants (Salati et al. 1990: 487).

Metals, of course, occur naturally throughout the biosphere. They are not altogether alien or inimical to living creatures. Some are so essential to life in trace quantities that their absence is manifested in illness. The "coast disease" that stunted sheep and cattle in South Australian grasslands reflected a paucity of copper and cobalt in the soil (Williams 1974: 275–79, 321–23). Endemic goiter long plagued inland populations that did not obtain enough iodine in their diets. But excessive rather than deficient doses have posed more of a problem ever since the Iron and Bronze Ages. Some of the earliest concerns of occupational medicine were with the symptoms characteristic of metalworkers of various kinds. Those who applied mercury to headwear, to remove stray hairs and discourage bacterial decay, developed the trembling and other manifestations of brain damage that won them the name "mad hatters." The same symptoms appeared among mirror makers when mercury was used as a surfacing agent. Past

169

and present concern over metal pollution has occasionally exceeded real impact. Early nineteenth-century American farmers feared that the new cast-iron plow would "poison the soil" (Brown 1948: 3).

Blasted landscapes have long testified at the local scale to the concentrated environmental impacts of releases from metal industries – copper smelters in particular. Poisonous metal and sulfur emissions from the processing of sulfide ores have killed off the vegetation, creating, to borrow a phrase of George Perkins Marsh's from a different context, "a desolation almost as complete as that of the moon" (Marsh [1864] 1965: 42). During the eighteenth century when Sweden's Falu mine was the world's largest producer of copper, "the famed botanist Linnaeus noted damage to the vegetation within reach of the smoke" (Hägerstrand and Lohm 1990: 618). Farmers harmed by the emissions have actively protested in many parts of the world. But until recent times, these hot spots of chemical pollution largely escaped stringent regulation just as did the physical devastation of the soil and the stream channels by mining excavation and debris. So opulent have been the rewards offered by rich ore fields that they have usually outcompeted the other possible uses of the land, even when they foreclose on possible alternative uses for the future.

Such hot spots of concentrated damage, then, have long existed. They have grown, however, in number and expanse, and more diffuse global levels of metal concentration have also risen. Extraction of many important metals has mounted exponentially since 1700 (see Figure 6.10). Human releases in many cases far outstrip natural flows; "the contribution from natural sources . . . most likely represents only a small fraction of the total anthropogenic loading." While trace releases from fossil-fuel combustion contribute significantly to total mobilization of a few metals, the direct activities of extraction, processing, and industrial and consumer use are much more important for the rest. Concentrated industrial point sources have long been the main target of regulation. Only recently has dissipation through consumptive uses begun to attract scientific attention as another major route of entry into the environment. A pioneering study of the Hudson-Raritan Basin (including the New York City metropolitan area) in the northeastern United States concludes (Tarr and Ayres 1990: 635, 638): "Success in controlling pollution from processes of production has not been matched by control of pollution from now widely dispersed processes of consumption." The latter "have now become the principal source of heavy-metals emissions." For a number of metals of concern – lead, cadmium, copper, mercury, arsenic, silver, chromium, and zinc – "consumption-related emissions in the Basin have dominated production-related emissions by a large factor" in recent decades (see Table 6.1). This pattern seems to be characteristic of the developed world generally and a higher share of production sources to be typical of developing countries.

Human activities release metals variously into the atmosphere, the water, and the soil, and exchanges occur among some of these compartments. Most metals released first to the atmosphere, especially as particulates, stay in it for only a

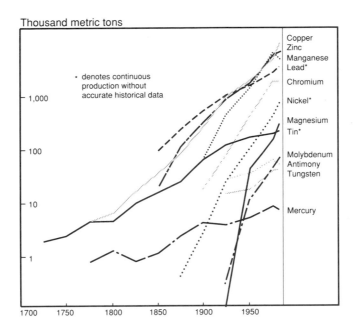

Figure 6.10 Annual worldwide production of selected metals, 1700–1983. Source: Brown, Kasperson, and Raymond 1990.

short time and do not travel far – although long-range transport also does occur, especially of releases in gaseous form. The typical short time scale of transport also means that changes in releases are reflected quite rapidly in changes in atmospheric and freshwater concentration. Contamination of soil, sediment (via water), the oceans, and the food chain, on the other hand, lasts longer, and curbs on emissions erase it far more slowly.

Lead stands out among the metals of environmental importance for two reasons. Its harmfulness to human health is well established (a status it shares among metals with mercury and cadmium), and no other heavy metal has been released in equal quantity into the environment by human action. Large-scale emissions of lead began in 1922. An American scientist, by adding the compound tetraethyl lead to gasoline, solved the problem of engine knock that had plagued automobiles since their invention. Its use as an additive, making possible a much improved efficiency of combustion and less wear on engines, was a clear advance from a conservationist point of view. Even at that time some environmentalist concerns were expressed over the heightened exposure of chemical workers and garage employees, and also of the public in general, to releases of lead and of the poisonous gas in which it was being used. Three factory accidents involving tetraethyl lead occurred in the fall of 1924, the worst of which, at the Bayview, N.J., plant of the Standard Oil Company, killed five workers and

Table 6.1. Emissions of copper, mercury, and lead in the Hudson-Raritan Basin (in tons)

(a) Average Annual Copper Emissions

| Year | Metallurgical Operations | | Fossil Fuel Combustion | Consumptive Uses | Total Emissions | |
	low	high			low	high
1980	0.9	1.8	10.1	1,109	1,120.0	1,120.8
1970	3.3	12.5	16.4	1,222	1,241.7	1,250.9
1960	7.7	28.0	16.4	973	997.1	1,017.4
1950	10.3	52.7	30.7	1,145	1,186.0	1,228.4
1940	9.8	43.8	66.0	1,309	1,384.9	1,418.9
1930	9.7	40.3	96.3	550	656.0	686.7
1920	9.9	37.8	326.8	541	877.8	905.7
1900	6.6	18.4	408.0	309	723.6	735.4
1880	2.3	3.7	125.1	109	236.4	237.8

(b) Average Annual Mercury Emission

Year	Metallurgical Operations		Fossil Fuel Combustion	Consumptive Uses	Total Emissions	
	low	high			low	high
1980	0.00	0.00	0.03	64.1	64.2	64.2
1970	0.01	0.02	0.10	106.3	106.4	106.4
1960	0.03	0.04	0.16	56.6	56.8	56.8
1950	0.04	0.06	0.32	66.4	66.7	66.8
1940	0.04	0.05	0.71	66.0	66.7	66.8
1930	0.11	0.16	1.04	57.8	58.9	58.9
1920	0.16	0.31	3.54	48.9	52.6	52.7
1900	0.05	0.08	4.21	27.7	31.9	31.9
1880	0.01	0.01	1.28	27.9	29.2	29.2

(c) Average Annual Lead Emission

Year	Metallurgical Operations		Fossil Fuel Combustion	Consumptive Uses	Total Emissions	
	low	high			low	high
1980	43	51	5,312	95	5,451	5,458
1970	112	261	9,684	199	9,994	10,143
1960	295	688	7,203	126	7,625	8,017
1950	564	2,173	4,884	81	5,529	7,138
1940	957	3,163	2,504	18	3,480	5,685
1930	864	2,306	266	13	1,144	2,586
1920	1,254	2,902	74	14	1,342	2,991
1900	1,470	1,708	92	0	1,562	1,800
1880	16	23	29	0	45	53

Source: Tarr and Ayres 1990.

injured several dozen. The resulting outcry led to an official inquiry by the U.S. surgeon general, with the product withdrawn pending its report – but the report, issued in January 1926, cleared the substance of any hazard to health (Graebner 1986). Only with mounting evidence of widespread diffuse increases in lead levels as a result of automobile emissions did the government, in the 1970s, order the gradual withdrawal of leaded gasoline from sale in the United States.

Lead is the one metal whose diffuse releases have become strictly managed beyond the workplace in some parts of the world – and with striking success. Concentrations in the ambient air and in blood levels in the United States fell sharply following the onset of controls on leaded gasoline (see Figure 6.11). A longer-term record of lead concentration in corals from the Florida Keys (see Figure 6.12) maps the rise as well as the quite recent fall of automotive lead emissions; both are reflected quite rapidly in this index of biotic uptake, a rate of change that also reflects the short spatial range of the emissions. Releases of other metals, though, remain very lightly if at all controlled. While the consequences of high exposure to a few metals have long been readily apparent, it is much more difficult to assess the health significance for humans and other species of the lower but more pervasive levels now common in the environment.

ORGANIC CHEMICALS

The modern organic chemical industry both mimics the natural production of some substances and creates new and ever more complex organic compounds not known to exist in nature. Like many of the other human activities examined in this chapter, chemical technology first disrupted the environment at the local scale, not originally with novel synthetic substances but with the accumulation of natural compounds as by-products. Gasworks became common features of Western cities in the early nineteenth century; they made coal gas and pumped it to consumers for illumination. The gas was obtained by heating coal to a high enough temperature that the gas was given off and could be collected for use. Unfortunately, the process released other substances as well: some merely offensive, some toxic. As a result, gasworks became prominent among the innumerable "not-in-my-backyard" facilities of the gaslight era; they aroused the wrath of neighbors less even for their occasional habit of exploding than for the repulsive-smelling wastes that they gave off in their day-to-day operations. Yet technical innovation transformed one of these by-products, coal tar, from a noxious pollutant hard to dispose of to a scarce and valuable output of the generating process, when mid-nineteenth-century German chemists devised ways of making multi-colored aniline dyes from it. Suburban farmers found ammonia, another gasworks waste, a useful fertilizer.

Each is an exemplary – and unfortunately exceptional – tale of the rationalizing of industrial metabolism. After cataloging the wastefulness of many human activities, George Perkins Marsh added hopefully in 1864 that:

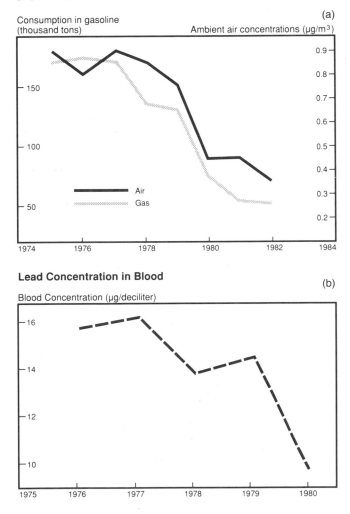

Figure 6.11 U.S. trends in (a) consumption of lead in gasoline and ambient air concentrations of lead (in micrograms per cubic m) and (b) lead concentration in blood (in micrograms per deciliter), 1975–82. Source: Brown, Kasperson, and Raymond 1990.

We are beginning to learn a better economy in dealing with the natural world. The utilization – or as the Germans call it, the *Verwerthung*, the *beworthing* – of waste from metallurgical, chemical, and manufacturing establishments, is one of the most important results of the application of science to industrial purposes. The incidental products from the laboratories of manufacturing chemists often become more valuable than those for the preparation of which they were erected. (Marsh [1864] 1965: 37n)

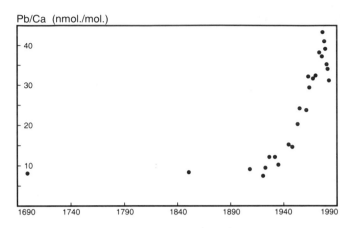

Figure 6.12 Lead concentrations in year bands of coral from the Florida Keys. Source: Jickells, Carpenter, and Liss 1990.

Often, but not often enough; things have not turned out nearly so well across the board. The ease with which generators of wastes can dispose of them for free into common media of air and running water has afforded a means to pass on the costs of nuisance or toxicity without which a far greater incentive would have existed for the discovery of incidental uses. Increasingly important dispersed emissions from consumption, moreover, are not as conducive as concentrated production ones to such recycling.

Environmental releases of numerous forms of synthetic organic compounds are important in a variety of ways. Their effects range from short-term acute episodes of atmospheric release to much longer-lived contamination of ground-water supplies that are only very slowly cleansed by natural recharge. There is space here to tell the stories of only two of the best-known and potentially most significant classes, chlorofluorocarbons (CFCs) and pesticides.

Chlorofluorocarbons were introduced in 1931 as refrigerants and subse-quently used also as solvents and propellants. They were not adopted hastily or irresponsibly. Testing showed them to pose no health hazards in workplace or home use, owing to their extreme chemical stability, which made them far supe-rior to the chemicals that had been used until then as refrigerants (Stern, Young, and Druckman 1992: 56). What has only become clear in the past decade or so is that that very stability, with a lifetime rivaling or exceeding that of a human being, makes them an extraordinarily dangerous addition to the global environ-ment. Persistent enough on release to find their way up into the stratosphere, they there catalyze reactions that break down ozone (O_3) molecules and thin out the layer of ozone that blocks much of the sun's high-energy ultraviolet radiation from the earth's surface. Emissions continued to accelerate even as evidence for

176

this process grew. The total release of CFC-11 and CFC-12 during the 1970s exceeded by more than five times the cumulative releases before 1970 (Brown et al. 1990: 446). Evidence arising in the mid-1980s that the ozone layer over the Antarctic was being significantly eroded (see Chapter 7) has only in the past few years led to international agreements aimed at reducing and eventually phasing out CFC production.

Pesticides are released deliberately into the air, water, and soil, not incidentally. But they have many incidental effects; if they are aimed at pests, they hit the environment generally. Crude chemical pesticides of the nineteenth century were metal compounds toxic to insects or to fungi (Headrick 1990: 63). Farmers used such poisonous substances as Paris green (lead arsenate) against farm insects, but not in massive quantities or to any great net environmental effect. Such added damage as they caused took the form of local incidents of poisoning caused by careless application. The first of the synthetic organic pesticides, DDT, dates back to the 1930s. The United Nations launched it in quantity upon the world at the close of World War II as a major tool in a campaign to eradicate malaria from the tropics. For a time it seemed a brilliant success. It is easy to forget the magnitude of the short-term achievement that DDT brought about and the miracle-working image that it briefly enjoyed. A knowledgeable observer writing in 1957 described a "transformation" of the previously malaria-ridden Dry Zone of Ceylon that was "truly spectacular" (Farmer 1957: 22). Death rates in affected areas had fallen by more than half and settlement had expanded successfully into once disease-ridden areas.

World annual production of DDT peaked around 1960 at close to a hundred thousand tons, only to begin a precipitous fall. The immediate cause was the publication of Carson's *Silent Spring*, which detailed the evidence for the harmful accumulation of the pesticide and its residues in other species, notably songbirds. Carson's monumentally effective polemic posed a broader question – that of the gap between narrowly focused intentions and widely dispersed effects: "How could intelligent beings seek to control a few unwanted species by a method that contaminated the entire environment?" (Lowenthal 1990: 129). The decline in use began in the developed world and spread to the developing. Globally, the abandonment of DDT use is still not complete, but current use is less than 2% of the 1960 level. Yet its diffusion throughout the earth's physical systems, promoted by its chemical stability, is reflected in its accumulation and persistence in biota and other environmental compartments. Levels of DDT and its decomposition residues in eastern Canadian seals did not peak and begin to decline until almost 20 years after the global peak in production.

The pesticides that have been introduced to replace DDT – carbamates and organophosphates – are much less chemically stable. As a result, they persist in the environment for a much shorter period and pose few of the problems of steady accumulation that were DDT's undoing. Instead, they have defects of their own, the mirror image of the defects of CFCs. Because of their higher reactivity, they create more acute health threats of toxicity, especially for farm workers handling them (Brown et al. 1990: 449–51).

THE IONIZING RADIATIONS

Certain forms of radiation in the environment are high enough in energy to disrupt molecular bonds with which they come in contact. These "ionizing radiations" include X-rays, gamma radiation, subatomic particles, and cosmic rays. Of the flows examined in this chapter, none has been significantly affected by human action for a shorter period, and awareness, concern, and management of the undesirable consequences have shorter histories still. Yet the ionizing radiations have become probably the most carefully regulated of substances in the environment today owing to widespread fears of the health risks of exposure.

Not long ago, exposure was thought a source not of risk but of benefit. The element radium after its discovery at the turn of the century looked less like a hazard than a phenomenon of almost magical virtues. As a real or pretended ingredient, it graced products as varied as health tonics and fertilizers. Recreational entrepreneurs developed springs boasting high radium content into health spas. X-rays were likewise overused for any number of purposes. Early concern represented conservationism in its classic form, worry over the waste of the world's radium supply in frivolous uses and not over the side effects of dispersing a dangerous substance through the human environment. Only after several decades – approximately the time scale on which many effects become apparent – did health concerns emerge. High cancer rates among researchers and among workers who applied luminous radioactive paint to watch and clock dials provided early clues to the medical dangers. With the first use of atomic weapons at the end of World War II and subsequent concern over worldwide fallout from atmospheric testing, popular awareness of the harmful effects of ionizing radiations completed the transformation in their image.

Because the environmental concerns over the ionizing radiations center on issues of human health, impacts are best quantified in terms of change in the dose received. Here we are again in a realm where natural flows are already sizable, even though some individual radionuclides very rare in nature have been greatly multiplied by human action. Today in the United States, on average, the natural and anthropogenic doses of ionizing radiations received are very roughly equal: some 80 millirems per year. The principal sources of each – cosmic rays on the natural side and medical technologies on the human – together make up about 90% of that average dose (see Figure 6.13). The natural contribution varies considerably over space and depends strongly on a person's location and way of life. It rises, for instance, with altitude. The closer to sea level, the better the atmosphere can screen out incoming cosmic rays; higher locations receive higher doses because of the thinner atmosphere. Inhabitants of the mile-high

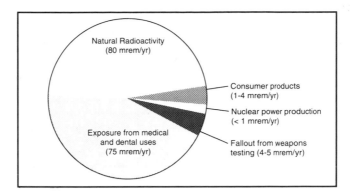

Figure 6.13 Estimated radiation dose (in millirems per year) received by the general population in the United States. Source: Eisenbud 1990.

city of Denver receive twice the dose of cosmic rays received at coastal ports. Frequent airline travel raises exposure for the same reason. Local geology also plays a role. Several areas in India and Brazil have extremely high exposure because of natural uranium and thorium content in the soil. Lesser hot spots exist where the earth's crust emits gases such as radon that may accumulate in enclosed spaces.

Most cultural exposure to ionizing radiations comes from medical-dental products and procedures. Radiant consumer items that once included luminous paint and glazes have been closely regulated as health risks became apparent. Regional variation in exposure remains considerable; so does personal variation with way of life. The nuclear fuel cycle, from mining and milling to waste disposal, does not yet contribute significantly to the dose received in the United States, though the extraction and disposal stages do locally. What gives nuclear power particular importance is the reaction that it evokes from the public and the government. The greatest degree of concern stems from the possibility of large releases from a catastrophic accident. So far, only two reactor accidents, at Britain's Windscale (1957) and the USSR's Chernobyl (1986) plants, have released "more than trace" amounts to the atmosphere. Only in the latter case did the releases cross national borders. About 1,000 reactors currently operate around the world, generating electricity, powering naval vessels, producing plutonium, and aiding in research. They produce both low- and high-level wastes whose safe disposal poses problems both technical and political.

Health effects of exposure depend on the level of the dose. Rare episodes of radiation release since World War II – most recently at Chernobyl – have involved episodes of high-dosage (greater than 50,000 millirems) exposure through accidents. Such levels of exposure produce clearly evident "nonstochastic" effects, including skin burns and suppression of bone marrow functioning. Under other

179

circumstances, the anthropogenic component of the dose received tends to be of the same order of magnitude as the natural. The consequences are "stochastic" effects, which must be identified statistically in the exposed population. The incidence of occurrence of these effects – notably cancer – increases with the degree of exposure. In an exposed population, roughly one case of cancer per 10,000 people per rem would be expected to occur.

Of all the human-induced biospheric flows, those of the ionizing radiations are now probably the most thoroughly regulated, even if in terms of mass they are also among the smallest. Treaties to limit atmospheric nuclear testing represented the first step ever taken toward the international regulation of global chemical flows. Concern over civilian uses of nuclear power has sharply restricted their spread. Such concern, though, has varied greatly even within particular world regions. Sweden voted in a 1984 referendum to phase out nuclear power altogether; in France, citizen opposition to its central role in the energy budget has been muted. Where opposition has been strong, it has scored some of the clearest successes of modern environmental politics. Expansion of nuclear energy in the United States has virtually come to a halt. Yet the victories are ambiguous ones. They have had, like most forms of management, their unintended as well as their deliberate consequences; in effect if not in intent they increase reliance on fossil fuels. The estimated cancer incidence from atomic energy facilities in the United States is considerably less than that from the ionizing radiation alone emitted from coal burned by power plants, to say nothing of the other damage that the latter cause.

CONCLUSION

Human-induced changes in the chemical flows of the biosphere have been profound but varied – in their magnitude, in their importance, and in the spatial and temporal scales at which they operate. Both agriculture and industry today depend heavily on activities that cause such changes. Evidence of unexpected adverse impacts, of the overtaxing of the ability of the biosphere to absorb emitted wastes, has made cases of human interference in such flows the stock in trade of environmentalism, supplementing earlier conservationist fears of exhaustion through wasteful use of the resources being used. Technological innovation, from the simple engines that burn fossil fuels to the sophisticated chemistry that creates new compounds, has been an important driving force (though it has also been the prerequisite for our knowledge and monitoring of the human impact and sometimes for its mitigation). Narrow technical successes have often been achieved at the eventual cost of wide-ranging, often quite persistent changes that were not foreseen.

Where the human impact has diminished, it has not always – perhaps not even usually – been as a result of deliberate environmental management. Increased oil prices are one of the main reasons global sulfur emissions have stabilized since the mid-1970s. Yet other improvements – declines in U.S. lead emissions, a decline or at least a slower growth in some urban concentrations of nitrogen oxides, the widespread abandonment of DDT – are largely due to regulatory policies. Problems have long been greatest in the industrialized developed world, but so has the capacity to respond. Yet heightened regulation in those regions may simply relocate the problems rather than solve them, shifting some of the impacts to developing areas less capable of bearing the costs of environmental regulation.

Management in the developed world has succeeded better in controlling "point sources" of pollution than "dispersed sources." Large and concentrated point sources, however much waste they pour out, are easy to locate and monitor and hence to control when control is sought. The same cannot be said of dispersed sources. Insignificant one by one, they can add up to an important cumulative effect, and being numerous and widespread they are not nearly so easily monitored and regulated as point sources. Yet the pathways of some dispersed sources have, fortunately, point bottlenecks at which it is possible to impose effective regulations. Emissions from leaded gasoline, released physically in a dispersed pattern, have been reduced and placed on the road to elimination by the regulation of gasoline manufacturing.

Water pollution and smoke emissions have been sporadically regulated for centuries, but their problems long remained local in scope. The question of whether or not to regulate was typically one of balancing different interests within a community. More recently, when acid rain has drifted from the United States to Canada and across many national boundaries in Europe, it has posed more complex political problems at higher scales. Action, of course, has had to await scientific recognition, which usually lags behind the reality; it has also had to await the identification and confirmation of the proximate sources and the cause-and-effect linkages at work. Even simple early international pollution disputes often took years to resolve. In disagreements involving only two or at most a few parties, the transaction costs posed by the problems of gaining information, bargaining over terms, and monitoring compliance are much more easily surmounted than in the truly global-scale and still scientifically uncertain issues now raised by the problems of carbon dioxide and CFC emissions. Yet the rapid progress since the mid-1980s of international initiatives to control the latter bode surprisingly well.

Only in the past few years have globally cooperative measures been suggested for the control of CO_2 and CFCs. Their relative chemical stability is a passport to circle the world, CO_2 in the troposphere and the especially long-lived CFCs even in the stratosphere. Their costs and effects are twice encouraged by being twice displaced; their spatial spillover, into the global system as a whole from single places of release, is matched by a temporal spillover that will extend their likely effects well into the future. Depending on the time scale of removal, past and present releases affect to varying degrees the world that we inherit and the world that we bequeath. Some transformations of chemical flows are hardly less reversible in practical terms than extinctions of species. Reforestation on a truly massive scale could absorb from the atmosphere some of the carbon dioxide released into it, but only by making land unavailable for other purposes, and deforestation is currently occurring because of high demand for those other purposes. And we know of no way to scour CFCs from the stratosphere, which cannot do the job itself; all that can be done is to mitigate the effects of ozone depletion and lessen continued CFC release. Mobilized for specific and narrow actions, chemical substances are then turned loose, still fully armed, to do as they will, and it is not surprising that the consequences are often unpleasant, long-lasting, and profound.

7

Oceans, Atmosphere, Climate

Not the least of the reasons for treating human impact on three environmental realms – the marine, the atmospheric, and the climatic – together is our tendency to equate them in other contexts. The pioneer makers of the barometer in the seventeenth century began by likening the atmosphere to "a sea of air." George Perkins Marsh used the same phrase to express his doubts that human action could much alter the chemical composition of either realm. But the association is not limited to scientific discourse. We speak interchangeably of the "climate" of opinion, of the intellectual "atmosphere," of "tides" and "sea changes" in thought. Such usage reflects a deeper sense of the likeness of these realms. They are our proverbial symbols of the vast, the fluid, and the undifferentiated. The view is partly accurate, and influential in our behavior even when not.

A few numbers suggest how the human realm is dwarfed by these three. The oceans cover more than twice the surface area that land does, and contain 1.35 billion cubic km of water, three dozen times the total fresh water of the lands, atmosphere, and ice sheets. An ordinary thunderstorm expends as much energy as did the first atomic bombs; an ordinary hurricane, several thousand times as much. Not only are the airs and waters vast, moreover, but they are fluid, as the land and its resources are not. Thus even severe human impacts can be spread and diluted in them to the point of invisibility. It would be a mistake, though, to treat this latter difference as one of kind and not of degree. As we shall see, localized impacts are by no means foreign to these realms.

A long-standing vacuum of authority over the air and ocean reflects their real and supposed qualities. While other realms have been brought under ever more careful supervision, they have been left largely to govern themselves. Both public and private controls have proliferated across the lands of the globe, but they have generally stopped at or near the water's edge. The freedom of the seas has been a commonplace of international law for centuries. It rested not only on the vital role of the ocean as a transportation route but on the supposed impossibility either of bounding and allotting its fluid contents or of exhausting its vast riches. Among these riches, a wealth of absorptive capacity has become ever more important. Nature may abhor a vacuum. Society, confronted with one, delights in a means for disposing of what is unwanted elsewhere. The atmosphere has had much the same regime as the oceans, one of free access for use and disposal. In recent times, the pressure of exploitation has made it clear that even these realms are finite and their resources highly concentrated in areas vulnerable to degradation. National jurisdiction of sorts has recently spread over most of the continental shelf, and international agreements now begin to establish rules for the atmosphere and climate. Yet large areas still lie outside effective governance, and fluidity distributes the consequences of actions far and wide: the classic conditions for "tragedies of the commons." That major human-induced changes are relatively new to the air and the oceans is a credit more to their size than to the care with which they have been managed.

Such changes are still newer in being recognized, at least with much accuracy. The oceans and the further reaches of the atmosphere are the earth's vast cellar and attic, useful for storing unwanted materials but rarely visited for long. Our acquaintance with them is less regular and less intimate than with many features on the land. Not only are oceanic and atmospheric processes distant, many are also invisible to the unaided eye. Even today, only doubly refracted – through sophisticated machinery and through theories and preconceptions hardly less complex – do we glimpse many of our effects. The chain connecting a human action with a physical impact that may occur far from its source is not always apparent. For the same reasons, to be sure, it has also been easy to attribute the frequent fluctuations in these areas, especially in the climate, incorrectly to human impact. All manner of wonders can be postulated in the invisible world. Drought and deluge have long been identified as supernatural retribution for improper behavior. If there is usually a vested interest for someone in denying that a particular social action is damaging the environment, there is also likely to be an interest for someone else in claiming that it is.

But if skepticism about alleged damage to these realms is appropriate, so in the end is a readiness to err on the side of caution. The very aspects that have diluted most human inputs to insignificance would spread larger ones throughout the systems. Here, moreover, raw correlations between gross levels of human activity and expected levels of environmental modification may entirely fail to capture the character of impact. A small change in the right place may produce secondary consequences far out of proportion to its own magnitude.

THE MARINE ENVIRONMENT

The human impact on the oceans, as distinct from their animal occupants, has been a recent and remains a relatively minor one. Human discipline and restraint have not been responsible. Even now, in many respects, the size of the seas compared to the scale of practical human action defies global change measurable in the terms that are appropriate for defining change in forests, land cover, or the sulfur and hydrologic cycles. A contributor to *Man's Role* could predict that the ocean, "the great matrix that man can hardly sully and cannot appreciably alter, . . . will remain much as it is and has been during the human epoch" (Graham 1956: 501–02). Since that statement was made in the 1950s, we have found ever more ingenious ways of detecting our imprints, to say nothing of new ways of inflicting them. Today, we would certainly wish to qualify that earlier verdict, but without, for the foreseeable future, overturning it altogether. The earth has been transformed by human action; the oceans have not. Our measurable traces extend widely over their expanse. Apart from the harvesting of fish and mammals discussed in an earlier chapter, though, the human impact has been significant primarily in the chemistry of coastal, enclosed, and estuarine waters. In these places, substantially cut off from the diluting powers of the larger ocean, humankind confronts the sea on approximately equal terms. Yet the very size and fluidity that have protected the broader marine realm until now make it essential to avoid profound damage and to monitor carefully those changes that suggest the onset of serious impacts.

PHYSICAL IMPACTS

Upon the physical outline of the oceans – the basins, shelf, and coastlines – the gross human impact has been minuscule. The prospect of a greenhouse warming threatens, through sea-level rise, to redraw the map of the world's coasts, just as natural climatic change did in the glacial periods. So far, the human impress on the global profile of the oceans has been a mere filling in at some margins and a nibbling away at others. Here, we have encroached a bit through polderization or landfill, adding up in some places to locally considerable areas; there, we have inadvertently worsened coastal erosion or deliberately carved canals. Such changes in the physical face of the seas have invited speculation about secondary impacts on key marine processes. Nineteenth-century journalists and scientists, George Perkins Marsh among them, worried in print that the Gulf Stream would follow a planned sea-level Panama Canal into the Pacific. They foresaw disastrous consequences for the climate, even the habitability, of Western Europe. Twentieth-century schemes for the deliberate rechanneling of this and other ocean currents to improve regional or global climates have occasionally made a stir, without yet finding a sustained existence outside the realm of the Sunday supplement.

Quite the opposite of such vast but improbable revolutions is the littering of the ocean bottom. Though less apparent than the same process on land, it remains a source of distress in its further restriction of the area that can be thought of as "wilderness" in a pristine or untouched state. In 1913, an American geologist enlivened a discussion of ocean-floor sedimentation to observe that here, man has become, as in many other regions of the earth, an important geological agent. The oxidized and inorganic debris which he throws overboard from ships must already mark out the steamer lanes across, especially the abyssal ocean bottoms. The unalterable materials which he contributes most abundantly to the deposits of the sea are coal ashes, broken dishes, and bottles. These are being permanently incorporated in the crust. . . . It is seen in light of these factors that the name being recorded most widely and indelibly on the earth at the present time is the name of him who made Milwaukee famous.

The apparent vastness of the marine realm has encouraged its use as a convenient and seemingly inexhaustible dump. Most of the material that humankind now deposits directly into the ocean is sediment dredged from inland and coastal navigational routes. The sea also offers a powerful temptation to maritime cities for easy disposal of other wastes whose storage on land would incur costs or offend neighbors. It can be a sound enough procedure for refuse that sinks to the bottom, if the water's depth is sufficient to absorb it, or for the creation of new land through fill.

Yet the capacity of nearshore areas for dredge spoil or urban trash has its limits. Shoaling of ship channels and damage to oyster beds in New York Harbor already led state and federal governments in the 1880s to curb dumping. In coastal areas, the sludge generated by sewage treatment plants has often been disposed of at sea to avoid the nightmarish problems of finding appropriate sites on land. The New York Bight, a shallow area of the continental shelf 12 km off the city's shore, received the sludge of the metropolis for decades, to the point where bottom-dwelling organisms over perhaps a hundred square km of the floor were severely affected. Occasional bacterial outbreaks occurred and a variety of trace pollutants were released. In the late 1980s, the city moved the dump site, at considerable cost, far out to the edge of the shelf, and more recently agreed to end ocean disposal altogether.

Floating debris causes different problems. The tides and currents may seem the efficient and clockwork janitors of the urbanized coastline who can be trusted to sweep each day's litter out of sight. Yet though their hours are fixed, their work is commonly more erratic than expected. Again New York's refuse history offers an illustration. A long-recurrent source of conflict has been the tendency of floating items dumped by the city's scows to find their way back onto the region's beaches. In 1886, a reporter at Coney Island found that a mass of washed-up refuse including "cut melons, decayed fruit, grease-coated barrel staves, old bottles, and an exhaustive assortment of cats and dogs in various postmortem stages appealed with staggering arguments to the senses of smell and sight." Dumping gave way at the turn of the century to incineration and landfill. It later resumed until New Jersey obtained relief for the region's coastline through a federal court order in 1934. Yet floating wastes either illegally or accidentally dumped, plus occasional masses of sludge, have sporadically plagued the metropolitan shores, culminating in the celebrated wave of beach closings in the summer of 1988 over fears of washed-up medical waste. Concerns associated with fouled beaches neatly track the changes in environmental public health from "filth" to germ theories of disease. If in 1988 they centered on contagion associated with the AIDS virus, fears in the late nineteenth century were over refuse that, "if left uncleaned, could not fail to send up unhealthy odors under the sun's rays."

Coastal refuse is disproportionately visible because of its location. To it is now added much floating waste in the open seas deposited as litter from ships (Jickells, Carpenter, and Liss 1990: 319–20). The extreme resistance of plastic to decomposition, its most useful quality, also makes it troublingly persistent. Some 500,000 plastic containers were dumped each day from merchant shipping in the 1980s, and 6 million tons of litter each year. Considerable lengths of plastic driftnet, perhaps hundreds of miles of it annually in the North Pacific, are also lost or discarded. To them is added "plastic sand," small granules a few millimeters or less in diameter, generated in the industrial production process.

Unaccustomed to its presence, the ocean has evolved no mechanism to digest away such a durable and buoyant substance as plastic. Some washes up on beaches. Some granules acquire a crust of biotic colonization and eventually sink under its weight. The rest accumulates. The inhabitants of the sea have not yet learned to avoid so new and innocuous-seeming an ingredient of their surroundings. Two processes have been widely observed. One is the entanglement of birds, fish, and marine mammals in abandoned driftnets. Steady decreases in the population of the northern fur seal on the Pribilof Islands since the mid-1970s, for example, have been attributed to entanglement of the young in plastic fishing debris routinely abandoned in the North Pacific. The second is the ingestion of plastic debris, which may block or damage the digestive tract. Reports of plastic granules found in the stomachs of marine animals have become commonplace. Regulations on plastics pollution in the legally free-access open seas – most recently, an international agreement to ban all disposal from ships under the registry of the signers – are inconvenient to obey and difficult to enforce.

Similar to plastic litter as a form of floating ocean waste are tar balls formed from spilled petroleum (Jickells, Carpenter, and Liss 1990: 318–19). Unlike plastics, they have a natural as well as a human source, if only a minor one. Underwater seeps added oil to the oceans long before the first tanker left port. Yet the amounts added by human action – not only dramatic and well-publicized spills, from the *Torrey Canyon* in 1967 to the *Exxon Valdez* in 1989, but far more routine kinds of discharges – are much greater, probably more than 90% of the current totals. The large-scale, long-distance ocean transportation of oil began in the 1920s, and the first reports of tar balls at sea date from the following decade. Modern surveys disclose clear spatial patterns in their concentration – highest in the Mediterranean, an enclosed ocean and a major tanker route, high along other tanker routes and in oceanic gyres, and quite low in the southern oceans. The residence time of tar balls on the surface seems to range from a few months to a few years. If plastics pollution is increasing, the concentration of tar balls, paralleling trends in other oil-related environmental problems, has apparently decreased in the past decade or so with a reduction in seaborne oil transportation.

CHEMICAL POLLUTION

Because plastic is not a natural component of the ocean nor tar a common one, their observed marine concentrations translate easily enough into a measure of human impact. Human-induced changes in many other aspects of ocean chemistry are harder to specify against a preexisting background presence of the substance involved. If, for example, salt were mined in large quantities from the earth for some purpose and were eventually disposed of in the seas, it might be some time before the impact became detectable. Background levels of ocean chemistry, moreover, are themselves hard to nail down with confidence because of their own considerable fluctuation over time and space – with the seasons, with the surroundings, with natural events such as the El Niño oscillations.

The difficulties lie less in measuring present levels than in establishing a reliable baseline of pre-impact composition with which they can be compared. Modern seawater samples are analyzed with enormous precision, but comparative historical research is hampered by a shortage of data on the past. Careful collection and analysis date back to the pioneering expedition of the British ship *Challenger* in the 1870s. Most early samples, though, have not been stored in a way that preserved them, free from contamination, for study with more sensitive modern techniques. Many trends must be inferred from indirect indicators. Among the most commonly employed are the concentrations of substances in the different layers of vertical sediment columns from the seafloor. Biological remains also record the chemical past both distant and recent. Some corals, for instance, yearly accrete growth bands like tree rings, the concentrations in which of a number of substances provide an index to their concentrations in the surrounding water. A confident and reliable assessment of trends in change can often be based only on the agreement of several independent sources of evidence.

Whether added to the oceans through the atmosphere, by dumping, or by runoff from the land, chemicals find an eventual resting place in the sediment on the seafloor. There, unless restored to the waters by disturbance, they lie under a soft rain of particles until hardened into rock and uplifted by tectonic activity over a scale of tens or hundreds of millions of years. They have opportunities for damage en route to the seafloor that depend on the paths and itineraries followed.

Dispersion occurs through the basic physical flows of the ocean. Land barriers retard outward spread from bays, estuaries, and enclosed seas. In open coastal areas, wave and tidal stirring can promote downward mixing, while currents throughout the oceans circulate water horizontally over wider areas. Vertical mixing is much slower away from the coasts, for reasons that we have seen assume a particular importance in the carbon cycle. Over most of the area of the ocean basins, a stable intermediate layer characterized by a sharp downward decrease in temperature and increase in density obstructs the ready blending of components of the surface with the deeper seawaters. Such mixing occurs over a span measured in perhaps hundreds to thousands of years, in contrast to a wide horizontal dispersion occurring over a decade or so. But other processes scour the surface waters. Biological uptake, followed by the sinking of biogenic particles or of the organism itself – whether as small as phytoplankton or as large as a whale – can accelerate the removal of substances to the deeper layers and the bottom sediments. The most reactive substances, being prone to uptake of some form, vanish most rapidly from the surface layers, and show the most uneven spatial pattern of distribution.

Remote from concentrated sources of input, and vast if erratic in the capacity for mixing and dilution, the open oceans, especially the deeper layers, have been little affected in their chemical composition by human inputs. Most of the substances whose concentrations have been detectably increased across the surface waters are those whose natural concentrations are either low or nonexistent. Synthetic organic chemicals are obvious examples. Atmospheric transport dispersed DDT widely at detectable levels across the ocean surface in mid-century. The concentration of sources and the pattern of winds produced levels in the Northern Hemisphere several times higher than in the Southern. Much the same occurred with polychlorinated biphenyls (PCBs). As both substances are rapidly removed through the sinking of biogenic particles, in each case the regulation of releases in the developed world was quickly reflected in decreases in ocean concentrations. Yet both have retreated not only to the ocean's basement but into the near-surface biota as well. The bioaccumulation of these substances is much more slowly reversed by decreased emissions. Atomic testing for two decades after World War II, plus Britain's Windscale and the Soviet Union's Chenobyl nuclear power plant accidents, introduced a number of radionuclides to the atmosphere and subsequently to the ocean. The high natural background of carbon 14 (^{14}C) dampened the magnitude of the human increase; the other radionuclides, much less abundant in nature, appeared in the oceans at vastly enhanced levels, though ones still tiny in absolute terms (Jickells, Carpenter, and Liss 1990: 318).

Among the trace metals, the natural presence of lead is unobtrusive because its removal from surface water is fairly rapid. Its modern human mobilization to the atmosphere, through leaded gasoline combustion and industrial smelting, has been enormous. Consequently, its concentration in the oceans is readily shown to have been much increased by anthropogenic processes. Human releases are concentrated in North America, Europe, and Southeast Asia, a pattern mimicked by the rough oceanic distribution of lead. Declines in some surface-water and coral-band lead concentrations, particularly in the North Atlantic, followed the onset of emissions controls in the developed world in the 1970s (Jickells, Carpenter, and Liss 1990: 320–21). It is not clear that human contributions of lead, iron, cadmium, or other metals to the oceans have caused significant damage. Though detectable, these inputs have been slight when assessed in absolute terms. Yet they at least should be viewed with concern because of their possible disruption of biological processes.

The most serious human impacts on marine chemistry occur close to land (Jickells, Carpenter, and Liss 1990: 330). They are especially concentrated in estuaries and in shallow, semi-enclosed regional seas along populous coastlines. Because of bars to circulation, these areas experience only a sluggish exchange with the open waters. Well-known estuaries are those of the Thames and the Hudson rivers and the Chesapeake Bay. Enclosed seas include the Mediterranean, the Baltic, the Black Sea, and the North Sea. The circulation of waters is further restricted in those enclosed seas that are divided into two or more deeper basins linked by much shallower areas. These nearshore waters receive inputs of the same trace pollutants, and from closer and more concentrated sources, that have been detectably increased in the open ocean. They also receive large quantities of nutrients from two types of sources. Point discharges, from sewer systems or sewage treatment plants, are combined with widely dispersed ones such as fertilizer runoff from farmlands. These nitrogen and phosphorus compounds, whose net anthropogenic increase in the open seas has been insignificant, are dangerous because of the end results, discussed in an earlier chapter, that they stimulate through biological activity. In particular, they enhance the growth of phytoplankton, whose decay through bacterial action consumes the dissolved oxygen vital for marine animal life. These conditions also promote the emission of hydrogen sulfide through anaerobic respiration by bacteria, driving out the fauna for whom it is poisonous. Extreme conditions of anoxia, or the entire loss of oxygen content in the water, can result from pollution, made still worse by smothering levels of hydrogen sulfide.

Estuaries are of prime economic importance. Their physical character as a meeting ground of salt and fresh water, land and sea, translates into high levels of diversity and biological productivity. More than two-thirds of the commercial fish caught in the United States are of estuarine origin. Yet the manifold human pursuits attracted to these locales – disruption not only by the familiar forms of effluent disposal from population, agriculture, and industry but by other activities ranging from oil and gas extraction to dredging for navigation – can easily foul such nests. In an estuary such as the Chesapeake Bay, long a synonym for piscatorial wealth, the denser, because more saline, lower layers of water are especially prone to oxygen depletion, and bottom-dwelling organisms are severely affected. Severe modern declines in the catch of oysters and rockfish in the bay have been attributed in large part to pollution.

Not only here but in the larger enclosed seas, the danger is mediated to a considerable extent through the details of the natural setting. So shielded is the Baltic Sea in northern Europe by the configuration of its floor from mixing with the waters of the Atlantic, and the several basins of the sea from one another, that the wastes of the 16 million people living on its coast and the more than 60 million more in its watershed area are only slowly diluted. The result has been a measurable increase in nutrient concentrations in the sea – though not uniform across all of its basins – and a consequent drop in dissolved oxygen in the deep waters, with possible incidents of anoxia during this century. On the other hand, Puget Sound, in the northwestern United States, has so far escaped major damage from the sewage of the million or so residents in its vicinity, including the Seattle-Tacoma metropolitan area. The depth of the glacially carved basin permits a large, rapid, and regular tidal influx of ocean water, diluting and dispersing the wastes. And in contrast to other areas, the water that enters the sound is already high in nutrients, so that the relative human addition through sewage is low. On the other hand, pollution inputs have been sufficient to enhance levels of trace metals and petroleum-related chemicals in the sediments of the sound (Jickells, Carpenter, and Liss 1990: 321–30).

Not only does the natural setting mediate the human impact; in some cases, it is such as to produce problems even without human impact. The Black Sea, for instance, is naturally anoxic below the surface layer, and a useful reminder that not all unproductive environments are the product of human action, except perhaps insofar as the very definition of productivity is a human one.

ATMOSPHERIC TRACE CONSTITUENTS

As in the marine environment, the human impact on the atmosphere has been slight when stated in terms of gross magnitudes. The ordinary composition of the atmosphere, excluding water vapor, is more or less fixed in its broad outlines: about 78% nitrogen gas (N_2), nearly 21% oxygen (O_2), plus some inert "noble gases," principally argon. These components add up to 99.9%, with a mere 0.1%, or one part per thousand, filled by the trace components, largely the portion, along with particulate impurities such as smoke and aerosols, open to human-induced change. Yet modifications of the atmosphere that seem small in their effect on its overall composition can all the same be quite significant in their results.

A catalog of natural realms compiled 300 years ago would surely have included such ones as the oceans and the climate. The very notion of distinct atmospheric components is a rather recent one, alien to the ancient and long-lived view of "air" as a basic, indivisible element. This is not to say that the presence of contaminants – smoke, for example, or the "miasma" that in classical times gave one disease the name of "malaria" after its supposed origin in "bad air" – has not long been a concern, just that they appeared to be extraneous substances, impurities mingled with but distinct from "air" itself. The widespread recognition of air as simply a mixture of independent though interacting gas molecules forming no larger unity, not unlike an economist's view of society, goes back only as far as the revolution in chemistry in the late eighteenth and early nineteenth centuries. Scientific knowledge is far newer still of most of the trace gases that are present at low concentrations in the atmosphere (Graedel and Crutzen 1990: 295). All but a dozen of the known trace species, which now number some 3,000, have been identified only since World War II. Such knowledge as we possess of their atmospheric roles is more recent yet, having been outstripped by advances in the techniques of monitoring and analysis. We know much about what substances are now present and at what levels, much less about what their presence means.

If the list of concerns about atmospheric composition has also lengthened greatly over this time, at least some of the items once prominent on it have disappeared. Many global disease epidemics in the early nineteenth century were blamed on vast world-circling waves of atmospheric impurity sometimes attributed to spates of earthquakes, volcanic eruptions, even comets. By 1866, a germ theory of cholera was winning acceptance, yet a U.S. senator could still ridicule a proposal for quarantine against an outbreak in Europe and Asia by saying, "If you could prevent the introduction of that air from which the disease arises, if you could prevent it from traversing its circle around the world every sixteen or eighteen years, and then coming into our atmosphere, perhaps something might be done" (*Congressional Globe*, 39th Cong., 1st sess., 2446). The nineteenth-century medical investigators of miasma, once it had been redefined as a trace gas of sorts, performed detailed quantitative studies of its emissions from both natural and human sources, the former including earthquake fissures and marshes, the latter embracing a diverse array of landscape features from sewers to cemeteries to mill ponds. The planting of trees as a protective measure both physically, in order to block the circulation of the dangerous gases, and chemically, to absorb and neutralize them, was proposed, just as it is today to soak up carbon and stave off global warming. George Perkins Marsh ([1864] 1965: 134–36) devoted several pages of *Man and Nature* to a laudatory account of "Trees as a Protection Against Malaria." The eucalyptus, the "Australian fever tree," was widely planted to banish the "fever and ague" and apparently with some success, though not because (as was thought) its emanations neutralized miasma; rather, its voracious thirst dried the soil and made it a less hospitable ground for disease-bearing insects, who also found its odor repellent (Thompson 1970).

Of course, human actors need not understand the details or even the rudiments of an aspect of the environment to have an effect on it. Such understanding does, though, enhance the likelihood that purposeful management can stave off degradation. Accurate awareness of human impact on the composition of the atmosphere is relatively novel, but has existed long enough for at least some benefits to have been reaped from it through the deliberate introduction of remedies. Yet the typical global pattern for the trace species that human action has affected has been a slow change – generally an increase and an undesirable

192

one – in concentration from early times, followed by an acceleration in the change in this century, whether at the local or the global scale (Graedel and Crutzen 1990). A typical pattern at the local – in this case, urban – scale has been one of rapid degradation of air quality with industrialization and development, followed by some improvement if and when incomes rise, governments regulate, and industries innovate or move elsewhere.

The scarcity of data on past atmospheric, like oceanic, composition hampers the assessment of human-induced changes, but a variety of sources can be studied to fill some of the gaps. Indicators preserved in sealed spaces can, if extracted with care, furnish direct evidence of the state of the atmosphere in that area at a past point in time. Substances dissolved in columns of Antarctic or Greenland ice, and air bubbles trapped inside, have become prime sources on contaminants widely enough distributed to have reached the ends of the earth. Calculations of the masses released to the skies by human activity can be used for estimates of some substances, and have proven valuable for assessing sulfur dioxide levels in early industrial cities such as London. Research can also reason from the effects back to the causes; corrosion rates on urban statues and monuments provide indications of pollution levels, especially in European cities rich in such features.

Even each of these sources provides only local data, possibly not representative of wider conditions. The study of human impact, as in the oceans, is complicated by the structure and the flows of the atmosphere. More fluid than the oceans and more prone to rapid diffusion, it still contains barriers to the even and automatic spread of inputs. The troposphere, roughly the first 12 km above the earth's surface, is sometimes termed the weather sphere; it is a realm of turbulence and mixing, quite distinct in that regard from the far thinner and more stable stratosphere immediately above. Yet temperature inversions, notorious in their connection with air pollution episodes, can impose an unusual degree of stability on even the air near the ground and produce the atmospheric equivalent of an enclosed sea. Much the same principles apply as in the ocean in the patterns of distribution and hence of impact. The more reactive the component, in general, the more localized its distribution and the less the consequences for areas distant from the point of release. Many of the more reactive pollutants are concentrated in the northern mid-latitudes, where sources have been concentrated, or, at an even finer scale, in and around cities (Graedel and Crutzen 1990). The more stable components added by human action tend to spread more evenly across the atmosphere because they persist longer. The reactive elements that are more quickly removed are those whose concentrations, if worrisome, can be readily reduced by controls on the human activities responsible for their increase.

THE THREE FACES OF OZONE

Less than 10 parts per billion of the troposphere and a few parts per million of the stratosphere under natural conditions, and little increased or diminished by

193

human action before this century, ozone has still had a far longer and richer history of recognition as an important trace component than one would expect from the size of its presence. Like any triangular relationship, the molecule (O_3) tends to be unstable and short-lived, but its effects while it holds together illustrate well the potential importance of even small concentrations of atmospheric components.

Ozone, upon its discovery in the 1840s, was thought, from its peculiar qualities (an acrid odor and a blighting effect on plant and animal tissue) and from the apparent pattern of its distribution, to be highly effective at low concentrations in destroying the gases of decay in the atmosphere then held responsible for epidemic disease. That it appeared to be more plentiful in mountains than in valleys, by the seashore than inland, in the countryside than in cities, outdoors than indoors, during the early morning than later in the day, and during the spring than by the end of the summer, all seemed to suggest that where and when it abounded, so did health and vigor, and that it was depleted in neutralizing the miasma that built up in confined, warm, and densely populated areas. A prominent nineteenth-century American physician observed that ozone, "one of Nature's great purifiers . . . in disinfecting and purifying decaying and putrid matter, is itself destroyed. It dies that others may live" (Beard 1874: 464). Some hospitals installed artificial ozone generators. The medical theories on which these early concerns about depletion were based were eroded by both better testing and the onset of germ theories of disease. In fact, while records of ozone concentrations from the nineteenth century abound, most were flawed, taken with the only simple means for measurement then widely available, and few are deemed reliable enough to be used in modern studies of trends in atmospheric change.

The next issue arose in the mid-twentieth century with the onset of smog in sprawling, automobile-dependent cities. Observations accumulated in the Los Angeles area of widespread damage to vegetation, of irritation to human tissues, and of such lesser annoyances as the cracking of tires. Research pinpointed ozone as the common culprit. A reaction chain was identified by which nitrogen dioxide from automobile exhaust could be broken down by sunlight, releasing oxygen atoms that combined with oxygen molecules to form ozone. Emissions controls in U.S. cities have brought ozone concentrations down a bit from their peak levels. Yet, in cities throughout the developed world, they remain high when compared to the preindustrial background – two to four times higher in Western Europe, for instance, and as much as ten times higher during smog episodes. In other places the problem has continued to worsen. Ironically, it has sometimes worsened because of measures taken for pollution control. In London, progress in the control of coal-smoke pollution after the "Great Smog" of the early 1950s let in more sunlight, a critical partner in the photochemical ozone-formation reactions, causing a new problem to appear in place of the old

(Brimblecombe 1987: 175–76). The natural paucity of sunshine in London has moderated photochemical smog formation, however, an advantage not shared by some dry and sunny megalopolises of lower latitudes, where ozone is a particularly severe problem. Mexico City and Los Angeles are cases in point. Efforts in Mexico City to control lead emissions greatly worsened the ozone problem. A new additive contained in the lead-free gasoline mandated by the government in 1986 promoted ozone formation, such that atmospheric concentrations quickly began to exceed the maximum allowable standard as many days as not. The average level during the late 1980s exceeded the normal background level by ten times (Ezcurra 1990).

Yet even as ozone was being cast as one of the heavies of the troposphere, it was also assuming a hero's role as a vital natural component of the next layer above. The gas is produced at high altitudes when O_2 molecules are broken apart by solar radiation and each of the two free atoms combines with another molecule of O_2. This stratospheric ozone reservoir absorbs most of the shortwave, high-energy ultraviolet rays from the sun, shielding the inhabitants of the earth's surface from their damaging effects, which in humans include eye damage and skin cancers, and which may also include serious harm to crops and livestock. The parallel destruction of ozone molecules in this layer is promoted by the presence of several catalysts. Under natural conditions, these are principally oxides of nitrogen, to an extent that balances production and loss and maintains the size of the ozone shield.

Much more powerful as catalysts for ozone destruction, however, are chlorine and chlorine monoxide. Both are released when artificially produced chlorofluorocarbons make their way into the stratosphere and, above an altitude of 25 km, are fragmented by shortwave solar radiation. As noted in the previous chapter, the low reactivity of these compounds makes them attractive for certain industrial uses; as with plastics, this stability is also what makes them a dangerously persistent addition to the biosphere. As no processes in the troposphere break down the CFCs, virtually all remain intact for their eventual upward migration. The increase in these chlorine gases in the middle and upper stratosphere is estimated at about 5% per year. Despite reduced rates of production, CFC releases from the earth still are higher than their rates of natural withdrawal.

The impact on the stratosphere, expected to involve a net ozone depletion on the order of 5% in coming decades, will not be evenly distributed. The processes of CFC fragmentation will concentrate the loss in the upper reaches of the layer and in the higher latitudes, even as ozone actually increases in abundance in the lower stratosphere. In the early 1980s, it was believed that stratospheric depletion by CFCs, while a worrisome prospect, had not so far been substantial. This view was abruptly revised by the discovery in the mid-1980s that the ozone layer over Antarctica was showing large and yearly increasing depletions during the spring months of the Southern Hemisphere. The depletions, reaching or exceeding 50% of the concentrations recorded in the late 1970s, are now convincingly ascribed by scientists to the action of CFCs, and Northern Hemisphere O_3 losses have since become apparent as well.

Nothing illustrates so well some major themes in global change: the physical transfer of impacts from the areas of their sources to far distant ones, the major and unforeseen secondary consequences of some human actions in the physical environment, and the essential irreversibility on a human time scale of many changes that have already been effected and others that are predicted. Tropospheric ozone, because of its reactivity, can be brought down relatively rapidly in concentration by appropriate management measures, but no measures that we know of will so quickly restore stratospheric ozone or destroy the CFCs that have been released in the troposphere and, beyond recall, like letters dropped into the mailbox, await a slow but certain delivery to their destination. An international agreement reached in Vienna in 1985 established a preliminary framework for defining national responsibilities in curbing CFC emissions. It was followed by a 1987 Montreal agreement committing the signatory countries to halving their CFC use by the end of the century, in turn succeeded by further pacts, adding further signatories, that have set still tighter limits (Rowlands 1993). These major achievements in international management notwithstanding, the CFCs already and still to be emitted will do further damage for many years to come. Precisely how much ozone depletion will occur is not clear, and relatively little is known about the results of increased ultraviolet penetration of the atmosphere. No ready historical analogies exist for evaluating so possibly profound a change in the workings of the biosphere.

TROPOSPHERIC CHANGES

Ozone depletion is the principal stratospheric change in which human actions are implicated. A much wider array of tropospheric impacts has been cataloged at the global, regional, and local scales. Many of the increases in the global cycles and flows, both the major ones of carbon, sulfur, nitrogen, and phosphorus, and lesser ones enhanced or entirely created by human action, have been felt in changes in the tropospheric concentrations of various trace components (Graedel and Crutzen 1990).

Carbon has been added in the form of several gases. Methane (CH_4), the most abundant reactive trace gas, has doubled in its average global concentration since 1750, largely as a result of human activity. A slight difference in concentrations of about 7% between the Northern and Southern Hemispheres, the former the source of most emissions, reflects the gas's reactivity. Carbon monoxide (CO), more reactive yet, has also increased, mainly across the northern midlatitudes. If the methane and carbon monoxide molecules are relatively transient lodgers in the atmosphere, with residence times of several years and a few months respectively, the more stable CO_2 becomes almost part of the furniture.

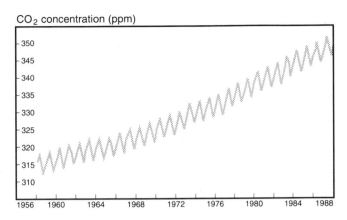

Figure 7.1 Concentration of atmospheric carbon dioxide (in parts per million) measured at Mauna Loa, Hawaii, 1957–88.

It has increased by some 25%, from a level of 280–90 parts per million through the early nineteenth century to about 350 today. Careful monitoring begun in the 1950s documents the clear upward trend (see Figure 7.1), though it has recently been interrupted by a still-mysterious leveling trend in the early 1990s. The regular sawtooth pattern in the climb in level represents what has been termed the "biospheric breath" (Smil 1987: 264), where the earth's lungs are the concentration of land area and hence of vegetation in the Northern Hemisphere. During the northern winter, the predominance of respiration over photosynthesis releases more CO_2 than is taken up; the reverse is true in the summer.

The nitrogen and sulfur compounds emitted from a variety of human sources, significant in acid rain and other impacts reviewed in the previous chapter, have assumed a much higher atmospheric profile. Nitrous oxide (N_2O) appears from ice-core records to have increased by only about 8% over the past three centuries, but to have attained a much faster modern rate of increase now averaging more than 1% per decade. The nitrate ion began an increase in the 1950s that has accelerated more recently, though the sulfate ion record, once the contributions of volcanic eruptions are combed out, displays in common with other portions of the sulfur cycle a more erratic path of increase that has leveled out to relatively constant values in the past 20 years.

Natural fluctuations almost entirely overwhelm the human contribution to some other components. Ice-core data from Greenland have made possible the reconstruction of a global record of hydrogen ion (H^+) concentration, or acidity (see Figure 7.2). It shows the influence of volcanic eruptions on atmospheric aerosol particles more clearly than that of human inputs. The major modern eruptions – Tambora (1815), Krakatoa (1883), Katmai (1912), and Agung, on the island of Bali (1963) – are apparent, yet more careful analysis has

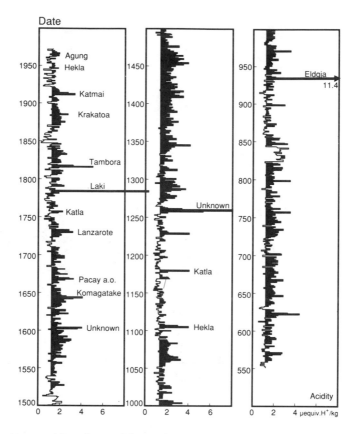

Figure 7.2 Mean acidity of annual layers from A.D. 553 to 1972 in an ice core from central Greenland. Source: Hammer, Clausen, and Dansgaard 1980; redrawn for Graedel and Crutzen 1990.

indicated a detectable though small anthropogenic increase over this time as well. Much the same pattern shows up in ice-core data on the aerosol levels of the atmosphere, where any human increase is even more fully hidden behind the natural perturbations. For lead, on the other hand, often a component of particles, the pattern in the atmosphere is the same as seen in emissions and in marine concentrations – a massive increase with the human mobilization of the metal for service in gasoline, and a sizable decrease after the onset of regulation.

At lower scales than the global, other patterns become evident. If particulate matter has not been much affected at the global level by human action, the story in individual cities has been a different one. The history of urban air pollution has allowed some authors to emphasize the element of improvement, rather than degradation, in modern environmental history, but only by focusing on the cities of the developed world. There the combination of regulatory measures made possible by relative affluence and the relocation of many polluting indus-

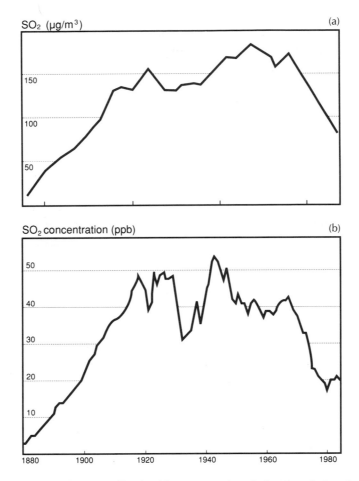

Figure 7.3 (a) Decadal mean sulfur dioxide concentrations in London air, in micrograms per cubic m. Redrawn from Brimblecombe 1977. (b) Sulfur dioxide concentrations in New York City, in parts per billion. Source: Graedel and Crutzen 1990.

tries makes it possible to draw a vivid picture of improvement by comparison with the worst of earlier conditions. No one can see pictures or read descriptions of the smoke-laden air of such British and American capitals of the Industrial Revolution as Manchester, London, and Pittsburgh without the sense that here, at least, is an exception to the downward environmental spiral that we all but take for granted. Improvement in many aspects of the atmosphere – such coal-derived pollutants as sulfur dioxide and particulate matter – has occurred in developed-world cities both through air-quality legislation and through the departure for other reasons of pollution-generating activities (see Figure 7.3).

Even in the nineteenth century, the annoying effects of coal smoke and chemical emissions were sufficient to prompt legal advances in pollution control based on the principle – though one shot through with exceptions for established in-dustrial districts and exceptionally valuable industries – that one's property could not be used in such a way as to damage the property of another. Yet coal smoke was then thought a violation primarily of the comfort and cleanliness of the urban population. It seemed either innocuous in terms of health or pos-itively beneficial. An authoritative American medical treatise in the 1870s de-clared that "the presence of smoke in the atmosphere does not seem to produce any injurious effect on the public health" (Buck 1879: II, 465), and British expert opinion as canvassed by the urban reformer Henry Mayhew had the same con-clusion. Coal smoke was often thought to neutralize miasmatic contaminants and protect urban populations, as was tobacco. Fumigation held a time-honored place in the European cabinet of remedies for urban disease epidemics.

Modern trends in air quality, if encouraging in the developed world, are less so elsewhere – in Eastern Europe and the Third World. In Mexico City, mass automobile use, industrialization, and a natural environment highly prone to trap emissions within a mountain basin have produced a crisis that is only deep-ening with time. Atmospheric levels of ozone, sulfur dioxide, and nitrogen ox-ides continue to rise. Recent estimates have particulate matter in the air increas-ing at 6% per year. If the natural setting accounts for part of the basin's pollution problem, it also has much in common with other industrializing primate cities plagued by ill-controlled emissions from factories and automobiles and heavily dependent on coal as a fuel. In Holdgate's (1990) words, such congested mega-lopolises may in the near future face conditions "even worse than those of Victo-rian England at its foulest."

At the lowest spatial scale, indoor pollution is at once the most contemporary and the most ancient of air quality problems. As Brimblecombe (1987: 3) writes, anthracosis, or the blackening of the respiratory tract, "is the rule rather than the exception in mummified lung tissue," reflecting the smoky, ill-ventilated inte-riors of prehistoric huts. A modern study of the Semang of Malaysia, a tribe of swidden agriculturalists, found that they too "achieve quite respectable pollution levels in terms of the immediate life space of the individual and the household," particularly in interior smoke. If forced to breathe air as bad, the population of the capital city of Kuala Lumpur, itself by no means atmospherically pristine, "would rise up in outrage" (Rambo 1985: 48–51, 79). Yet the Semang, and many others who inhabit similar environments, see the smoke – with some reason – less as a pollutant than as a protection, for it keeps mosquitoes that are both an annoyance and the carriers of malaria away from the living quarters to an extent that may more than compensate for any long-term harm done.

Many of today's well-insulated indoor spaces in developed countries, long since freed of such noxious-smelling components, harbor elevated levels of far more subtle trace pollutants, such as radon gas and the products of its decay, asbestos, and formaldehyde. Here conservationism and environmentalism work at cross-purposes. Modern concern with insulation to improve energy efficiency has lowered the speed with which pollutants are dispersed by ventilation. As the more enclosed portions of the oceans suffer severely from the loss of the vast diluting capacity, so do the portions of the atmosphere that we enclose deliberately with the aim of warding off the elements.

CLIMATE

Nowhere even in the natural world is cause and effect a matter of simple observation, but making the link is easier in some fields than in others. In climatology, the distance in space and time between causes and effects and their connection through a web or loop of invisible mechanisms pose particularly formidable obstacles to fitting the pieces of the puzzle together, or rather to solving what is less a jigsaw than a connect-the-dots puzzle. Lines can be drawn from a wide range of events regarded as possible causes to a wide range of subsequent possible effects, to produce any number of plausible patterns, yet only a few of which can be correct.

That the earth's climates had changed in the distant past was evident to observers at a relatively early time. Fossil remains of tropical vegetation found in now-temperate and cold lands could not be plausibly explained otherwise, and evidence also accumulated, beginning in the middle of the nineteenth century, for the occurrence of the glacial period that is now dated as having ended 10,000 years ago. If the climate system was so unstable as to have undergone changes like these in geologic time, might it not also be vulnerable even to relatively small human intervention, made deliberately or otherwise? Thus did the immemorial popular sense of a link between human deeds and misdeeds and the behavior of the weather acquire some scientific respectability. At the same time, though, scientists recognized the importance of natural weather and climate fluctuation, which has always greatly hampered any attempt to specify what portion of any change was human-induced and what was not.

The fuzziness of the data and of the governing processes necessarily instills a large element of guesswork in this area, and the result has been an exceptional degree of intellectual instability and controversy. The cyclic nature of many climatic phenomena is hardly more oscillatory than the history of climatological thought. Some of the major swings are apparent in a comparison of Marsh's *Man and Nature*, which in the spirit of its time is pervaded by discussions of human impact on climatic conditions, with the relevant papers in *Man's Role* and with those in *The Earth as Transformed by Human Action*. The treatment given the subject in 1955 reflected the Western scientific consensus of the first half of the twentieth century, which largely dismissed the possibility of human impact on the climate. One paper dealt with the climates of cities and another with artificial rainmaking, a prospect then much in the news; but otherwise the tone at Princeton was set by C. W. Thornthwaite's (1956: 582) pronouncement "that man is incapable of making any significant change in the climatic pattern on the earth;

that the changes in microclimate for which he is responsible are so local and some so trivial that special instruments are often required to detect them." These words reached print just as empirical and theoretical advances were building up into a renewed wave of concern over human impacts on climate that has continued to grow to the present day.

THE CLIMATIC RECORD

The climate of a place is defined by the character of its weather conditions – with particular attention to temperature and precipitation but also such variables as humidity, cloudiness, and windiness – over a given period. Where a particular purpose has not dictated some other scale, 30 years is often taken as the span for defining present climate, but there is no time scale, nor any particular average, that defines the one and only real climate independent of the questions being asked. So depending on the period of comparison, present climates, globally and in particular areas, are at once warmer and colder, wetter and drier, and becoming more and less so, than before. For the present purposes, the appropriate questions are whether human activity has significantly changed the climate of the globe, of its regions, and of their localities, over the past 300 years.

One cannot identify change without specifying an initial climate from which the change occurred. An enormous amount of data is needed to do so – to calculate a scientifically reliable profile of "climate" for any area at a given time. The systematic collection of data is quite novel even within the last three centuries, and has been more complete for some areas than for others. For most earlier places and periods there are no such data. The most seemingly straightforward human testimony to weather and climate events, numerical records of temperature and rainfall, is a trap that has snared many an unwary research effort. Even when taken with care such records show only local conditions, and early ones in particular may have been strongly distorted by the placing of the thermometer or the rain gauge without regard to the variations that can occur over a range of a few meters. George Perkins Marsh warned in 1864 of "the great influence of slight changes of station upon the results of observations of temperature and precipitation" as an element of uncertainty in meteorological knowledge. Records taken in cities, where weather stations or observers are apt to be located, are especially suspect because of the effects of cities on the local climate. The mistaken extrapolation of urban readings to the regions in which they lie is of long standing; so, too, is its recognition. In 1799, the great lexicographer Noah Webster noticed a pronounced and well-defined difference "between the real temperature of open country, and the artificial one of a city," and he cautioned against "the great error of determining the temperature of a climate, by observations made in a large city."

Direct measurements, though the most convenient data to use, are scanty or untrustworthy over long time periods and large regions. Many supplemental sources of information, such as records of agricultural production and prices, of settlements, and of other social phenomena loosely tied to climate, have been drawn upon and interpreted with increasing sophistication to fill the gaps. The demonstration of important natural climatic variations even in historic times is a major, if in its details still a controversial, advance. What is known as the Little Ice Age was a period of unusually low temperatures – best documented in Western Europe – that lasted from approximately 600 to 100 years ago. Entirely indirect "proxy" data, the circumstantial evidence on which most long-term climatic research depends, provide evidence for change that is clearer than the evidence for its precise nature. Tree-ring widths, or the advance and retreat of mountain glaciers, for instance, reflect the sum of temperature and precipitation patterns in the particular locale. These factors may be hard to disentangle further and may not have been representative of wider conditions. What caused the Pleistocene continental glaciations, eight of which occurred in the last two million or so years, has long been a matter of debate. The original commonsense idea that they stemmed simply from a uniform cooling of the globe has not survived a closer scrutiny. A decrease in temperature in the polar regions, in fact, would most likely have diminished the already scant precipitation there, thus slowing glacial accumulation. It is thought more likely that a combination of changes – of warmer winters, allowing increased snowfall in the high latitudes, and cooler summers, with less melting of the previous winter's deposits – probably provided the trigger under broadly favorable conditions set by the changing geography of world landmasses and ocean flows. At an intermediate scale of analysis the glaciations are thought, because of correlations now well established, to be connected through a complex net of mechanisms to recurrent orbital variations in the earth's receipt of solar radiation.

Even significant change within the last three centuries may, if evidence for natural fluctuations of similar magnitude before the time of possible human impact is strong, be plausibly ascribed to more natural fluctuation rather than to a human source. The widely accepted curve of global mean temperatures (see Figure 7.4) for the past century and a half shows a gradual net warming of about one degree Celsius, though interrupted by a brief and smaller cooling for some decades after 1940. Standing alone it would make a strong bit of evidence for human impact through changes in the "greenhouse gas" content of the atmosphere. But even these data are not uncontroversial; the curve required recalculation after some scientists suggested that the rise might merely be the artifact of a tradition of stationing weather observatories near cities that have grown considerably during the same period. And place this curve, with its relatively small fluctuations, next to one of natural temperature changes over the last 20,000 years (see Figure 7.5), and one might well despair of hearing any human impacts against so noisy a background. Was the rise a result of a greenhouse warming, or was it merely a still unaccountable natural change, one of many, and a comparatively small one at that? Similar patterns, even when accepted, can be

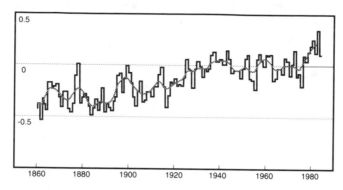

Figure 7.4   Global mean annual surface temperature changes, in degrees Celsius. Source: Wigley, Jones, and Kelly 1986; redrawn for Jäger and Barry 1990.

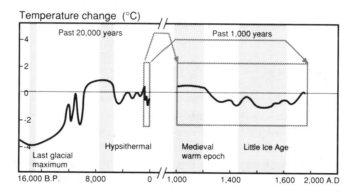

Figure 7.5   Schematic representation of the temperature changes during the past 20,000 years. Redrawn from Jäger 1983 for Jäger and Barry 1990.

compatible with quite different postulated underlying processes. Data are essential, but are by themselves insufficient to resolve the issues of causation. Only by adding a theoretical explanation of the workings of the climate system, the processes that generate the events that we experience as weather and the order that we discern as climate, can we suggest with some confidence what would have been or would be the consequences of particular human activities.

THE CLIMATE SYSTEM

The very word "climate" is a descriptive term with explanatory roots. The Greek word *klimata*, from which it stems, denotes parallel bands, reflecting the belief that weather conditions were fixed by latitude. Marking as it does the location of a place within the geometry of earth–sun relationships, latitude is indeed the dominant factor in climate, governing the initial availability of the solar radiation that powers the weather. The growth of atmospheric science has been the expansion of the list of modifying factors, in the interactions of the atmosphere with the oceans and land cover, that disrupt this neat picture.

Energy from the sun drives the weather system. About 50% of the total incoming solar radiation is absorbed at the earth's surface, 31% has been reflected away by the atmosphere, mainly by clouds, and on a global average 4% more is reflected away by the surface. Only about 15% is originally absorbed by the atmosphere, which is largely transparent to the wavelengths of radiation received from the sun. The ground reradiates upward its absorbed energy in longer (lower-energy) wavelengths. To these rays the atmosphere is somewhat more opaque, because of the presence of water vapor and carbon dioxide, both of which absorb energy at these frequencies. Hence the air is largely warmed from the ground, and not the ground from the air; its absorption of this energy is what is known as the greenhouse effect.

Variations enter in several ways. The sun's radiation output may fluctuate in subtle but significant ways. Different fractions of the total radiation received are reflected away by the land cover – this is known as that cover's albedo. Snow cover has a very high albedo; that is, it reflects much of the incident radiation, well over half. For forests or wet earth, the albedo values are very low; most of the radiation is absorbed. Another variable is the state of the atmosphere. Airborne particulates can, depending on circumstances, change the heat balance either way – by reflecting away or trapping more of the incoming radiation. The prospect, much discussed during the 1980s, of a "nuclear winter" invokes the former effect to predict a severe cooling across the globe from the vast amounts of dust and soot that a nuclear exchange would throw into the air.

The fluid media of air and ocean then redistribute the global energy income, easing some of the latitudinal inequities. The most important cell of atmospheric circulation is driven by the high energy of the equatorial latitudes. It creates a band of unstable, rising air and high precipitation that is flanked by bands of relative drought and stability where the air descends at roughly 30 degrees north and south. Mid-latitude and polar cells take a similar form.Their surface flows, deflected by the earth's rotation, form the prevailing winds – roughly from the east within the tropics, from the west in the mid-latitudes. Ocean currents also route heat poleward from the tropics, and the ocean waters further affect the climates along the coasts. Proximity to the seas, which warm and cool more slowly, moderates land temperatures at both extremes; the continental interiors experience much harsher, and also dryer, summers and winters.

Precipitation depends on three basic processes, all related to the ability of warm air to hold more water vapor than cold. Colder, denser air masses in the continental-scale circulation underrun warmer ones and force them upward to a level of lower pressure, where they cool through expansion. As the air's capacity for vapor diminishes and the saturation point is reached, some of the vapor may condense into cloud and fall as rain. Mountain barriers to the prevailing winds produce what is called orographic precipitation by the same kind of vertical forcing. Finally, in convective storms – summer thunderstorms, for example – it is the heating of air at the ground that makes it rise, and the steady upward release of heat through the condensation of vapor into rain that fuels its continued ascent. All, of course, depend on an adequate initial content of water vapor in the air, and of condensation nuclei on which raindrops or snowflakes can form.

If this is the way the system works, most of it stands, at least for the time being, beyond direct human manipulation – if we set aside the rich literature of grandiose projects to reshape the climate by raising or leveling mountains or redirecting ocean currents, or if we ignore efforts at rainmaking as a kind of climate control purchased at newsstand rather than subscription rates. There exist three sets of ways in which ordinary human actions can effect significant changes. First, they may alter the trace-component composition of the atmosphere, as discussed in the previous section, thereby affecting the radiation balance. Second, they may change the properties of the land surface in any of three ways: by altering the surface albedo (and hence the absorption of heat), roughness (and hence the wind patterns), or moisture (and hence evaporation and heat balance in the local air). Third, they may add heat directly to the atmosphere. The flows of the atmosphere present the possibility that any of these changes may be more widely distributed, or, on the contrary, may be obliterated by dilution in wider natural currents. It is important to distinguish the variety of spatial scales on which change can occur, here distinguished as the global, regional, and local.

The importance of particular human activities differs across these scales. Carbon dioxide, diffusing rapidly throughout the atmosphere, has little to do with local-scale variations in climate, though the impacts of a global greenhouse warming would indeed be quite diverse locally and regionally. Heat releases show another pattern (Jäger and Barry 1990). Averaged annually over the entire globe, the human release of energy is a trivial one – one ten-thousandth of the solar radiation absorbed at the earth's surface – and has a correspondingly negligible effect on global climate. At the other end of the spatial scale, though, in major urban-industrial areas in the United States and Europe the human release during the year is of roughly the same magnitude as the solar radiation absorbed, and combines with other factors to give cities their distinctive climates.

GLOBAL CHANGES

Perhaps no human impact on the biosphere, observed or forecast, now attracts so much attention as global climatic change brought about through an intensification of what is called the greenhouse effect. Scientific awareness of the thermal activity of carbon dioxide and water vapor in the atmosphere dates from the middle to late nineteenth century, and so does awareness that their increased concentrations might increase the absorption of heat and the temperature of the world. A few scientists in the early 1900s discussed the effects that the accelerating combustion of coal might have, through carbon dioxide releases, on the world's climate; for the most part they looked upon such a warming as the world's gain. It would, one geologist argued, produce "a much more abundant and widespread vegetation," speed the breakdown of rock into soil, and make life generally more pleasant; the consumption of coal for heating now, he expected, would reduce the need for it in the future (Van Hise 1904). For the most part, through, the predicted effect was disregarded, perhaps because it seemed both distant and unthreatening, and it did not regain a prominent place on the scientific agenda until the 1950s. Then new data showing increased CO_2 levels combined with new arguments that a warming, and possibly an undesirable one, would occur, renewed scientific interest in the matter.

Not only CO_2 and water vapor, but tropospheric ozone, nitrous oxide, methane, and CFCs are now known to act as greenhouse gases. Indeed, the last two, though present in much smaller concentrations than carbon dioxide is, absorb radiation far more efficiently, molecule for molecule. Though still the most important single gas among those influenced by human action (water vapor being the most important of all), CO_2 no longer accounts for more than half of the predicted anthropogenic trace-gas impact on temperatures. Sulfate aerosols released from coal combustion, on the other hand, appear to have a net cooling effect – deflecting incoming rays from the sun – that in part offsets the operation of greenhouse gases.

The rise of mean temperatures to 1940 has seemed to some clear confirmation of the onset of a human-induced change in the global climate, though the matter is still open to debate. The effects, direct and indirect, of a greenhouse-induced temperature rise would vary by location. The high latitudes are expected to experience a greater warming than the tropics. Across the globe, changes in temperature would be reflected, in complex ways, in the migration of rainfall patterns, with enhancement in some areas and drying in others. Short-term weather events might become more variable and severe and unusual storms occur more frequently. Forests, sensitive to temperature, might be severely damaged if the rate of warming exceeded the rate at which the forest species could migrate toward more suitable conditions, and such migration would be widely obstructed where other land uses stood in the way.

The probable release of water melted from the continental ice sheets of Greenland and Antarctica and the thermal expansion of the water already in the oceans would combine to raise global sea level. Again, the magnitude of rise to be expected is uncertain, and it has even been suggested on good scientific grounds that a warming of the polar regions would produce not a rise but a drop in sea level. By increasing the capacity of the air for moisture and hence for snowfall, a warming would lead to a net growth of the ice sheets and subtract water from the oceans. The two ice sheets contain enough water to raise world-wide sea level by 100 m, though there is no prediction of any catastrophe on that scale in the foreseeable future. Rather, what is expected is a slow rise on the order of several centimeters per decade, depending on the rate of warming itself. Such an increase would within a century flood some very low-lying coastal areas; particularly severe damage would occur in such polderized lands as the Sundarbans of Bangladesh and in low-lying atolls. It would also raise erosion and stress on shorelines more widely. The riches of the coastline have attracted settlement more than its risks have deterred it, which means damage, or the costs of either defending against a rising sea or relocating, disproportionately large for the land area affected.

To such direct effects of a global warming must be added, though even more tentatively, the secondary processes that might be set in motion. Some could run counter to the primary ones and some could reinforce them; all illustrate the complexity of global changes in key aspects of the biosphere. The higher temperatures and higher levels of carbon dioxide could enhance the growth of vegetation, thereby removing some of the excess gas from the air and reducing the greenhouse effect. On the other hand, higher temperatures and a richer vegetation would probably raise the terrestrial emissions of methane, producing a positive rather than a negative feedback. Increased temperatures also would most likely increase the content of water vapor in the atmosphere, thereby increasing the amount of heat retained and adding still further, perhaps by more than 50%, to the warming effect produced by the greenhouse gases alone. Yet if the rise in water vapor increased the cloud cover, the reflection of incoming radiation would be significantly heightened, now working against the primary process. Net global changes that have accompanied the industrial and agricultural augmentation of CO_2 have included, as we have seen, deforestation of considerable magnitude. This change, it has been argued, by increasing the net global albedo, may promote a cooling tendency counter to the greenhouse warming, like the one sulfate particulates bring with them; yet its importance too is disputed.

There is good reason to believe that our past contributions of carbon to the atmosphere will bear fruit in a warming of significant proportions, but its size and physical and social consequences are issues still up in the air. Such consequences belong more in a projection of future environments than in a historical account of the earth as thus far transformed, save as possible explanations for a century and a half of net temperature rise.

REGIONAL CHANGES

If global effects would stem largely from changes in atmospheric composition, at the regional scale we find ourselves almost exclusively in the territory of land-cover influences. Modern scientific ideas in this realm have a long if somewhat shady popular pedigree. The nineteenth century gave us that classic observation that while everybody talks about the weather, nobody does anything about it; but neither the Victorians nor earlier generations ever shrank from the latter task when a suitable opportunity seemed at hand. The principal tool employed, that of "landscape meteorology" (Kollmorgen and Kollmorgen 1973), finds its commonsense basis in the fact that certain types of climate tend to go along with certain land covers. Landscape meteorology turns on its head the usual ascription of the land cover to the climate. Thus, that today we commonly find forests or lakes or rain-fed agriculture in humid areas does not make it clear which came first: the climate, or the forests or lakes or farms. One so predisposed may see not the land cover determined by the climate, but the climate created or maintained by the land cover, which implies that the former can be manipulated by changing the latter.

Thus nineteenth-century French lawmakers, presented with the claim that deserts receive little rainfall because they are dry, not the other way around, debated a plan to cool and moisten the climate of the Sahara by letting the waters of the Mediterranean into a large depression in it thought to lie below sea level (Heffernan 1990). Not long after, the Brazilian government began building reservoirs in the drought-plagued *sertão* region in the hope that they would produce rainfall (Cunniff 1970). During the same decades, settlers moving onto the American Great Plains under the banner "Rain Follows the Plow" expected, by afforestation and cultivation, to guarantee an increase in the unreliable precipitation of the area (Riebsame 1990). In the Sahara and the *sertão,* it was hoped that high evaporation from the new seas would both absorb heat and generate rain; on the Plains, that planting trees and breaking the prairie sod would cause what rain did fall to collect and re-evaporate locally, rather than be lost to the region through river runoff. More involved theories predicted the enhancement of showers through the effects of these land-cover changes on the heat balance. The director of the U.S. Geological Survey, John Wesley Powell, quite unsympathetic to most notions of climate modification (Powell 1891), argued nonetheless along similar lines that irrigation, if widely adopted on the Plains, "will increase the humidity of the climate . . . and as the lands gain more and more water from the heavens by rains, they will need less and less water from canals and reservoirs" (quoted in Kollmorgen and Kollmorgen 1973: 439). Not to all did such prospects seem desirable. Opponents of the Sahara sea and of irrigation in many places advanced as their crowning argument the possibility that pestilential vapors arising from stagnant, heated waters would debilitate the human population. Open-range stockmen on the Great Plains feared an influx of farmers attracted by a more humid climate.

These early episodes raised, in a naive but direct way, many of the issues still central to regional-scale climatology. More sophisticated modern studies avoid such oversimplified and one-directional causal reasoning. They emphasize the importance that surface–atmosphere interactions, now more rigorously measured and modeled, can have in altering the conditions that latitude and position would otherwise be expected to produce. Generalizations about the nature and reality of regional changes remain elusive. Existing lakes and inland seas do have some measurable effects on temperature and humidity in the ribbon of land along their shores, but not so large and so widespread as ordinarily to justify creating new ones as climatic generators. The climatic consequences of hydrological diversions are debatable. The Jonglei Canal project to drain the vast Sudd swampland of the upper Nile Basin aims to increase the river flow by lowering evaporation loss. It might, in doing so, lessen the already scanty precipitation in its surrounding region. Similar speculation about the climatic consequences of the proposed diversion toward the Caspian and Aral Seas of north-flowing rivers in the former Soviet Union has escaped experimental testing because of the abandonment of the scheme. The desiccation of the Aral Sea itself has affected the climate of the surrounding region, making temperatures more extreme and lessening precipitation.

The claim has also been advanced, though it remains highly controversial (Jäger and Barry 1990), that desertification in some lands – the Sahel zone of northern Africa, Rajasthan in northwestern India, and portions of the Middle East – in part represents a climatic effect of human actions. It is argued that overgrazing by livestock both raised the albedo of the surface and injected dust into the air, thus altering the regional heat balance by reflecting away more solar radiation. A net cooling from these processes then promoted atmospheric stability and suppressed rainfall; the vegetation withered under the lessened rainfall and more dust swirled upward, magnifying the original impact. In a very different environment, part of the concern over the clearing of the tropical forest, especially in the Amazon Basin, now stems from the claim that the forest itself is a major factor in the regional hydrological cycle. Detailed studies show that the amount of water vapor brought into Amazonia by the prevailing easterly winds from the Atlantic is equaled by the amount recycled to the atmosphere by evapotranspiration, largely from the rainforest, within the region. Some 75% of the precipitation that falls in Amazonia is thus returned to the regional atmosphere. Deforestation, it is argued, would disrupt this flow and diminish the total rainfall; it is also thought likely that with less heat taken up through evaporation the climate would grow hotter (Salati et al. 1990).

Profound changes occur in the microclimate when a tropical forest is cleared, with daily temperature varying over a much wider range of extremes and humidity considerably diminished; smaller but real changes follow the loss of temperate forests and the adoption of irrigation. Yet the whole question of scale in climate is bound up with the question of whether such local changes can be extrapolated accurately to wider effects, or whether they are swallowed up in the processes dominant at higher scales; in short, whether, to borrow a phrase of John Wesley Powell's, "in the presence of the grand effects of nature [they] es-

Table 7.1. *Maximum heat island effect of 11 metropolitan areas*

	Maximum heat-island effect (urban-rural temperature) (°C)	Population[a] (× 10⁶)
Louisville, KY (SDF)	6.5	0.89
Baltimore, MD (BAL)	5.2	2.14
Washington, D.C. (DCA)	5.2	3.02
Cincinnati, OH (CVG)	5.1	1.38
Indianapolis, IN (IND)	4.5	1.14
Dayton, OH (DAY)	4.5	0.84
St. Louis, MO (STL)	4.4	2.37
Richmond, VA (RIC)	3.8	0.57
Columbus, OH (CMH)	3.3	1.07
Kansas City, MO (MCI)	3.2	1.30
Petersburg, VA —	2.6	0.04

*Source:*Matson et al. 1978; reprinted from Jäger and Barry 1990.
[a] 1974 metropolitan populations based on U.S. Census Standard Metropolitan Statistical Areas (SMSAs) as defined in the 1970 census.

cape discernment." Though the climate system can operate at a global scale, some of its processes are resolutely parochial.

LOCAL CHANGES

More firmly established than global or regional changes are human impacts on climate on the local scale. They are the most easily studied because of the opportunity to control important variables that is all but absent for larger areas.

The city represents the most transformed of landscapes; so is the urban climate the one most clearly and significantly affected by human action. Its principal manifestation is the "heat island" effect, a net elevation of city temperatures above those found in the surrounding countryside. It stems particularly from changes in the land surface and the energy budget. Cities themselves generate much of the heat in which they bask or swelter. The roughness of the urban land surface retards the speed of the winds, and thus lessens the dispersion of heat; the impermeable and well-drained surface is less moist, and so less heat is lost through evaporation; and the structures and surfaces typical of the city absorb and retain heat at high rates. Temperatures within a city thus show a marked increase over those outside (see Table 7.1), one roughly proportional to the city's size.

These figures represent average differences, and the magnitude of change varies further depending on location within the city. The typical urban heat island resembles a jagged, eroded, irregular volcanic isle rather than a flat-topped atoll or a shapely pyramid. But its altitudes also fluctuate, with extreme city–country degree differences sometimes quite subdued, and often reaching double digits under other circumstances, and tropical cities displaying different patterns of daily and seasonal heating from temperate ones.

Secondary effects may follow, such as an increase in fog, cloudiness, storms, and precipitation brought on by convective heating and perhaps also by increased turbulence and the addition of condensation nuclei by pollution. James Pollard Espy, the American meteorologist who pioneered the theory of convective rainfall, found support for his case in the 1840s in the apparent generation of storms over heated industrial cities: "rains are common in London & some other cities of England, while the adjacent country remains dry" (quoted in Ludlum 1970: 164). Some wider effects transcend the urbanized area. The adjacent country, at least for some distance downwind, Espy notwithstanding, often does not remain dry, but is unusually well watered by virtue of its location. Scientific controversy arose in the 1960s over the claim that La Porte, Indiana, 48 km east of Chicago, had experienced a striking rise in rainfall and in stormy weather, presumably as the spillover of convective effects from the urban warming. Lingering skepticism about the results prompted a more thorough study. This investigation, known as the Metropolitan Meteorological Experiment (METRO-MEX), demonstrated a clear increase in rainfall (especially in the summer months), hail, and thunderstorm frequency over a sizable area downwind of St. Louis, Missouri (see Figure 7.6). Similar patterns are found outside other large metropolitan areas (Jäger and Barry 1990).

Deliberate and successful modification of climate at the microscale predates these concerns about unintended effects. House types and even urban form in many areas of the world reflect an adaptation to climatic conditions. The narrow, often covered streets and high, windowless walls of Middle Eastern cities function in part to block the sun and to minimize ventilation that would rapidly heat the indoor air. The modification of the microclimate for agriculture is another venerable form of folk environmental technology. For most people, writes Wilken (1972: 544), "linking the terms 'traditional farmer' and 'climate' conjures up the image of a fetish-bound native in the far corner of a parched field mumbling incantations to an impotent rain god." Yet he and others have amply documented an array of techniques that traditional farmers use – mounding to diminish frost, constructing windbreaks, manipulating shade and the absorption and reradiation of heat – to control the conditions in which their crops grow.

CONCLUSION

Human impact on some components of the oceans, atmosphere, and climate has increased in scale to reach the global level and in magnitude to exceed some

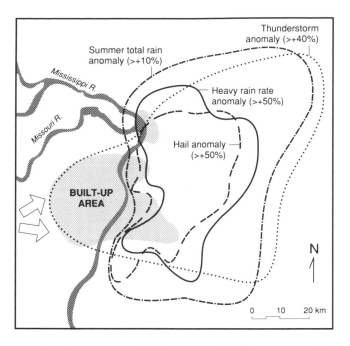

Figure 7.6 Anomalies of summer rainfall, heavy rains, hail frequency, and thunderstorm frequency downwind of the St. Louis metropolitan area. Arrows show the prevailing motion of summer rain systems. Redrawn from Barry and Chorley 1987 for Jäger and Barry 1990.

natural rates of change or fluctuation during the past three centuries. Some local air and coastal pollution and some managed or unintended microclimate change have long accompanied human settlement, but the major impacts have been recent. Most, despite the fluidity of these spheres, have intensified while remaining confined to the local or regional scale. Urbanization has transformed the climatic environment in which a large share of the world's population now dwells; coastal pollution has worsened not only with increased population, but with sewage systems that more rapidly transfer wastes from the land to the water. But some effects have diffused more broadly through fluid global systems, actions taken in one locale having potential consequences around the earth. Changes in such trace gases of the atmosphere as ozone, carbon dioxide, and methane, and through them, in the earth's radiation balance, are the foremost global consequences of human actions, while new substances of a persistence and durability previously unknown – plastics and CFCs – have been widely circulated in the waters, sediments, and atmosphere. The fact that much of the ocean and atmosphere has been, de jure or de facto, a free-access realm has contributed immeasurably to its attractiveness as a dumping ground for unwanted substances.

213

The secondary effects of many of these recent changes brought about by human activity can be predicted from theory or theories but cannot yet be confirmed. Only after time do such experiments with the biosphere begin to announce their consequences. The early results, as with global warming, may be ambiguous and difficult to understand, given nature's unconquerable tendency to mumble its answers to even the most pressing and clearly phrased questions. Surprising new impacts are always possible and even probable, as shown in the unpredicted appearance of the Antarctic ozone hole, a classic instance of the unforeseen consequences of technical innovation. Future activities will no doubt raise concerns that will turn out to have been exaggerated or baseless, but the careful monitoring of even remote possibilities is a vital task.

The fluidity of oceans, atmosphere, and climate, however imperfect, comports uneasily with a social system organized by sharply demarcated boundaries. Victorian faith in the power of landscape change to transform the climate prompted one of the first discussions of externalities and market failure in the literature of economics. Henry Sidgwick observed in 1883 that although it is "advantageous to a nation to keep up forests, on account of their beneficial effect in moderating and increasing rainfall, the advantage is one which private enterprise has no tendency to provide; since no one could appropriate and sell improvements in the climate" (1883: 413). The last comment is not strictly true. Architects, landlords, and realtors have been selling such improvements for ages. But Sidgwick's point still holds true at all scales higher than that of the built environment. And fluidity imposes external problems as well. Even the successful enhancement of precipitation can generate floods of costs as readily as showers of benefits, for climatic interests are not uniform even within regions or places, and such modification might also diminish rainfall elsewhere. A character in Samuel Johnson's eighteenth-century philosophical fable *Rasselas* had contemplated the control of the weather, but "found it impossible to make a disposition by which the world may be advantaged; what one region gains, another loses by any imaginable alteration" ([1759] 1990: 148).

Threats from global processes have slowly begun to expand into the air the mechanisms of international cooperation first proposed for other realms. Yet both remain in large part areas of free access and use. The Third United Nations Conference on the Law of the Sea (1976–82) proposed to substitute for the age-old regime of free access one of joint ownership and management of the open oceans and the riches of their floor, redefined as the "common heritage of mankind." It has waited for more than a decade, however, to gain international assent even in modified form. Proposals for an equally comprehensive "law of the air" remain tentative, though they have been given new credibility by concern over global climate change and ozone depletion. The latter has evoked a series of international agreements; the former, an international "Framework Convention" to develop measures to control greenhouse-gas emissions.

Voluntary international cooperation against perceived threats to a general good remains the only portal through which goals of global environmental amelioration can be reached. The evidence already exists and continues to accumulate that countries can cooperate in setting rules for the use of a common pool. The atmosphere is a pool, however, in which they have interests differing in degree and in kind. The diversity of the earth's surface translates into a diversity of physical impacts of global changes, different social impacts even of similar physical ones, different expectations of their impacts – which, of course, have often been wide of the mark – and different costs that any globally uniform change in behavior would incur. Landlocked countries have little reason to fear a greenhouse-induced rise in sea level to which their actions may contribute. Areas now deficient in rainfall or warmth may expect, rightly or wrongly, to gain from climatic change. Nations dependent on agriculture, forestry, and fisheries are more dependent on climate, and hence more vulnerable to changes in it, than those specializing in the industrial, information, and service sectors. Climate change may create opportunities for gain as well as for loss, but countries with different endowments of skills and capital will differ in their ability to exploit those opportunities.

Because climate itself is so noisy and chaotic, identifying any human sources of change in it is a challenging task. And once we seek the consequences of those changes for human society, we confront the inverse problem: that of identifying those consequences against the noisy and chaotic background of economic, social, and political change. Thus we come full circle, from these most fluid and global of earth systems to the social forces with which we began; the latter are not only sources of human-induced change in the environment but the media through which its impacts are felt and the means by which it is responded to, and in ways that may give rise to new changes again.

8

Three Centuries That
Shook the Earth

How can the modern human impact on the globe be summed up? First, in a tabulation of the individual changes that have occurred. Such a tabulation shows that in many realms of the biosphere, the changes that had occurred thoughout human history to the beginning of the twentieth century have been dwarfed by the changes that have taken place since. Stating 10 major forms of human impact in numerical form, we find that most have accelerated relentlessly (see Figure 8.1). The net emission of carbon to the atmosphere by human action dates back at least to the origins of agriculture, but half of the total amount released has been released since 1920. Half of the sulfur and half of the lead ever mobilized by humankind have been emitted since 1960; half of the phosphorus and nitrogen, since 1975. The annual human releases of many heavy metals now vastly exceed their natural flows from weathering: those of lead, for example, by more than 20 times. Land used for farming has expanded 400% since 1700, obliterating onetime forests, grasslands, and wetlands, and the area of irrigated cropland has grown by several thousand percent. The annual loss of organic carbon from the soil has more than doubled from its average rate over the past three centuries to its rate over the past 50 years. The losses in biodiversity now occurring as a consequence of land-cover change appear comparable to those of the greatest natural extinction episodes in the geologic record. If Marsh in 1864 could correctly describe the earth as modified by human action, we can now say that it has been transformed.

To be sure, some human sources of change have weakened in recent years as compared to earlier periods. Releases of sulfur and lead are among them. So are those of such organic chemicals as DDT and carbon tetrachloride. Much of the change in these cases can be credited to deliberate environmental management, an encouraging sign for the management of future problems. And as the trajectories of change have varied in time, not all of them rising ever more steeply, so

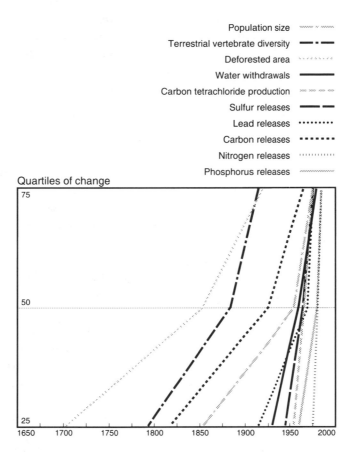

Population size
Terrestrial vertebrate diversity
Deforested area
Water withdrawals
Carbon tetrachloride production
Sulfur releases
Lead releases
Carbon releases
Nitrogen releases
Phosphorus releases

Figure 8.1 Trends in selected forms of human-induced transformation of environmental components. The vertical axis represents percentage of change between 10,000 B.P. and the mid-1980s. The steeper the slope of a component's line, the greater the rate at which the change (whatever its absolute value) in that component has occurred. Source: Kates, Turner, and Clark 1990.

have the patterns of change varied over space. Forests have returned in some regions although worldwide forest area has shrunk, and though air and water quality are deteriorating in many urban areas, the air and water in others are much cleaner than they were a century or even a quarter-century ago.

To make some order out of the variety of environmental paths, three broad regional modes of human transformation of the environment can be distinguished in the contemporary world: the agricultural, the industrial, and the advanced industrial (Kates, Turner, and Clark 1990). In the agricultural mode, the principal impacts are on the landscapes and on the materials flows associated with them. Forests, grasslands, and wetlands are converted to crop and pasture, soil is eroded and sediment flows are increased, biodiversity is lost as habitats are destroyed or degraded. The type, of course, has its subtypes. Changes and im-

217

pacts in agricultural frontier zones are likely to differ from those in long- and heavily settled zones of agricultural intensification, as Brazilian Amazonia (Salati et al. 1990) or the heavily forested, thinly peopled island of Borneo (Brookfield et al. 1990) differs from the densely populated and intensively farmed East African Highlands (Berry, Lewis, and Williams 1990). Either is likely to vary according to the wealth and technological capacity of the society in which it is embedded.

In the industrial mode, landscape modifications continue, but to them are added many more changes in materials and energy flows. Industrialization and urbanization raise the pollution load on the environment far beyond its capacity for absorption, and the demands that they make may also overstress the resources of the local ecosystem – water supply in arid or semi-arid lands, for example. Rural–urban migration keeps population growth in centers of transformation rapid, and those centers affect their surroundings in ever-widening circles. The Basin of Mexico (Ezcurra 1990) displays all of these features in as dramatic and pronounced a form as can be found anywhere, but many other regions in the developing world and the former Eastern Bloc show them hardly less clearly.

Advanced industrial transformation is characteristic of much of the contemporary developed world, particularly its more densely settled regions. Many were nineteenth-century sites of intensive industrial and/or agricultural transformation. Today, forests and biota recover and expand save where suburban sprawl converts rural land to settlement. The more obvious forms of air and water pollution are lessened, in part by environmental regulation and abatement technologies and in part by the migration of heavily polluting industries elsewhere. New forms of pollution, however, appear in the form of the waste emissions of a mass-consuming society – some of them affecting the global systems of climate and stratospheric ozone, some driving more localized processes such as groundwater pollution and acid precipitation. Population growth rates are low to near-zero, but per capita affluence, enormously high by world standards, translates into high resource demands, some of their impacts registered far away. Sweden (Hägerstrand and Lohm 1990), Switzerland (Pfister and Messerli 1990), and the New York City region (Tarr and Ayres 1990) are representative examples of this pattern.

The regional variety of change (and there is much local variety as well within regions, of course) complicates matters. Vulnerability to the impacts of change likewise differs enormously. Resource systems that are closely connected to the climate – agriculture, forestry, and fisheries, all more significant in Third World economies than in the First World – are obviously the most vulnerable to climate change, though at the same time more capable of reaping benefits if changes prove to be beneficial. Regions and groups within them well equipped with wealth, social and technical infrastructure, and skills are the ones that can adapt best to the same changes and even take advantage of them. All global environmental changes, in process or in prospect, are viewed and assessed from regions of differing physical and socioeconomic characteristics. "Thus the view from Sahelian Africa is not that from the northern plains of Canada, in regard to both current and projected transformation" (Kates, Turner, and Clark 1990: 13), and there is no "view from nowhere" (Sack 1990).

The challenge of a global assessment, of course, is to produce something that seems like a view from nowhere. It can at least be asserted that an overall picture is apparent of unsettlingly rapid, sizable, and escalating change in the global environment. If regions differ in their immediate vulnerability to it, their increasing interdependence in a world economy more tightly knit than ever before may make them unprecedentedly vulnerable in the long term. Most unsettling perhaps about contemporary human impact is the range and variety of changes, seemingly unrelated, that may turn out to be related in new and surprising ways. Changes, of course, may dampen each other's effects; sulfur particulates released from coal burning have a cooling effect on the atmosphere counter to the warming effect of the carbon dioxide released by the same activity. Everything cannot be expected to cancel out in this way, and particular changes are equally likely to amplify the harm that others do; the growing scale of impacts means a growing potential for huge disruptions and hugely unpleasant surprises. Ozone depletion is the classic example, but it is apt before long to be joined by many others. The steady growth of population, resource demand, and technological innovation threatens to bring about more such unforeseen catastrophes. Further fundamental changes in the biosphere may arise far more rapidly than we can recognize them and certainly than we can understand their implications, adapt to them, or repair them.

At first glance, these findings, themselves the product of a careful study of environmental history, may seem to make history irrelevant. If contemporary global change is of a scale, rate, and character quite different from anything previously experienced, what lessons but misleading ones can previous experience teach? Much the same is sometimes said of the relations of history in general to contemporary events by those who emphasize the element of discontinuity. And certainly caution is in order. Simple lessons cannot be drawn from the past. Environmental history no more repeats itself than history does, and it cannot be read as a user's manual for the biosphere. The study of human–nature relations over the long term offers no direct answers to our questions. It does offer information, insight, and illumination that can help in answering them. Past human dealings with the environment, however they may have differed from those that we are now conducting, offer the only empirical basis that exists for a better understanding. The alternative to drawing on them in an intelligent way is theorizing uninhibited by anything that personal experience does not make plausible. Our experience of the past, in the broadest sense to be sure, is the only guide we have to the future.

There is no clearer proof that the environmental past does not teach clear and unambiguous lessons than the fact that directly opposed ones have been drawn from it. Here the extreme global assessments make a useful starting point. From one, the earth has entered an accelerating spiral of degradation under the pressure of human use. It is already vastly overpopulated and overexploited, and the likely doubling of human numbers – with probably much more than a doubling of their pressure on the environment – before growth ceases can spell nothing but global catastrophe. From another point of view, the earth has been steadily improved as a home for humankind and never more efficiently than in recent times – as witness the once inconceivable levels of population that it now holds or is expected to hold in the future. That population has doubled since 1950 and will most likely double again proves as conclusively as anything could that we have finally burst the surly bonds of the earth, making the age-old checks of war, famine, and pestilence at last impotent to keep down numbers at the global scale. "Catastrophists" point to the natural finiteness of resources as setting absolute physical limits to sustainable expansion that have already been exceeded. "Cornucopians" emphasize the power of innovation as a response to apparent scarcity; every generation, they assert, far from living at the expense of the future, has made future generations richer by its investment in modifying the earth. That the real price of most metals, classic nonrenewable resources, has steadily fallen even as their use increases demonstrates to some the fallaciousness of the notion of "limits to growth." To others it proves only the ineffectiveness of the market in rationing vital resources. The world's rapid growth in human numbers, technological capacity, and affluence are from one perspective the causes of environmental destruction, from the other the proof of environmental improvement. To one school of thought, the limits of sustainability have long since been exceeded, and rapid action must be taken to shrink the scale of human activities and demands back within them. To the other, sustainability is a problem only to the extent that the idea itself may constrain and discourage the responses, adaptations, and inventions needed to keep humankind progressing.

Both views usefully call attention to what might otherwise be ignored. They do not exhaust the possibilities for making order out of the past. Another approach is to see the past few centuries of global environmental history not as steady or accelerating progression up or down but as a series of coherent epochs separated by revolutionary changes in nature–society relations: eras of colonial, capitalist, and global environmental change (Merchant 1990). It is also possible, of course, to see the historical record as much messier than any of these frameworks allows – which is not necessarily to give up seeking lessons from the past, for it can teach the ubiquity and inevitability of surprise as just such a lesson, and prescribe the cultivation of flexibility and capacity for coping with the unexpected as the route to a more secure environmental future.

But it is reasonable to conclude with what can be generally agreed upon, and to do so to recur to what George Perkins Marsh in the nineteenth century and V. I. Vernadsky in the early twentieth tried to teach their contemporaries: the vast, novel, and growing human power to transform the earth, whether for better or for worse. Both understood that humankind unavoidably alters the earth in the process of inhabiting it and making a living from it. Marsh documented the changes in the earth's landscapes, Vernadsky those in the globe's chemical metabolism. Both were acutely aware of the damage that human activities could do and often did, particularly of the unforeseen impacts produced by interference in a vastly complex web of connected environmental processes. Neither was inclined to see all human-induced change as damage or human-induced change as incapable of improving the earth rather than degrading it, but neither saw improvement as easy or guaranteed.

The great modern revolutions in human thought are often said by historians of ideas to be the Copernican, the Darwinian, and the Freudian, and each is said to have lowered in its turn humankind's sense of its own importance and distinction. If the seriousness of global environmental change effects, as it may, a comparable change in worldview, one could do worse than call it the Marshian or the Vernadskian revolution. In a sense, its lesson runs counter to the pattern, for above all it stresses the extraordinary strength that humankind possesses. Marsh wrote that his point in *Man and Nature* was to show that "man made the Earth" against the prevalent belief that "the earth made man." But at bottom he was hardly more flattering than Copernicus or Darwin to human vanity. For he showed that strength is not necessarily accompanied by skill, and that if we achieve vast effects by our actions it is frequently without intending to do so or understanding what we are doing. The development of that understanding is essential:

> With today's growing, though still far from adequate, knowledge of the earth system and our role in it comes a responsibility to reflect on and be accountable for our actions. The task of understanding global change, anticipating impacts, and keeping human activity in some harmony with the physical environment looms as a test that our species could easily fail. It can only be hoped that the next century will turn out to be the one in which humankind learns to manage its global and growing power to transform planet earth. (Clark and Mathews 1990: 141)

References

Adams, R. McC. 1990. Foreword: The relativity of time and transformation. In *The Earth as Transformed by Human Action* (see Turner et al. 1990), vii–x.

Alayev, E. B., Yu. P. Badenkov, and N. A. Karavaeva. 1990. The Russian Plain. In *The Earth as Transformed by Human Action* (see Turner et al. 1990), 543–60.

Anon. 1860. Will the coal beds last? *The New England Farmer*, n.s., 12: 295.

    1874. Review of G. P. Marsh, *The Earth as Modified by Human Action. The Nation* 19: 223–24.

Ayres, R. U. 1989. Industrial metabolism. In *Technology and Environment*, eds. J. H. Ausubel and H. E. Sladovich, 23–49. Washington, DC: National Academy Press.

Badenkov, Yu. P., A. K. Borunov, A. F. Mandych, A. I. Romashkevich, and V. O. Targulian. 1990. Caucasia. In *The Earth as Transformed by Human Action* (see Turner et al. 1990), 513–31.

Bairoch, P. 1982. International industrialization levels from 1705 to 1980. *Journal of European Economic History* 11: 269–333.

Baker, B. 1894. The Nile reservoirs and Philae. *The Nineteenth Century* 35: 863–72.

Baker, B. J. and G. J. Armelagos. 1988. The origin and antiquity of syphilis. *Current Anthropology* 29: 703–37.

Balée, W. 1989. The culture of Amazonian forests. *Advances in Economic Botany* 7: 78–96.

Barr, B. M., and K. E. Braden. 1988. *The Disappearing Russian Forest*. Totowa, NJ: Rowman and Littlefield.

Barry, R. G., and R. J. Chorley. 1987. *Atmosphere, Weather and Climate*. 5th ed. London: Methuen.

Beard, G. M. 1874. Atmospheric electricity and ozone: Their relation to health and disease. *Popular Science Monthly* 4: 456–69.

Bennett, J. W., and K. A. Dahlberg. 1990. Institutions, social organization, and cultural values. In *The Earth as Transformed by Human Action* (see Turner et al. 1990), 69–86.

REFERENCES

Berry, B. J. L. 1990. Urbanization. In *The Earth as Transformed by Human Action* (see Turner et al. 1990), 103–19.

Berry, L. W., L. A. Lewis, and C. Williams. 1990. East African Highlands. In *The Earth as Transformed by Human Action* (see Turner et al. 1990), 533–42.

Biswas, A. K. 1970. *History of Hydrology.* New York: American Elsevier.

Blaikie, P., and H. Brookfeld. 1987. *Land Degradation and Society.* London: Methuen.

Blake, N. M. 1956. *Water for the Cities: A History of the Urban Water Supply Problem in the United States.* Syracuse, NY: Syracuse University Press.

Bowden, M. J. 1992. The invention of American tradition. *Journal of Historical Geography* 18: 3–26.

Brimblecombe, P. 1977. London air pollution, 1500–1900. *Atmospheric Environment* 11: 1157–62.

  1987. *The Great Smoke: A History of Air Pollution in London since Medieval Times.* London: Methuen.

Brookfield, H. C. 1989. Sensitivity to global change: A new task for old/new geographers. Norma Wilkinson Memorial Lecture, University of Reading, Reading, UK.

Brookfield, H. C., F. J. Lian, K.-S. Low, and L. Potter. 1990. Borneo and the Malay Peninsula. In *The Earth as Transformed by Human Action* (see Turner et al. 1990), 495–512.

Browder, J. O. 1988. The social costs of rain forest destruction: A critique and economic analysis of the "hamburger debate." *Interciencia* 13: 115–20.

Brown, H. S., R. E. Kasperson, and S. Raymond. 1990. Trace pollutants. In *The Earth as Transformed by Human Action* (see Turner et al. 1990), 437–54.

Brown, R. H. 1948. *Historical Geography of the United States.* New York: Harcourt, Brace.

Buck, A. H., ed. 1879. *A Treatise on Hygiene and Public Health.* 2 vols. New York: William Wood.

Bunyan, J. [1678] 1960. *The Pilgrim's Progress from this World to that Which is to Come,* ed. J. B. Whaley. 2nd ed. Oxford: Clarendon Press.

Buol, S. W. 1994. Soils. In *Changes in Land Use and Land Cover: A Global Perspective,* eds. W. B. Meyer and B. L. Turner II, 211–29. Cambridge University Press.

Butzer, K. W. 1990. The realm of cultural-human ecology: Adaptation and change in historical perspective. In *The Earth as Transformed by Human Action* (see Turner et al. 1990), 685–701.

Callendar, G. S. 1938. The artificial production of carbon dioxide and its influence on temperature. *Quarterly Journal of the Royal Meteorological Society* 64: 223–37.

Carey, J., and A. Fowler, eds. 1968. *The Poems of John Milton.* London: Longmans, Green.

Carson, R. 1962. *Silent Spring.* Boston: Houghton Mifflin.

Carter, F. W., and D. Turnock, eds. 1993. *Environmental Problems in Eastern Europe.* New York: Routledge.

Chapman, G. C., and M. Thompson, eds. 1995. *Water and the Quest for Sustainable Development in the Ganges Valley.* London: Mansell.

Chisholm, M. 1990. The increasing separation of production and consumption. In *The Earth as Transformed by Human Action* (see Turner et al. 1990), 87–101.

REFERENCES

Clark, W. C. 1986. Sustainable development of the biosphere: Themes for a research program. In *Sustainable Development of the Biosphere,* eds. W. C. Clark and R. E. Munn, 5–48. Cambridge University Press.

Clark, W. C., and J. T. Mathews. 1990. Editorial introduction: Section II. In *The Earth as Transformed by Human Action* (see Turner et al. 1990), pp. 139–41.

Coase, R. H. 1960. The problem of social cost. *Journal of Law and Economics* 3: 1–44.

Cobban, A. 1964. *The Social Interpretation of the French Revolution.* Cambridge University Press.

Commoner, B. 1994. Population, development and the environment: Trends and key issues in the developed countries. In *Population, Environment and Development: Proceedings of the United Nations Expert Group Meeting on Population, Environment and Development,* 64–77. New York: United Nations.

Cox, S. J. B. 1985. No tragedy on the commons. *Environmental Ethics* 7: 49–61.

Crookes, W. C. 1898. Inaugural address by Sir William Crookes, F.R.S., V.P.C.S., President of the Association. *Nature* 58: 438–48.

Crosson, P. R. (with A. T. Stout). 1983. *Productivity Effects of Cropland Erosion in the United States.* Washington, DC: Resources for the Future.

Cunniff, R. L. 1970. The great drought: Northeast Brazil, 1877–1880. Ph.D. dissertation, University of Texas at Austin.

Cushing, D. 1975. *Fisheries Resources of the Sea and their Management.* Oxford: Oxford University Press.

Daiber, F. C. 1992. Review of M. Williams, ed., *Wetlands: A Threatened Landscape. Global Environmental Change: Human and Policy Dimensions* 2: 164–65.

Darwin, C. [1839] 1952. *Journal of Researches into the Geology and Natural History of the Various Countries Visited by H.M.S. Beagle.* New York: Hafner.

Davis, S. D., S. J. M. Droop, P. Grejerson, L. Henson, C. L. Leon, J. L. Villa-Lobos, H. Synge, and J. Zantouska. 1986. *Plants in Danger: What De We Know?* Gland, Switzerland: IUCN.

Dean, W. 1987. *Brazil and the Struggle for Rubber: A Study in Environmental History.* Cambridge University Press.

Deevey, E. S., Jr. 1960. The human population. *Scientific American* 203(3): 194–204.

Demeny, P. 1990. Population. In *The Earth as Transformed by Human Action* (see Turner et al. 1990), 41–54.

Denevan, W. M. 1992. The pristine myth: The landscape of the Americas in 1492. *Annals of the Association of American Geographers* 82: 369–85.

Dillon, F. 1894. The proposed Nile reservoir: The submergence of Philae. *The Nineteenth Century* 35: 1019–25.

Dodds, G. B. 1969. The stream-flow controversy: A conservation turning point. *Journal of American History* 56: 59–69.

Douglas, I. 1990. Sediment transfer and siltation. In *The Earth as Transformed by Human Action* (see Turner et al. 1990), 215–34.

    1994. Human settlements. In *Changes in Land Use and Land Cover: A Global Perspective,* eds. W. B. Meyer and B. L. Turner II, 149–69. Cambridge University Press.

Douglas, M. 1975. *Implicit Meanings: Essays in Anthropology.* London: Routledge & Kegan Paul.

225

REFERENCES

Ehrlich, P. R. 1968. *The Population Bomb.* New York: Ballantine.

Ehrlich, P. R., and A. H. Ehrlich. 1990. *The Population Explosion.* New York: Simon and Schuster.

Ehrlich, P. R., and J. P. Holdren. 1971. Impact of population growth. *Science* 171: 1212–17.

Eisenbud, M. 1990. The ionizing radiations. In *The Earth as Transformed by Human Action* (see Turner et al. 1990), 455–66.

Ezcurra, E. 1990. The Basin of Mexico. In *The Earth as Transformed by Human Action* (see Turner et al. 1990), 577–88.

Farmer, B. H. 1957. *Pioneer Peasant Colonization in Ceylon: A Study in Asian Agrarian Problems.* Oxford: Oxford University Press.

Farvar, M. T., and J. P. Milton, eds. 1972. *The Careless Technology: Ecology and International Development.* London: Stacey.

Francis, C., E. Boyes, A. Qualter, and M. Stanisstreet. 1993. Ideas of elementary students about reducing the "greenhouse effect." *Science Education* 77: 375–92.

Freeman, D. B. 1992. Prickly pear menace in eastern Australia, 1880–1940. *Geographical Review* 82: 413–29.

French, R. A. 1964. Drainage and economic development in pre-Revolutionary Russia. *Transactions, Institute of British Geographers* 34: 175–88.

Glacken, C. J. 1956. Changing ideas of the habitable world. In *Man's Role in Changing the Face of the Earth*, ed. W. L. Thomas, Jr., 70–92. Chicago: University of Chicago Press.

——— 1967. *Traces on the Rhodian Shore: Nature and Culture in Western Thought from Ancient Times to the End of the Nineteenth Century.* Berkeley: University of California Press.

Goudie, A. 1990. *The Human Impact on the Natural Environment.* 3rd ed. Cambridge, MA: MIT Press.

Graebner, W. 1986. Ethyl in Manhattan: A note on the science and politics of leaded gasoline. *New York History* 57: 436–43.

Graedel, T. E., and P. J. Crutzen. 1990. Atmospheric trace constituents. In *The Earth as Transformed by Human Action* (see Turner et al. 1990), 295–311.

Graetz, D. 1994. Grasslands. In *Changes in Land Use and Land Cover: A Global Perspective*, eds. W. B. Meyer and B. L. Turner II, 125–47. Cambridge University Press.

Graham, M. 1956. Harvests of the seas. In *Man's Role in Changing the Face of the Earth*, ed. W. L. Thomas, Jr., 487–503. Chicago: University of Chicago Press.

Gray, P. 1989. The paradox of technological development. In *Technology and Environment*, eds. J. H. Ausubel and H. E. Sladovich, 192–204. Washington, DC: National Academy Press.

Grigg, D. 1993. International variations in food consumption in the 1980s. *Geography* 78: 251–66.

Grove, R. H. 1990. Colonial conservation, ecological hegemony, and popular resistance: Towards a global synthesis. In *Imperialism and the Natural World*, ed. J. M. MacKenzie, pp. 15–50. Manchester, England: Manchester University Press.

Hägerstrand, T., and U. Lohm. 1990. Sweden. In *The Earth as Transformed by Human Action* (see Turner et al. 1990), 605–22.

Hammer, C. U., H. B. Clausen, and W. Dansgaard. 1980. Greenland ice sheet evidence of postglacial volcanism and its climatic impact. *Nature* 288: 230–35.

REFERENCES

Hardin, G. 1968. The tragedy of the commons. *Science* 162: 1243–48.

Headrick, D. R. 1990. Technological change. In *The Earth as Transformed by Human Action* (see Turner et al. 1990), 55–67.

Hellden, U. 1991. Desertification: Time for an assessment. *Ambio* 20: 372–83.

Hilborn, R. 1990. Marine biota. In *The Earth as Transformed by Human Action* (see Turner et al. 1990), 371–85.

Holdgate, M. 1990. Postscript. In *The Earth as Transformed by Human Action* (see Turner et al. 1990), 703–06.

Holmgren, P., E. J. Masakha, and H. Sjöholm. 1994. Not all African land is being degraded. *Ambio* 23: 390–95.

Houghton, R. A., and D. L. Skole. 1990. Carbon. In *The Earth as Transformed by Human Action* (see Turner et al. 1990), 393–408.

Hume, D. [1739–40] 1985. *A Treatise of Human Nature.* New York: Penguin Books.
  [1752] 1907. On the populousness of ancient nations. In *Essays Moral, Political, and Literary,* vol. 1, eds. T. H. Green and T. H. Grose, 381–443. London: Longmans, Green.

Husar, R. B., and J. D. Husar. 1990. Sulfur. In *The Earth as Transformed by Human Action* (see Turner et al. 1990), 409–21.

Ives, J. D., and Messerli, B. 1990. *The Himalayan Dilemma: Reconciling Development and Conservation.* London: Routledge.

Jacobs, W. 1978. The great despoilation: Environmental themes in American frontier history. *Pacific Historical Review* 47: 1–26.

Jacobsen, T., and R. McC. Adams. 1958. Salt and silt in ancient Mesopotamian agriculture. *Science* 128: 1251–58.

Jäger, J. 1983. *Climate and Energy Systems.* Chichester: Wiley.

Jäger, J., and R. G. Barry. 1990. Climate. In *The Earth as Transformed by Human Action* (see Turner et al. 1990), 335–51.

Jickells, T. D., R. Carpenter, and P. S. Liss. 1990. Marine environment. In *The Earth as Transformed by Human Action* (see Turner et al. 1990), 313–34.

Johnson, S. [1759] 1990. *Rasselas and Other Tales,* ed. G. J. Kolb. New Haven, CT: Yale University Press.

Kasperson, R. E., and J. X. Kasperson, eds. 1977. *Water Re-use and the Cities.* Hanover, NH: University Press of New England for Clark University Press.

Kates, R. W., B. L. Turner II, and W. C. Clark. 1990. The great transformation. In *The Earth as Transformed by Human Action* (see Turner et al. 1990), 1–17.

Kempton, W. 1991. Lay perspectives on global climate change. *Global Environmental Change: Human and Policy Dimensions* 1: 183–208.

Keynes, J. M. [1936] 1972. William Stanley Jevons. In *Essays in Biography: The Collected Writings of John Maynard Keynes,* v. 10, 109–50. London: St. Martin's Press for the Royal Economic Society.

Klein, I. 1973. Death in India, 1871–1921. *Journal of Asian Studies* 32: 639–59.

Knight, F. H. 1921. *Risk, Uncertainty and Profit.* Boston: Houghton Mifflin.

Knorr, K. E. 1944. *British Colonial Theories, 1570–1850.* Toronto: University of Toronto Press.

Kollmorgen, W., and J. Kollmorgen. 1973. Landscape meteorology on the Great Plains. *Annals of the Association of American Geographers* 63: 424–41.

REFERENCES

Kosarev, A. N., and R. E. Makarova. 1988. Changes in the level of the Caspian Sea and the possibility of forecasting them. *Soviet Geography* 29: 617–24.

Kotlyakov, V. M. 1991. The Aral Sea Basin: a critical environmental zone. *Environment* 33(1): 4–9, 36–38.

Krutch, J. W. 1958. *Grand Canyon: Today and All Its Yesterdays.* New York: W. Sloane.

Leont'yev, O. K. 1988. Problems of the level of the Caspian and the stability of its shoreline. *Soviet Geography* 29: 608–16.

Leopold, L. A. 1956. Land use and sediment yield. In *Man's Role in Changing the Face of the Earth,* ed. W. L. Thomas, Jr., 639–47. Chicago: University of Chicago Press.

Lewis, M. W. 1992. *Green Delusions: An Environmentalist Critique of Radical Environmentalism.* Durham, NC: Duke University Press.

Lindlay, K. 1982. *Fenland Riots and the English Revolution.* London: Heinemann.

Lovejoy, A. O. [1936] 1964. *The Great Chain of Being.* New York: Harper.

Lowell, P. 1908. *Mars and its Canals.* New York: Macmillan.

Lowenthal, D. 1958. *George Perkins Marsh: Versatile Vermonter.* New York: Columbia University Press.

——— 1962. Not every prospect pleases. *Landscape* 12(2): 19–23.

——— 1990. Awareness of human impacts: Changing attitudes and emphases. In *The Earth as Transformed by Human Action* (see Turner et al. 1990), 121–35.

Ludlum, D. 1970. *Early American Tornadoes.* Boston: American Meteorological Society.

L'vovich, M. I. [1974] 1979. *World Water Resources and Their Future.* Trans. R. L. Nace for the American Geophysical Union. Chelsea, MI: Litho Crafters.

L'vovich, M. I., and G. F. White. 1990. Use and transformation of terrestrial water systems. In *The Earth as Transformed by Human Action* (see Turner et al. 1990), 235–52.

McDowell, P. F., T. Webb III, and P. J. Bartlein. 1990. Long-term environmental change. In *The Earth as Transformed by Human Action* (see Turner et al. 1990), 143–62.

McNeill, W. H. 1976. *Plagues and Peoples.* Garden City, NY: Anchor Press.

——— 1989. Control and catastrophe in human affairs. *Daedalus* 118(1): 1–12.

Malin, J. C. 1956. The grassland of North America: Its occupance and the challenge of continuous reappraisals. In *Man's Role in Changing the Face of the Earth,* ed. W. L. Thomas, Jr., 350–66. Chicago: University of Chicago Press.

Marsh, G. P. [1864] 1965. *Man and Nature; or, Physical Geography as Modified by Human Action.* Cambridge, MA: Belknap Press of Harvard University Press.

——— 1885. *The Earth as Modified by Human Action: A Last Revision of "Man and Nature."* New York: Charles Scribner's Sons.

Matson, M., E. P. McClain, D. F. McGinnis, Jr., and J. A. Pritchard. 1978. Satellite detection of urban heat islands. *Monthly Weather Review* 106: 1725–34.

Merchant, C. 1990. The realm of social relations: Production, reproduction, and gender in environmental transformations. In *The Earth as Transformed by Human Action* (see Turner et al. 1990), 673–84.

Meyer, W. B. 1987. Vernacular American theories of earth science. *Journal of Geological Education* 34: 20–25.

——— 1994. When dismal swamps became priceless wetlands. *American Heritage* 45(3): 108–16.

REFERENCES

Meyer, W. B., and B. L. Turner II. 1990. Editorial introduction: Section III. In *The Earth as Transformed by Human Action* (see Turner et al. 1990), pp. 469–71.

Micklin, P. P. 1988. Desiccation of the Aral Sea: A water management disaster in the Soviet Union. *Science* 241: 1170–76.

Mill, J. S. [1852] 1967. The regulation of the London water supply. In *Essays in Economics and Society: Collected Works of John Stuart Mill*, vol. 5, ed. J. M. Robson, 431–37. Toronto: University of Toronto Press and Routledge & Kegan Paul.

———. [1874] 1969. Nature. In *Essays on Ethics, Religion, and Society: Collected Works of John Stuart Mill*, vol. 10, ed. J. M. Robson, 373–402. Toronto: University of Toronto Press and Routledge & Kegan Paul.

Moran, J. H., and A. Gode, trans. and ed. 1966. *On the Origins of Language.* New York: Frederick Unger.

Morrisette, P. M. 1988. The stability bias and adjustment to climatic variability: The case of the rising level of the Great Salt Lake. *Applied Geography* 8: 171–89.

Mortimore, M. 1989. *Adapting to Drought: Farmers, Famines and Desertification in West Africa.* Cambridge University Press.

Nash, R. 1967. *Wilderness and the American Mind.* New Haven, CT: Yale University Press.

Nations, J. D., and D. I. Komer. 1982. Indians, immigrants and beef exports: Deforestation in Central America. *Cultural Survival Quarterly* 6: 8–12.

Needham, J. 1971. *Science and Civilization in China*, vol. 4: *Physics and Physical Technology.* Cambridge University Press.

Newell, N. D., and L. Marcus. 1987. Carbon dioxide and people. *Palaios* 2: 101–03.

Nilson, G. 1986. *The Endangered Species Handbook.* Washington, DC: Animal Welfare Institute.

Oedekoven, K. 1980. The vanishing forest. *Environ. Pol. Law* 6(4): 184–85.

Olson, S. 1971. *The Depletion Myth: A History of Railroad Use of Timber.* Cambridge, MA: Harvard University Press.

O'Riordan, T. 1988. Special report: The Earth as Transformed by Human Action. *Environment* 30(1): 25–28.

Ostrom, E. 1990. *Governing the Commons: The Evolution of Institutions for Collective Action.* Cambridge University Press.

Peters, R. L., and T. E. Lovejoy. 1990. Terrestrial fauna. In *The Earth as Transformed by Human Action* (see Turner et al. 1990), 353–69.

Peterson, D. J. 1993. *Troubled Lands: The Legacy of Soviet Environmental Destruction.* Boulder, CO: Westview Press.

Pfister, C., and P. Messerli. 1990. Switzerland. In *The Earth as Transformed by Human Action* (see Turner et al. 1990), 641–52.

Pielou, E. C. 1991. *After the Ice Age: The Return of Life to Glaciated North America.* Chicago: University of Chicago Press.

Platt, R. H. 1991. *Land Use Control: Geography, Law, and Public Policy.* Englewood Cliffs, NJ: Prentice-Hall.

Powell, J. W. 1891. The new lake in the desert. *Scribner's Magazine* 10: 463–68.

Prance, G. T. 1990. Flora. In *The Earth as Transformed by Human Action* (see Turner et al. 1990), 387–91.

REFERENCES

Rambo, A. T. 1985. *Primitive Polluters: Semang Impact on the Malaysian Tropical Rain Forest Ecosystem.* Anthropological Papers #76, Museum of Anthropology, University of Michigan, Ann Arbor.

Repetto, R., and M. Gillis, eds. 1988. *Public Policies and the Misuse of Forest Resources.* Cambridge University Press.

Rhodes, S. L. 1991. Rethinking desertification: What do we know and what have we learned? *World Development* 19: 1137–43.

Richards, J. F. 1986. World environmental history and economic development. In *Sustainable Development of the Biosphere,* eds. W. C. Clark and R. E. Munn, 53–71. Cambridge University Press.

1990. Land transformation. In *The Earth as Transformed by Human Action* (see Turner et al. 1990), 163–78.

Richey, J. E., C. Nobre, and C. Deser. 1989. Amazon River discharge and climate variability, 1903 to 1985. *Science* 246: 101–03.

Riebsame, W. E. 1990. The United States Great Plains. In *The Earth as Transformed by Human Action* (see Turner et al. 1990), 561–75.

Rockwell, R. C. 1994. Culture and cultural change. In *Changes in Land Use and Land Cover: A Global Perspective,* eds. W. B. Meyer and B. L. Turner II, 357–82. Cambridge University Press.

Rogers, E. C. 1962. *Diffusion of Innovations.* New York: Free Press.

Rogers, P. 1994. Hydrology and water quality. In *Changes in Land Use and Land Cover: A Global Perspective,* eds. W. B. Meyer and B. L. Turner II, 231–57. Cambridge University Press.

Rowlands, I. H. 1993. The Fourth Meeting of the Parties to the Montreal Protocol: Report and reflection. *Environment* 35(6): 25–33.

Rozanov, B. G., V. Targulian, and D. S. Orlov. 1990. Soils. In *The Earth as Transformed by Human Action* (see Turner et al. 1990), 203–14.

Sack, R. D. 1990. The realm of meaning: The inadequacy of human–nature theory, and the view of mass consumption. In *The Earth as Transformed by Human Action* (see Turner et al. 1990), 659–71.

Salati, E., M. J. Dourojeanni, F. C. Novaes, A. Engrácia de Oliveira, R. W. Perritt, H. O. R. Schubart, and J. C. Umana. 1990. Amazonia. In *The Earth as Transformed by Human Action* (see Turner et al. 1990), 479–93.

Scarff, J. E. 1977. The international management of whales, dolphins, and porpoises: An interdisciplinary assessment. *Ecology Law Quarterly* 6: 323–426, 571–638.

Schama, S. 1986. *The Embarrassment of Riches: An Interpretation of Dutch Culture in the Golden Age.* New York: Alfred A. Knopf.

Schumpeter, J. 1939. *Business Cycles: A Theoretical, Historical, and Statistical Analysis of the Capitalist Process.* 2 vols. New York: McGraw-Hill.

Schwarz, H. E., J. Emel, W. J. Dickens, P. Rogers, and J. Thompson. 1990. Water quality and flows. In *The Earth as Transformed by Human Action* (see Turner et al. 1990), 253–70.

Seidenstecker, E. 1983. *Low City, High City: Tokyo from Edo to the Earthquake.* New York: Alfred A. Knopf.

Servheen, C. 1985. The grizzly bear. In *Audubon Wildlife Report,* 1985, ed. R. L. Di Silvestro, 401–15. New York: National Audubon Society.

REFERENCES

Sidgwick, H. 1883. *The Principles of Political Economy.* London: Macmillan.

Simmons, I. G. 1991. *Earth, Air and Water: Resources and Environment in the Late 20th Century.* London: Edward Arnold.

Simon, J. O. 1981. *The Ultimate Resource.* Princeton, NJ: Princeton University Press.

Skole, D. L. 1994. Data on global land-cover change: Acquisition, assessment, and analysis. In *Changes in Land Use and Land Cover: A Global Perspective,* eds. W. B. Meyer and B. L. Turner II, 437–71. Cambridge University Press.

Skole, D. L., and C. Tucker. 1993. Tropical deforestation and habitat fragmentation in the Amazon: Satellite data from 1978 to 1988. *Science* 260: 1905–10.

Smil, V. 1987. *Energy, Food, Environment: Realities, Myths, Options.* Oxford: Clarendon Press.

———. 1990. Nitrogen and phosphorus. In *The Earth as Transformed by Human Action* (see Turner et al. 1990), 423–36.

———. 1992. China's environment in the 1980s: Some critical changes. *Ambio* 21: 431–36.

Solley, W. B., C. F. Merk, and R. R. Pierce. 1988. *Estimated Use of Water in the United States in 1985.* United States Geological Society Circular 1004. Washington, DC: U.S. Government Printing Office.

Solow, R. M. 1974. The economics of resources or the resources of economics. *American Economic Review* 64(2): 1–14.

Soroos, M. S. 1992. The odyssey of Arctic haze: Toward a global atmospheric regime. *Environment* 34(10): 6–11, 25–27.

Soutar, A., and J. D. Isaacs. 1969. A history of fish populations inferred from fish scales in anaerobic sediments off California. *California Marine Research Commission CalCOFI* 13: 63–70.

Stern, P. C., O. R. Young, and D. Druckman, eds. 1992. *Global Environmental Change: Understanding the Human Dimensions.* Washington, DC: National Academy Press.

Sternberg, H. O'R. 1987. Aggravation of floods in the Amazon River as a consequence of deforestation? *Geografiska Annaler* 69A: 201–19.

Stewart, O. C. 1956. Fire as the first great force employed by man. In *Man's Role in Changing the Face of the Earth,* ed. W. L.. Thomas, Jr., 115–33. Chicago: University of Chicago Press.

Tarr, J. A. 1971. Urban pollution – many long years ago. *American Heritage* 22 (6): 65–69, 106.

Tarr, J. A., and R. U. Ayres. 1990. The Hudson-Raritan Basin. In *The Earth as Transformed by Human Action* (see Turner et al. 1990), 623–39.

Thomas, D. S. G., and N. Middleton. 1994. *Desertification: Exploding the Myth.* New York: John Wiley.

Thomas, W. L., Jr., ed. 1956. *Man's Role in Changing the Face of the Earth.* Chicago: University of Chicago Press.

Thompson, K. 1970. The Australian fever tree in California: Eucalypts and malaria prophylaxis. *Annals of the Association of American Geographers* 60: 230–44.

Thornthwaite, C. W. 1956. Modification of rural microclimates. In *Man's Role in Changing the Face of the Earth,* ed. W. L. Thomas, Jr., 567–83. Chicago: University of Chicago Press.

Tiffen, M., M. Mortimore, and F. N. Gichuki. 1994. *More People, Less Erosion: Environmental Recovery in Kenya.* New York: John Wiley.

REFERENCES

Tomasevich, J. 1943. *International Agreements on Conservation of Marine Resources, with Special Reference to the North Pacific.* Stanford, CA: Food Research Institute.

Tuan, Y.-F. 1968. Discrepancies between environmental attitude and behavior: Examples from Europe and China. *Canadian Geographer* 12: 176–91.

Tucker, C. J., H. E. Dregne, and W. W. Newcomb. 1991. Expansion and contraction of the Sahara Desert from 1980 to 1990. *Science* 253: 299–301.

Turner, B. L., II, and K. W. Butzer. 1992. The Columbian Encounter and land-use change. *Environment* 43(8): 16–20.

Turner, B. L., II, W. C. Clark, R. W. Kates, J. F. Richards, J. T. Mathews, and W. B. Meyer, eds. 1990. *The Earth as Transformed by Human Action.* Cambridge University Press.

Turner, B. L., II, and W. B. Meyer. 1994. Global land-use and land-cover change: An overview. In *Changes in Land Use and Land Cover: A Global Perspective,* eds. W. B. Meyer and B. L. Turner II, 3–10. Cambridge University Press.

Udo, R. K., O. O. Areola, J. O. Ayoade, and A. A. Afolayan. 1990. Nigeria. In *The Earth as Transformed by Human Action* (see Turner et al. 1990), 589–603.

U. S. Geological Survey. 1985. *National Water Summary 1984 – Hydrologic Events, Selected Water-Quality Trends, and Groundwater Resources.* U.S.G.S. Water Supply Paper 2275. Washington, DC: U.S. Government Printing Office.

Van Hise, C. R. 1904. *A Treatise on Metamorphism.* Washington, DC: U. S. Geological Survey.

Walker, H. J. 1990. The coastal zone. In *The Earth as Transformed by Human Action* (see Turner et al. 1990), 271–94.

Wallace, A. R. 1911. *Island Life: or, the Phenomena and Causes of Insular Faunas and Floras.* 3rd ed. London: Macmillan.

Watts, D. G. 1987. *The West Indies: Patterns of Development, Culture, and Environmental Change since 1492.* Cambridge University Press.

WCED (World Commission on Environment and Development). 1987. *Our Common Future.* Oxford: Oxford University Press.

Webb, S., and B. Webb. 1922. *English Local Government: Statutory Authorities for Special Purposes.* London: Longmans, Green.

White, G. F. 1988. The environmental effects of the high dam at Aswan. *Environment* 30(7): 4–11, 34–40.

Whitmore, T. M. 1992. *Disease and Death in Early Colonial Mexico.* Boulder, CO: Westview Press.

Whitmore, T. M., B. L. Turner II, D. L. Johnson, R. W. Kates, and T. R. Gottschang. 1990. Long-term population change. In *The Earth as Transformed by Human Action* (see Turner et al. 1990), 25–39.

Wigley, T. M. L., P. D. Jones, and P. M. Kelly. 1986. Empirical climate studies. In *The Greenhouse Effect, Climatic Change and Ecosystems,* ed. B. Bolin. SCOPE 29. Chichester: Wiley.

Wilken, G. 1972. Microclimate management by traditional farmers. *Geographical Review* 62: 544–60.

Wilkinson, R. G. 1973. *Poverty and Progress: An Ecological Perspective on Economic Development.* New York: Praeger.

REFERENCES

Williams, M. 1974. *The Making of the South Australian Landscape: A Study in the Historical Geography of Australia.* London: Academic Press.

———. 1990a. Forests. In *The Earth as Transformed by Human Action* (see Turner et al. 1990), 179–201.

———. 1990b. Understanding wetlands. In *Wetlands: A Threatened Landscape,* ed. M. Williams, 1–41. Oxford: Basil Blackwell.

Williams, R. 1976. *Keywords: A Vocabulary of Culture and Society.* New York: Oxford University Press.

Wood, L. B. 1982. *The Restoration of the Tidal Thames.* Bristol, England: Adam Higher.

Zimmerman, E. W. 1951. *World Resources and Industries: A Functional Appraisal of the Availability of Agricultural and Industrial Materials,* rev. ed. New York: Harper & Brothers.

Zuo, D., and P. Zhang. 1990. The Huang-Huai-Hai Plain. In *The Earth as Transformed by Human Action* (see Turner et al. 1990), 473–77.

Index

developed countries (*cont.*)
land in, 58; daily food supply in, 34; export of environmental damage from, 48–9; forest change in, 61; low vulnerability of to climatic change, 218; near-zero population growth in, 28; urban air quality improvement in, 199–200

developing countries: cultivated land in, 58; daily food supply in, 34; export of environmental damage to, 48–9; forest change in, 61; high vulnerability of to climatic change, 218; population growth in, 28, 34; rapid urbanization in, 75–6; urban air quality deterioration in, 200

Dickens, Charles: 8

Dinka: 74

discounting: *see* costs and benefits

distribution: *see* costs and benefits

disturbance, natural: 12

Dnieper River: 90

dodo: 90

dogs: as introduced species, 89

domestication, species: 2, 92

Donbass: 80

Doyle, Sir Arthur Conan: 8

drainage: *see* wetlands

drought: and desertification, 71; Sahelian of 1970s and 1980s, 71; and wind erosion, 79, 80; *see also* rainfall

dry farming: and wind erosion, 80

dust: natural transport of, 79; storms, 79–80; *see also* erosion

Dust Bowl: 70, 79–80

Dutch elm disease: 110

earth: axis of, 5, 22; long-term history of, 2; magnetic field of, 5

Earth as Modified by Human Action, The: 6

Earth as Transformed by Human Action, The: 21, 32, 113, 118, 201

Earth Day: 10

earthquakes: 5

East Africa: 218; lakes of, 115; soil erosion in highlands of, 78

East Asia: aquaculture and mariculture in, 109; polders in, 74; sewage farming in, 133, 165; *see also names of individual countries*

East Bloc: 218; pollution and resource waste in, 47

Eastern Europe: air pollution in, 200; forest clearing in, 64; *see also* East Bloc; *names of individual countries*

ecological revolutions: 220

economics: analysis of environmental change, 40–6; as prime mover of history, 49–50

Ecuador: Amazonian rainforest of, 55; decline of cinchona tree in, 96; plant species lost in, 95

Edinburgh: 165

EEZs: 108

Egypt: irrigation development in, 123, 125; soil salinization in, 77, 81; see also Aswan Dam; Aswan High Dam; Nile River; Nile Valley

Ehrlich, Paul E.: 23, 32

El Niño: 106, 116, 188

enclosed basins: 117–18

enclosed seas: pollution in, 190–1

enclosure: 43, 52–3

endangered species: protection of 16, 92–3, 102; *see also* animals; plants; species

endemic species: defined, 89; *see also* animals; plants

energy: 7; generation, environmental impacts of, 38–9; heat releases from use, 206; national disparities in consumption of, 34; trends in per capita global use, 23, 35; *see also* fossil fuels; hydropower; nuclear energy

England: forest regulation in Elizabethan, 53; population thought in, 31; wetland drainage in, 74; *see also* Great Britain

English Channel: 89

environment: as research topic, 11

environmental catastrophism: 22, 220

environmental degradation: 16; defined, 3; deforestation not necessarily, 63;

distinguished from environmental improvement, 17–18, 221; early concerns about, 4

environmental history: lessons from, 219

environmental improvement: belief in, 4; distinguished from degradation, 17–18, 221

environmentalism: and biodiversity loss, 113; and chemical flows, 145, 146; defined, 13; and indoor air pollution, 200–1; and water, 114

environmental literacy: 11

environmental management: *see* regulation

environmental movement: 10

environmental transformation: human driving forces of, 22–50; modes of, 218–19; regional variety of, 218

Erie, Lake: 166

erosion: 77–80; agriculture and, 78; coastal, 81, 82; downstream from dams, 81; measures to prevent, 78–9; overgrazing and, 78; by water 78–9; by wind, 79–80; *see also* soil

Espy, James Pollard: 212

Essay on the Principle of Population: 31

estuaries: pollution in, 190–1

eucalyptus: 192

Europe: 192; air pollution in, 193, 200; change in farmland in, 58; decline of water-borne diseases in, 132; domestic-municipal water withdrawal in, 131, 132; forest decline in, 168; frontiers of deforestation in, 64; lead releases in, 189; population history of, 27, 28; sewage farming in, 165; sulfur emissions in, 157; syphilis in 15th-century, 110; urban heat releases in, 206; urban ozone levels in, 194; water withdrawal in, 121, 129; wetland drainage in, 72; *see also* Mediterranean region; Western Europe; *names of individual countries*

eutrophication: in enclosed seas and estuaries, 190–1; in freshwater systems, 166–7

Evelyn, John: 63

Exclusive Economic Zones (EEZs): 108

exotic species: *see* species transfers

externalities: and climate modification, 41, 214; defined, 41–2; of deforestation, 63; of drainage, 73; of land use, 53–4

extinctions: *see* species

Exxon Valdez: 10, 145, 187

faces, earth's: modified by human action, 3, 5

fadama agriculture: 140

Falu: 170

farmland: *see* cultivation

fauna: *see* animals

Fenland: wetland drainage in, 74

fertility rate: 29–31

fertilizer: 59, 127; eutrophication and, 165–7; manures as, 163; nitrogen and phosphorus, 164–5; and nitrogen releases, 160, 165; sewage as, 133, 162, 164–5

filth theory of disease: *see* anticontagionism

Finland: wood exports from, 67

fire: use by early hunter-gatherers: 3–4, 64

First World: *see* developed countries

fish, freshwater: of Amazonia, 97–8; of Aral Sea, 98, 126; of Caspian Sea, 125; in reservoirs, 138; in southwestern US, 98; in Thames River, 133; vulnerability to human impact, 97–8; *see also* mariculture; marine fish; *names of specific fish*

fishponds: 9

floods: 5; control of, 139–40; *fadama* agriculture based on, 140; insurance against in US, 139–40; resulting from dam failures, 138; resulting from river sedimentation, 81; role of land-cover change in, 127–9; *see also* streamflow

flora: *see* plants

Florida: lead records in corals from, 174; spread of water hyacinth in, 96

flows, earth's material and energy: natural and modified, 3, 6; V. I. Vernadsky on global changes in, 9, 221